Raising
Lifelong
Learners

Other books by Lucy McCormick Calkins

The Art of Teaching Writing

A Writer's Shelf: Literature in the Writing Workshop
(coauthored by Katherine Bearden)

Living between the Lines
(with Shelley Harwayne)

Lessons from a Child

The Writing Workshop: A World of Difference
(coauthored by Shelley Harwayne)

Raising Lifelong Learners

A PARENT'S GUIDE

Lucy Calkins
with
Appendices by Lydia Bellino

ADDISON-WESLEY
Reading, Massachusetts

Many of the designations used by manufacturers and sellers to distinguish their products are claimed as trademarks. Where those designations appear in this book and Addison-Wesley was aware of a trademark claim, the designations have been printed in initial capital letters.

Library of Congress Cataloging-in-Publication Data

Calkins, Lucy.
    Raising lifelong learners : a parent's guide / Lucy Calkins
with Lydia Bellino.
       p.   cm.
    Includes bibliographical references and index.
    ISBN 0-201-12749-0 (alk. paper)
    1. Education—Parent participation.   2. Reading—Parent participation.
3. Home and school.   4. Child rearing.   I. Bellino, Lydia.   II. Title.
LB1048.5C35   1997
371.19'2—dc21   97-18548
                                                          CIP

Find us on the World Wide Web at
http://www.aw.com/gb/
Addison-Wesley is an imprint of Addison Wesley Longman, Inc.

Jacket design by Suzanne Heiser
Text design by Dede Cummings Design
Set in 11½-point Janson by Pagesetters, Inc.

1 2 3 4 5 6 7 8 9-MA-0100999897
First printing, August 1997

Dedicated to my parents, Evan and Virginia Calkins, who are present on every page of this book and in every moment of my parenting.

Lucy Calkins

Dedicated to Tony, Michael, Marissa, Michelle, and Kristyn for always knowing when I needed solitude to write and when I needed their company to listen.

Lydia Bellino

CONTENTS

ACKNOWLEDGMENTS

When my sons Miles and Evan were born, my friends and family sent gifts, and for each, I wrote a thank-you letter. This is a thank-you letter for the gifts that have mattered even more.

John, thank you for being my companion, soulmate, and counselor in the project of raising our boys. You revel in Miles and Evan, in their idiosyncrasies, their spirit, their inventiveness. How the boys adore you! You let them ski black diamond trails and scale giant rock cliffs; and you let them hold your hand when the trails are too steep, too slippery. You watch for and celebrate moments when Miles and Evan are industrious, spunky, and compassionate, and the boys have grown in the sunlight of your approving attention. I also have grown in this sunlight. Thank you for reveling in me during the moments when my parenting has been wise, energetic, and compassionate.

Mum, thank you for being there to supervise the nine of us kids on the piano, to join us on long horseback rides across the creek, to give out popsicles and interested attention to the troops of neighborhood kids who regarded our rambling farmhouse as their playground. Thank you for giving me and my sons the most beautiful childhood world a kid could ever dream of having. Thank you also for teaching us to take pleasure in the small, the ordinary, the everyday.

Dad, how grateful I am for your high-spirited and tenacious enthusiasm for all that you value: for adventure, tradition, music, projects, and family. Thank you especially for teaching me and my sons the joy of working hard in the service of a calling. For our clan, you have been Keeper of the Values.

Thanks also to each of my brothers and sisters, especially my sister Ellen. How grateful I am, Ellen, that you and I are traveling the bumpy road of parenting together.

Miles and Evan both attend Wooster Lower School in Danbury, Connecticut. At Wooster, they read books, plant gardens, write poems, and explore the world in the company of passionate, respectful friends and teachers. I am grateful to all the grown-ups at Wooster, but especially to Annemarie Powers, Beth Hamilton, Gillian White, Liz Lynn and to Cathy Grimes. For three years now, our family has had the privilege of having Cathy as a teacher. Her extraordinary influence is a testimony to the gifts a teacher can bring not only to a child but also to an entire family.

This is a thank-you letter not only to those who've supported me in the project of learning to parent, but also to those who've assisted me in the project of this book. My thanks go first and foremost to Lydia Bellino. Lydia gave her wise attention to the beginning, middle, and ends of each chapter. She talked me through the ideas and the structure of every section of the book. She has been consistently generous, wise, balanced, and patient. I couldn't have written this without her.

All that I know and believe about education grows out of the extraordinary community of educators comprising the Teachers College Reading and Writing Project. A few people from this community have helped specifically with this book; Pam Allyn wrote pages of wise response to an early draft, Kathleen Tolan unpacked her childhood for me, and Kate Montgomery has been an astute coach.

Susan Forrest functions as my third hand. She has invested loving, thoughtful attention and many days of hard work into this book. She has also guided and cared for me as I wrote the book, seeing in her astute and brilliant way what it was that I needed in order to do and to be all that I can. I'm more grateful to her than she could ever know. Kathy Collins and Laurie Roddy have joined Susan in giving me the back-up support I needed in order to write this book, and I'm grateful to them all. I am also thankful to Laurie Pessah, codirector of the Teachers College Reading and Writing Project, who has helped with both the book and with leadership of the Teachers College Reading and Writing Project.

Finally, my thanks go to Sharon Broll, my editor, who gave close and courageous guidance to me as I drafted and revised the manuscript. Sharon has had to say "No" to me, to wrest stories of my children from my text, and to nudge me to imagine alternative trails of thought. She has done this difficult work with warmth, patience, and wisdom, and the book is far better because of her. I am also grateful to John Wright, my agent and advisor, and to Liz Maguire who supported this project with enthusiasm from the beginning.

L. M. C.

LIFELONG LEARNING: AN INTRODUCTION

In the fairy tale story of Rapunzel, a child is born at long last to the king and queen. To celebrate, they invite the entire village to a banquet on the day of their infant's christening. Seven good fairies come as guests of honor, and at the banquet, each bestows a gift upon the baby. One gives the gift of wisdom, another, the gift of generosity.

In my ideal version of this beloved fairy tale, the good fairies would come to every family when a child is born. And in my fairy tale world, the gifts would be given not to the newborn infant, but to the parents on their child's behalf. Each of the seven fairies would sprinkle her fairy dust on us, giving us wisdom, generosity, tenacity, laughter, initiative, imagination, and love. We parents would hold these gifts in custody, and in time, would pass them on to our children. And because we were generous, they would become generous as well.

But in real life, there is no magic wand which turns us into the parents we long to become. No job requires more intelligence, knowledge, and energy than the job of parenting. Yet most of us do not take classes or attend conferences, join study groups or receive on-site supervision in this, the most challenging job of our lives. We're on our own. Sometimes it seems more support is given to people buying Tupperware than to those of us who want to parent wisely.

When a baby is newborn, friends, family, and even strangers deluge us with moral support and advice. Everywhere we turn, people inquire about our baby's progress. "Is she teething?" they ask; and everyone has suggestions for this and every other real or

1

imagined problem. It seems as if the entire world is ready to help and support us when our children are babies. But by the time our kids have joined Little League and begun getting allowances, having friends sleep over, and carrying knapsacks to school, all this changes. The same people who asked "Is she sleeping through the night?" do not ask, "Is she practicing her piano regularly?" Or "Does she remember to bring her schoolwork home?"

Parenting the school-aged child is complicated by the fact that once a child heads off to school, he or she is now part of a split family. Kids come home saying things, thinking things, and being things that are completely alien to us. "This is *my* child?" we wonder. "Where's this stuff coming from?"

I'll never forget the evening of Miles's first day of kindergarten. After we finished dinner, he looked up and said, "Who wants a popsicle? Raise your hand." After Evan, Miles, and our niece Charlotte had dutifully raised their hands, Miles said, "Line up, girls first." I was flabbergasted. He had been to school *one day* and already he was using phrases and assuming roles that belonged to a different world.

Lydia Bellino and I have written this book because we recognize that long after the umbilical cord has fallen off and the child has been sleeping through the night, parents need support and guidance. Whereas once we needed help with diaper rashes, pacifiers, and sleep habits, now we need help educating our child's mind and character. How can we live up to the awesome responsibility of being our child's first and most important teachers?

This, then, is a book about parents as educators. We offer ways to support a child's early reading and writing endeavors, suggest methods to decipher current math expectations, and give advice on what teachers want to see in our children's book reports. But this book does *not* focus specifically on ways parents can help children with their schoolwork. Rather, our definition of education includes our children's explorations alongside a creek, the social graces they need to use when we parents have company over for dinner, and the mind-work of play.

We hope this book helps all of us keep in mind the profound impact we can have on our children as readers, writers, mathematicians, and scientists. We teach these disciplines even when we don't realize we are doing so.

Some parents will say, "It turns out my kid isn't the sort who loves reading"; or "My child has no particular interest in science"; as if the paths our children take in life are coded in their genes or are the result of random coincidence. This book shows ways in which we can co-create our children's lives as readers, writers, and players, while helping us feel less alone in this work.

Lydia and I are not child psychologists, clinicians, or therapists who want to help parents deal with all the disasters that can happen in a child's development. This is not a book about what to do when the sky falls down on us as parents. Its chapters are not titled "Unspoiling the Spoiled Child," or "Disciplining the Angry Child," or even "Reforming the Reluctant Reader." This is not a book about what to do when everything goes wrong. Rather, it is a book about trying to do things right. It's about the mistakes we have made, the lessons we have learned, and the discoveries that have surprised us as we tried to draw on what we know about education in general and literacy in particular in order to do the best for our children.

It is fitting that Lydia and I are not clinicians or child psychologists but are instead teacher-educators. At Teachers College, Columbia University, we have worked with thousands of teachers and principals throughout the world who are turning schools and classrooms into richly literate environments in which children can flourish as readers, writers, scientists, and inquirers. Now we want to share with parents the principles and techniques that inform those classrooms, and, more than that, we want to help parents consider ways they can use these principles and techniques as they build rich learning environments in their homes.

When I speak of turning homes into rich learning environments, I am not suggesting that we clear off the kitchen table and put away our child's drawings and baseball cards to bring out the worksheets and flash cards. Instead I am saying that the qualities that matter most in science and math, reading and writing—initiative, thoughtfulness, curiosity, resourcefulness, perseverance, and imagination—are best nurtured through the "everydayness" of our shared lives at home. Our children can learn to develop the curiosity and tenacity of scientists as they watch a new patio being built, or play with Legos in the bathtub.

In my town, every May and October, the Women's League sells tickets for a home tour. People from all over town buy tickets for a tour through the homes of five or six citizens. The odd thing is that before the Home Tour, the host families put the "home stuff" away. The cupboards are closed, the toys are out of sight, the tables are cleared. How I'd love to tour through other people's homes just after breakfast on a school day; to spy on how other people navigate through the congestion of several kids, each running in a different direction as they pack up their knapsacks, brush their teeth, double back for their permission slips. How I'd love to peek in during homework time, to see whether other parents supervise math and piano as I do, and to learn how they glean information about what their child's teacher has assigned. How I'd love to look through the bookcases and toy chests in these homes, to listen in on the disciplinary talks and the bedtime conversations. But in my town, the home tours are all about furniture and decorations, not homework, weekly allowances, toys, chores, traditions, and relationships.

In this book, I open *my* home to my readers. I invite you to listen in to what I say when my sons give one-word answers to my "How was school?" questions. You'll read about Evan getting out the ironing board and the iron to smooth the creases in his sloppy math paper. You'll hear the ways I prompt my children and my nieces and nephews to write with more detail, grace, and clarity. You'll learn how I react when Miles, on his homemade map, represents Connecticut and New York as larger than all the western states combined. You'll peek in on our family's policies regarding chores, homework, allowance, manners, television, Little League, spelling, pets, music lessons, and a million other things.

I open my home with some trepidation and humility. When I give keynote addresses at teachers' conferences, or lead summer institutes on the teaching of reading and of writing, I leave home. I dress up, I package myself, and I head off to speak with clarity and confidence about methods for teaching children to grow as readers and writers. But at home, everything is not neatly packaged and put together, and I do not always feel clear or confident. We forget to feed the rabbit.

My youngest son's penmanship is illegible. I'm writing about parenting and about my parenting, not because it's perfect (which it isn't) but because it's important. It doesn't make sense for me to continue to write only for teachers when the work that matters most is the teaching I try to do at home with my children.

I know that my passions, priorities, and philosophies will not always be congruent with those of my readers, and that is how it should be. There is nothing more personal than the choices we make about how to raise our children. I know, too, that the decisions I've made as a parent are affected, in ways I can't even imagine, by my circumstances. Readers who live in city apartments rather than in a rambling, rustic home such as ours may sometimes feel distant from my images of how children play and work. Although I teach as much in city classrooms as in suburban ones, I do not have a true sense of what it's like to live in city homes. I haven't tried to disguise this. And, readers who are parents of daughters will no doubt find that, despite my efforts to achieve a balance, my thinking has been skewed by the fact that my own children are both boys. I apologize in advance for this.

Finally, I'm somewhat concerned that because I've gathered together lots of ways we can be wise parents, readers may feel intimidated by the parenting I describe. No doubt I have created an image of parenting that may seem beyond your grasp—or mine. I've written chapters on how to support reading and writing, play, and chores, but I know that, in the end, we each have areas that matter most to us. Although I invite you inside my home, the truth is, I've cleaned it up a bit first. I've omitted some of the "home stuff", but not the dirty underwear. I don't talk much about the times when my parenting is hurtful, impatient, and wrong. This doesn't mean those times don't exist, but they are hard to accept, and it seemed unnecessary to publicize them. Writing this book has made me more aware of the parent I want to be, and more aware also of the ways I don't live up to my hopes.

A great Jewish philosopher was wise indeed when he said, "The decision to have a child is the decision to forever have one's heart walking around outside our bodies." For me there is no greater joy than this.

CHAPTER 1

Talk: The Foundation of Literacy

When my son Miles was three, I visited all the preschools in our town in search of the perfect one. I was particularly intrigued by a place about which I'd heard both rave reviews and critical comments. I couldn't wait to see it for myself. I arrived at the school very early that autumn morning. The classroom was almost empty, save for a cluster of little girls who sat at one table rolling and pummeling clay. The director was nowhere in sight, so I pulled my chair near the girls and listened.

One girl was drumming her fingers on the surface of what appeared to be a pond. "The wind is whooshing the waves," she said. The next girl plopped three blobs of clay onto the now-dappled surface of the pond. "The baby ducks are looking for their mom," she added. Then, in a high-pitched baby duck voice, she called, "Mommy! Mommy!"

At this point, the director of the school arrived and motioned for me to join her. Together we stood, eavesdropping as the three girls spun their tale of the lost baby ducks. "They looked in the tall grass," one child said, moving her three blobs to the pond's edge. Then she shook her head despondently and sighed. "No mother."

At this point, the director of the school pointed to the girls and stage-whispered, "This is where it all starts, you know. *This* is essential for their writing."

My heart leapt. "Yes!" I thought. "She knows, she knows, she knows." I could have hugged her. But my heart leapt too soon.

The director held up her hand, and began to move her fingers in the air as if she were kneading bread. "Yep," she said, "It all starts

7

here. We begin exercising their fingers with soft playdough, then move on to the stiffer beeswax clay, then to the really stiff clay . . . and by that time, their fingers are strong enough to work the pencil." I stared at her, aghast, silent. "Yep." She nodded with assurance. "It's all in the fingers, it's all in the fingers."

I didn't even stay the morning. And from that day on, as I traveled from one nursery school to another, I looked with a new sense of direction. Whether children were building towers with blocks, making masks with paper bags, or sculpting duck ponds with playdough, I listened to hear whether the adults who were there were celebrating the talk, the emerging stories. When children gathered for juice and crackers, I watched for signs that this was a time for teachers and children to muse over plans for the day, to share family stories, to retell favorite movie plots, to swap yarns. During recess, I checked whether the big people were bending low to listen to the little people.

In one school after another, I paid particular attention to the teachers' attitudes toward children's talk. I did this because yes, indeed, that duck story was foundational to those girls' growth as writers, and as readers, thinkers, problem-solvers, and world builders. Had the director of that school meant what I initially thought she meant, had she truly understood that the story those girls created around their three blobs of clay was foundational to their later writing, reading, and learning, I would probably have enrolled my son in her school.

Parents spend an enormous amount of time worrying about their children's reading and writing development for they know those capabilities are at the foundation of learning. But talk is also at the foundation of a child's learning life. Through language, meaning is built. Playing with playdough can be a time to hammer, roll, smush, and pinch, and nothing more; but it can also be a time to spin stories, to elaborate and reflect on them, to live inside them.

In the end, it's not what we do that matters, it's what we do with what we do that matters. A child can pat a ball of playdough flat, and simply be squashing that ball into a pancake, or she can be inventing, exploring, hypothesizing, planning, connecting, analyzing, imagining, and deducting. For young children, the difference is in the talk.

A kindergarten teacher I admire often says, "I need my kids to talk. After all, these kids can't think with their mouths closed."

Yes, Ms. Nursery School Director. It all starts here, with those girls playing with clay, and with the rhythms and sounds of language. It all starts with those girls reenacting the age-old search for a place to call home; with them collaborating to make a story.

Oral Language in the Home: The Importance of Conversation and Shared Stories

Although I searched diligently for a nursery school that supported talk (and therefore, thought), I have always believed that, for oral language development, Dorothy from *The Wizard of Oz* was right: "There's no place like home." When our children are toddlers, most of us are aware of this. When they are first learning to talk, we support, watch over, and extend their oral language development. When my sons Miles and Evan were beginning to use identifiable words and to put these words together into phrases and sentences, I would report on their progress in phone conversations with my sisters. I noticed what the boys said and how they said it.

I even had a list of resolutions when my children were very young for supporting their talk. I remember telling myself, "You've got to resist giving him that pacifier! He doesn't need to suck anymore, and it's senseless to be clogging up his mouth, silencing his voice." I also tried to give my babies time to respond whenever I talked with them. If I took off Evan's diaper and cooed, "How does that feel?" I tried to wait, expecting him to respond with a gurgle or a chortle. Then, and only then, would I answer back. "Is that right!" I'd say, just as if he'd played his part in the conversation and I was responding to what he'd said. "Why'd you say so?" I'd inquire. Again, I tried to wait and to look expectantly at him, as if confident that my bare-bottomed, kicking infant would soon clarify or elaborate upon his initial comment. I tried, also, to accompany and chronicle whatever we did together with talk. So if we made playdough and one of my boys banged on a playdough ball, I'd say, "Bang it," and join him. "Bang it. Smush it." Then, if he picked up a now-flat pancake, I'd say, "It's flat!" and run my hand over the flatness. If he wiggled his finger through the pancake, making finger-sized holes I'd say, "You are making holes." My verbalizing whatever I thought was probably going on in my baby's mind wasn't an unusual practice. Many of us do this for babies. As the language researcher Frank Smith points out, "People see a baby and automatically start talking to it. If we don't have our own baby, we borrow someone else's. 'Hi there, Cutie!' we say."[1]

Of course, every adult in every community does *not* behave this way, providing running commentaries that chronicle the events surrounding a child. Linguistics scholar Shirley Brice Heath studied how members of different communities talk with their children. She concluded that a family's "way with words" matches (or does not match) those of their teachers', and this has a lot to do with a child's eventual success in school.[2] Children tend to do better in school if they live alongside adults who provide running commentaries of the child's experience. "So, let's get some breakfast. Here is some cereal. We'll need milk. . . ."

Once a child can talk, it's also helpful for adults to solicit these running commentaries from children. "What are you doing with those pots and pans?" the adult asks. Later, when the child is older, we can solicit retellings of the day's events. "Did you and Daddy go for a walk? Did you go to the park? What did you do at the park?" Heath points out, "These requests for running descriptions and cumulative accounts of past actions provide children in these families with endless hours of practice in all the sentence-level features necessary to provide successful narratives or recounts of experience." By giving a foundation for our child's stories, we teach them languages and structures, which underpin what they do in school. "Gradually children learn," Heath says, "to open and close stories, to give them a setting and movement of time, and occasionally, even to sum up the meaning of the story."[3]

With my sons, I wasn't conscious that I was chronicling our shared adventures or that I was speaking in the short sentences and exaggerated intonation that are so helpful to babies learning to talk. But I did know that whatever we did—setting the table, feeding the cat, grocery shopping, or washing our hands—was an opportunity for language development.

Interestingly, after our children learn to talk, this deliberate support for oral language development stops. Instead, we teach our children to talk quietly, to talk less, and to stay out of the way. One night, for example, we had friends over for dinner, and I asked Miles, who had recently turned nine years old, to clear the table while I chatted with the grown-ups. He was happy to clear the table but insisted on talking nonstop as he worked. He talked to himself even when none of us were listening. I interrupted him countless times to say, "Miles, Shhhhh! Do it without the talk!"

How the tables have turned! Whereas once I would have celebrated the running monologue that accompanied Miles's work, and his efforts to participate in our adult conversation, now I was essentially saying to him, "Children are to be seen and not heard."

This incident is representative of a larger pattern that takes place too often in too many of our homes. In his book, *Talk with Your Child*, Harvey Wiener reports on a U.S. Department of Education study that indicates that American mothers spend less than 30 minutes a day talking with their children; fathers spend even less. Some pollsters report that fathers spend an average of 15 minutes a day talking with their children.[4] Others have found that the average father spends less than 30 minutes *a week* talking to his children.[5] In his *The Read Aloud Handbook*, Jim Trelease points out that the average adult in this country spends 6 hours a week shopping and 30 hours a week watching the television, in contrast to daily time spent in one-to-one conversation in homes with school-age children. One-to-one conversation averaged 9.5 minutes for at-home mothers, 10.7 for working mothers, and less for fathers.[6]

> Most parents find the time to put in a full workday, take a full complement of coffee breaks, eat lunch and dinner, read the newspaper, watch the nightly newscast or ball game, do the dishes, talk on the phone for 30 minutes ... drive to the mall, and never miss that favorite prime-time show.[7]

Why then can't we also find time to talk with our children?

Part of the reason is that by the time our toddlers are of school age, we take their talk for granted. We have turned all our attention to their reading and writing, not realizing that talk is still the motor that propels their intellectual development. It is through talk that children learn to follow and tell stories, understand logical sequences, recognize causes, anticipate consequences, explore options, and consider motives. It is through talk that our children learn about barometers, mortgages, civil rights, psychotherapy, and the Roman Empire. It is through talk that our children learn that their observations, hunches, and insights are interesting and worth developing. It is through talk that our children learn about empathy, generosity, forgiveness—about walking a mile in another person's moccasins. Talk matters, and it's not happening enough in our homes.

I recently met with a group of second-grade teachers from a Long Island community. Ostensibly, we had gathered to brainstorm about ways we could encourage more parents to read to their children, but what really excited these teachers was the side topic, which focused on ways they might encourage parents to talk with their children.

"It'll be the day before vacation, and we ask a child, 'What will you be doing over vacation?' The child shrugs and says, 'I don't know. We're going on a trip somewhere.' 'Oh, where?' we ask. The child has no idea. And afterward, the child has no clue where she went. Or we ask her, 'Does your father have a job? What does he do?' And she says, 'He goes to the office.' That's all she knows about what her father does each day."

Of course, it's entirely possible that a child in such a situation is simply not telling her teacher what she knows, that she is responding to the teacher with the same lack of detail she gives her parents when they ask, "How was school?" But these second-grade teachers are convinced that the problem is that parents aren't talking over trip plans with their children, showing them maps of their journeys, or sharing tales of their days on the job. The media is full of stories of "Johnny who can't read," but perhaps the problem is more basic than that.

And if *we're* not talking with our children, then no one is, because study after study has shown that schools do not support our children's oral language development. Researcher Gordon Wells monitored closely the talk 20 children from a wide range of socio-economic backgrounds engaged in at home and school. He found that even children from the most "linguistically deprived" homes still got far more support at home for language development than in school. Wells writes, "Not only do children speak less with an adult at school. In those conversations they do have, they get fewer turns, express a narrower range of meanings, and in general, use gram-matically less complex utterances. They also ask fewer questions, make fewer requests, and initiate a much smaller proportion of conversations. . . . At school children are reduced . . . to the more passive role of respondent, trying to answer the teacher's many questions and carrying out his or her many requests."[8]

Clearly, then, we need to value the talking we do with our children in our homes and to create more opportunities for conversation.

Establishing Rituals for Conversation within Our Families

Later in this book, I'll talk about establishing rituals for reading within our homes. I'll argue that if we want our children to read a lot, it's wise to create predictable opportunities for reading within each day. The same is true for talk. If we want to be sure that we engage in extended conversations with our children, then it's wise to build rituals for talk into our shared lives.

I know of a man who takes his granddaughter out for ice cream every Sunday afternoon, just to have time to talk with her. I know a family that takes a Sunday morning walk together each week; it's their time to reconnect with each other and the world. When my eight brothers and sisters and I convene each summer at our family cabin, we bring the year's family photographs with us, and we sit side by side for many evenings, assembling albums and lives.

For some families, conversations center around mealtimes. I know that I'm delinquent in this aspect of life. My husband, John, is a psychotherapist and sees his patients until late in the evenings. During the week, then, it's usually just Miles, Evan, and I who have supper together—and I'm on a perpetual diet. All too often, I set the table for the boys only, and spend my time at the stove or the sink, nibbling out of the frying pan. I know enough to give the boys a balanced meal, but I forget that Miles and Evan need a different kind of nourishment as well. They need me to sit at the table with them, to use shared meals as times to retell moments of the day, to reenact and critique and plan and imagine.

In the Foreword to the book, *Awakening Your Child's Natural Genius* Shari Lewis writes, "A couple of years ago, there was a study to determine what caused children to get high scores on the SATs (Scholastic Aptitude Tests). I.Q., social circumstances, and economic states all seemed less important than another subtler factor. Youngsters who got the highest SAT scores all *regularly* had dinner with their parents."[9]

Of course, just sitting at the table to share a family dinner in no way guarantees shared conversation. Frequently, the rule, unspoken or not, is that adults talk only to each other. Children are expected to carry on their own separate conversation or to just be quiet. It makes all the difference in the world if children and parents expect that conversations will be shared. This means when I talk with my husband about my work at Teachers College, one of my sons will inevitably interrupt with questions. "What do you mean that the cost of benefits is going up? What are benefits?"

Miles's and Evan's incessant questions and their efforts to contribute solutions, can sometimes overwhelm me and others. When friends join our family for dinner or for a car ride, I know it's often surprising to them that Miles and Evan listen keenly to whatever we talk about. I admit, sometimes I find myself longing for my kids to be seen and not heard. But I know that John and I do a lot of educating simply by assuming that kids have the same right to participate in conversations as we adults.

Car rides, like mealtimes, can be perfect opportunities for conversations. The best are the long ones that go deep into the night. When my husband drove the boys on an 18-hour trip to our summer cabin in Traverse City, Michigan, I bought "trip toys" to punctuate their time; but more important, I set them up for long talks: "Miles," I said as they climbed into the car, "Have Dad tell you stories about when he was a kid. Ask him to tell you about his adventures taking the subway to school."

Earlier I had said to John, "Would you ask Evan to tell you his concerns about his friends at school? I know he's trying to figure out what to do now that Gregg has moved out of town."

In my family, we established traditions for talking on long drives. Whenever we drove home from our summer vacation in Traverse City, as soon as the sound of the wheels on the road changed, when we turned off the sandy dirt roads and onto the smooth pavement, our talk would change. "So what'd you like best?" my father would ask.

For the first hour or so of the long car ride, we'd spin stories about our shared memories. Of course everyone in the car had been present during most of the summer's highlights, but we still regaled each other with detailed descriptions of my sister Ellen's dramatic belly flop, the scary motorboat ride in the storm, the Scrabble tournament, the great kick-the-can game in the meadow. On one such family drive, my father, recalling a family wedding at the summer cabin, said, "What I loved most was the look on people's faces when they rounded the bend to the house and saw that elegant brunch all spread out. They were *astonished*, weren't they?" It's not an accident that my father selected a particular instant to extol. It's the tradition. One of us takes the tiniest moment and holds it in our hands, recalling it in all its particulars. Then the next person adds more details or more reactions.

I grew up listening to my parents swap stories at the end of each day. Dad would come home too late to eat supper with the rest of us, but he and my mother would review the day, recalling the little moments. John and I try to engage in a similar sort of talk when we go to each child's bedroom to say a final goodnight. This is long after the *first* goodnight, after the pajamas, and teeth-brushing, and storytime. The ostensible purpose for this final visit is to turn off the lights, but it often gives us a moment for one-to-one intimate talk.

I often lie beside Evan for a few minutes and we talk in a secret sort of way. It's private; it's intimate. It's no longer so easy with Miles, who lately has established a big-boy distance, compounded by the fact that he sleeps on a top bunk bed and is always lost in a book.

Perhaps bedtime is no longer the right moment for this sort of talk with him. Still, my resolution as I write this is to work hard to find a ritual time for intimate conversations with Miles.

Shared Stories: Education of the Heart

When we talk over a vacation or the events of a day, we're not only supporting our child's language development, we're also demonstrating ways of responding to life. If our child says, "Robert is always tattling on me for things I didn't do!" our response should be carefully thought out. If we say, "Robert is wrong! Your teacher shouldn't let him do that! She's got to stop Robert," then our child can and will be all the more entrenched and vocal in his efforts to blame everyone but himself. "It's Robert's fault," our child will think, or "It's the teacher's fault." If we later hear from our child's teacher that he seems insolent even toward the teacher, we may not realize that our responses to our child's stories will have profoundly influenced his responses to the people and events of his day.

What a difference it makes when we acknowledge that every step we take along the way, every sentence we utter, every reaction we have, is part of the education we give our child. What a lesson we would have given had we said to our child, "You often blame Robert as if *he's* the only one who does things wrong. But I bet that if Robert tattles on you, there is some reason. Perhaps there's *something* you're doing. Instead of always thinking about what *Robert* does wrong, maybe you need to think about the part you play in this."

When we encourage our children to retell a day's events, we help motivate them to rethink those events and their responses to those events. What extraordinary teaching moments these interactions can be!

The stories that are told and retold in families everywhere also provide teaching opportunities; they are theories, lessons, parables. The great language educator, Margaret Meek, writes of the power of these stories. "Stories . . . create our first memories. . . . From the stories we hear as children we inherit the ways we talk about how we feel, the values which we hold to be important, and what we regard as the truth."[10]

Very often in my family the stories we share are those in which we've tackled adversity with great spirit. We're apt to swap fond memories about a cousin who dove overboard from a boat with all her clothes on in order to save the day, or about the youngsters who ran out of gas in the motorboat and had to row the length of the lake, but did so singing through the night.

Recently I took my youngest son out to dinner and found, upon arriving at the restaurant, that I'd left my shoes at home! "Oh, well," I consoled Evan. "We can eat at the McDonald's drive-through." Evan was aghast at the idea that our dinner date would be at McDonald's, so in the end, I walked through the parking lot in stocking feet and held my head high as Evan and I seated ourselves in a booth at a Chinese restaurant. We chose Chinese because we believed (mistakenly) that people don't wear shoes indoors in China. Throughout the evening, Evan and I consoled ourselves by imagining the "Trouble Story" our evening would produce.

That we share and celebrate these "Trouble Stories," as we've come to call them, has probably influenced my children as much as anything in our family. Optimism and energy, especially in the face of adversity, are defining characteristics of our clan. There isn't a relative who doesn't have a "Singing in the Rain" attitude toward life, and I have no doubt that this attitude comes from the powerful lessons taught through these family stories.

Stories are a family's way of saying "this is who we are." Stories about family heroes teach youngsters what it means to be heroic. Stories about mishaps teach youngsters that families and friends stay together through tough times. Stories about hard times teach the value of perseverance and hard work. Stories build and illustrate and recall family values. For some families, stories illustrate that no matter what, the family is always there to love a family member, even a prodigal son or daughter. In other families, stories reveal the resourcefulness of family members who have made do with very little.

When we and our children head off into our separate lives—to summer camp, to school, to jobs, to create our own families—we bring our family stories along. We are weaving the tapestry not only of who we have been but of who we will be.

Teaching the Art of Conversation
throughout Our Children's Lives

When we return home after a vacation, to reunite with those who weren't with us, we encounter a great educational opportunity. Undoubtedly, someone will ask, "How was it?" For many children it might take some prodding to get a response beyond "It was great." But a moment like this can become a wonderful opportunity to support a child's language development. Try to narrow the question for your child. Ask her what in particular she liked best, and encourage her to give examples.

You've been on the trip, too. You could have answered the question yourself. You probably even knew what your daughter had enjoyed most. But I believe that children need to be inducted into the tradition of reliving and rethinking moments of their lives. This isn't a minor detail in a child's education; it's essential.

After conducting a 10-year-long study of oral language development in the home and school, Gordon Wells concluded that there is little doubt that in accounting for differences in children's mastery of literacy, the major influence is that of the home. He said there are many ways parents foster their children's development, but that "of all the activities that were characteristic of homes (that foster literacy), it was the sharing of stories that we found to be most important." He goes on to say,

> Constructing stories in the mind—or storying, as it has been called—is one of the most fundamental means of making meaning. Whether at home or at work, in the playground or in the club, it is very largely through such impromptu exchanges of stories that each of us is inducted into our culture and comes to take on its beliefs and values as our own.[11]

So invitations to tell stories matter. Openers such as, "How was your day?" and "What'd you do?" and "What have you been up to?" and "What's the news around here?" matter. Reminiscing about a family trip matters. Of course, the journeys that most need to be shared are the daily ones, and so we ask our children, "How was school today?" I don't think there is a child anywhere who gives us satisfactory answers to that question. Parents the world over agree, "She just tells me, 'fine.' She never fills me in on the details." You'd think we'd learn. If the question, "How was your day?" doesn't yield the details we're after, obviously we need to ask a different question, or to coach our children in ways of responding. Instead what we're apt to do is to shrug, and give up on the conversation. That's not okay. It's not acceptable to give up on an effort to hear about our child's day. Children live through so much each day. They may have been feeling rebuffed or humiliated or threatened by a classmate or teacher, and we don't hear about it. They may have felt intrigued by a subject, challenged by a way of reading or writing or calculating, exhilarated by a new sense of competency, comforted by a new friendship, and we don't hear about it.

A few fleeting years from now, our children will be confronted with major decisions about drugs, alcohol, sex, and violence, and we'll be desperate to find a way to talk things over with them. The conversational bridge must be built back in kindergarten, first, and second grades. Is it possible to convince a tenth grader who for a decade kept his or her school and social life private to suddenly talk about it? I doubt it.

It's a small decision, the decision to let a child respond, "Fine," when we ask about the child's day, but what profound implications! We need to hold tenaciously to our commitment to talk over the ups and downs of our days.

My boys have tried the standard "It was okay" answer when I ask about their days. Sometimes I tell them that such a response is not an acceptable answer. " 'It was okay' tells me nothing. I'm *dying* to know what you did. What happened when you first got to the classroom? Then what?" I might say.

I doubt I help matters when I tell them it isn't acceptable to simply tell me the day was okay. Pursuing the conversation does help. I also rely on a few strategies to nudge my children into telling stories of their days. Journalists often say, "The more you know, the more you can learn," and for me this holds true. I try to visit my children's classrooms often, and even if my visit is just a tour of whatever is new, I always glean a sense of what's been going on in the room. I use what I know to help me learn more. If I know that Summer and Dillon have been working on a dramatic reading of a poem, then I can ask about that. If I know that recently one of the class fish was found dead on the floor, I can ask about that. If I know that the teacher always reads aloud to her students, I can ask, "What did Mrs. Grimes read to you today?" Then, if Evan says, "Nothing," I can say, "I guess it *feels* like she read nothing, Evan, but I'm pretty sure she reads aloud every single day. Why do you think it *feels like* she didn't read today?" It's often easier for our children to respond to particular questions than to summarize the day's events. It's easier for them to tell us who they played with at recess, what they ate for lunch, what happened in art class, and whether Robert got into trouble, than to tell us what happened in school.

Of course, sometimes our questions will feel like an inquisition, at which point, the more we question, the more our child draws into a shell. When this happens, John and I try to remind each other that we probably need to listen more to the little tidbits our boys *do* reveal, and try to value and extend these.

I learned the value of such everyday, ordinary, little bits of news when I was a child. Every Sunday morning at church there was an awkward, painful moment called "sharing of concerns." The minister would stand informally in front of the congregation and ask, "So, what's been going on?"

Silence. We'd stir in our pews. More silence. Finally, one person might stand and tell about a congregation member who'd been born or died. The minister would nod. "He will be in our prayers," he'd say. Then, looking out at us, he'd ask, "So, what else?" Using his most chatty, informal tone, he'd add, "What's up in your lives?"

Silence. Then we'd hear of another birth, death, or of a fiftieth wedding anniversary and there would be more silence.

My mother decided that what the congregation needed was for people to stand and talk about everyday news. She figured the awkward silence was partly the result of people believing that only big topics were worthy of being discussed. She offered my brothers, sisters, and me $10 each if we'd stand and say "I'd like to say I'm concerned about the Buffalo Bills football game this afternoon. I hope they play well despite the awful cold," or to say "I'm concerned about the new hours for the town library. It feels sad not to have the library open on Tuesdays after school anymore."

"*Mum,*" we'd plead, blushing and squirming at her prods. "You can't say that stuff in *church*." But $10 was a powerful lure, and we did speak up about everyday concerns; and soon the tone of that Sunday morning interlude changed. Having conversations about seemingly little things is no small accomplishment.

I try, therefore, to be interested in the particulars of my sons' lives, because hidden behind the details of their day are all the important issues of their lives.

For example, I've learned to relish my sons' stories about recess, for they always reveal so much about their social network and values. "Last week the third graders made fun of me," Evan recently reported. "It was Tuesday, my grade's pick-up-trash day, so I was picking up the trash and they called me a Barbie. When I picked up a cigarette case they said, 'Ohh! Is that your makeup kit?' and when I found a wire they said, 'Is that a hairpin for your Barbie hair?' "

I asked Evan what he did when they taunted him. "Oh!" he said, positively glowing with delight. "I got Bri' and all the other first graders, about 15 of us, and we circled the big kids and I said, 'Here are some other weenies for you to pick on!' " Then Evan thought for a bit and added: "My class is like that, because we're a *community*." It was clear from his tone that he and his classmates had talked often about the importance of being a community. The term is not his own, but it has become very important to Evan. "We help each other during recess so we don't have to go tell the teacher. Because I hate it when the third graders have to come to our classroom and say 'I'm sorry' while their teacher watches. That's like a failure."

But our talk doesn't always proceed like that. Sometimes I ask a question and my children seem to physically recoil from the question and from me. When my kids withdraw from my questions, they usually have a good reason for doing so. Without realizing it, although I have acted as if I'm just chatting aimlessly, I may actually have been setting a trap beneath my question. "Who'd you sit with at lunch?" I ask Miles. Miles knows full well that my unspoken question is, "Are you *still* sitting with only the boys?" I don't like that Miles's third grade has begun to divide itself along gender lines, and

I somehow expect my son to challenge the unspoken morés of his peer group. Because Miles knows the motive behind my question, he responds with a sullen "I don't remember."

My children are more likely to tell me about their day when they know I'll be listening openly, which makes them want to talk to me. I have tried to be influenced by the wise ideas of Adele Faber and Elaine Mazlish, authors of *How to Talk So Kids Can Learn*. Their book helped me realize that if we want our children to talk to us, we need to accept what they say and to listen for what they are feeling. More than this, their book helped me realize when I wasn't doing this. The following illustrates how these ideas might alter a conversation with Miles.

THE OLD WAY . . .	THE NEW WAY . . .
MILES: I had a boring day	MILES: I had a boring day
ME: What do you mean, 'Your day was boring!' That couldn't be. What was interesting about it? Surely *something* was interesting.	ME: It felt like a really boring day? What was going on today?
MILES: We didn't really do much today. Only gym and art.	MILES: We didn't really do much today. Only gym and art.
ME: You did more than gym and art! What else did you do?	ME: Were *they* interesting?
MILES: I don't know.	MILES: They were just regular.
ME: Miles, if you'd paid attention, you wouldn't be saying this.	ME: It sounds like the whole day felt empty for you? Why do you suppose it was that way?

I try to put the feelings Miles and Evan imply into tentative words, or to acknowledge them with nods, with comments such as "wow." This is easy to do when I accept their feelings and not at all easy to do when I want my sons to feel differently than they do. For myself, the best way to work out a feeling is to have the chance to talk my way through it, and the only way I can give our kids that support is to allow them to voice what they are thinking and feeling, and to help them feel heard and understood.

Teaching Children to Listen

As parents, we might go to great lengths to lure our children to talk to us, but chances are we spend less time encouraging them to listen to others and participate in group discussions.

John and I each travel separately a lot, often returning home late at night after the kids are in bed. Typically, after I've been gone for a few days, the first morning of my return the kids will greet me with little more than "Hello, what's for breakfast?" So I've begun coaching them in the art of conversation. "Evan," I'll say, "I've been away! I'm so surprised you're not asking how my trip was."

If John is away and the phone rings, before Miles or Evan picks up the receiver, I might say, "If it's Dad, find out what he's been doing on his trip." If John will be coming home late at night, I'm apt to remind the boys as I tuck them into bed, "Your dad will be home in the morning. Won't it be great fun to hear all about his adventures! Ask him to tell the stories when you wake up."

If I've been away, and the boys *do* remember to ask about my trip, I remark on their thoughtfulness by saying, "Thanks for asking!" and then regale them with stories about my journey.

I also now coach my sons in the art of participating in discussions. Previously I believed this was best learned at school; after all, teachers are in the ideal position to help our children become constructive members of small discussion groups. Unfortunately, not enough teachers support small group discussions. In too many instances, what is called a discussion is the teacher asking questions and calling on children for answers. Then the teacher rephrases, corrects, or evaluates what a child says before asking a new question and calling on a new respondent. In these so-called discussions, children learn very little about what it means to "talk things over" with a group of people, and this can become a real disadvantage. Few capabilities are more necessary in life—in families, marriages, friendships, projects, work—than being able to participate well in a group discussion.

It's a marvelous thing, then, when families have discussions. To that end, I've begun bringing issues that I'm mulling over to the weekend dinner table, and trying to think aloud with my kids as well as my husband. The issue may be sparked by an article in the newspaper, a concern at work, or an earlier conversation.

When we're talking together, I might call attention to "the conversational moves" that occur. I suspect many parents are vigilant that their children not interrupt others, and surely this is worth attending to. But being a good conversational partner entails a lot more than not interrupting. For example, if John asks me to explain why I have a certain opinion or to give an example, I might say to Miles and Evan, "It's so nice when someone asks you to say more, isn't it? Dad's question is getting me to *think* more."

It's also important that children learn to listen not just out of politeness, not just because they are waiting for their turn, but that they listen, hoping their minds will be changed by what the other person has said. This is an important concept. So often, even in an adult conversation, it's clear that listeners are simply clasping their pre-made ideas close to their chests, enduring the comments others make while they wait their turn to release their ideas.

The mark of a good conversation is when our minds are awake, and we are *thinking with* the other person. Thus I try to highlight those discussions in which another person's ideas have changed my ideas. I want my sons to realize that a conversation is not a match in which the goal is to defend one's original idea; the goal is to gain new insight, to be surprised, to change one's mind. I'll say: "You're giving me a new idea! You've got me thinking. Hmmm . . . I'm beginning to see things differently." Then I'll add: "Don't you adore it when you get into a great talk and your mind gets totally changed?!"

Of course, my sons (like people the world over) will often say non sequiturs. The conversation will be on one thing, and they interject with a remark from left field. Invariably, we adults tend to think,

"Now where did that come from?" but essentially overlook the detour. I don't think this is wise. It's better to confront the sidetrack: "How does that fit with what I was saying?" then suggest it be saved for *after* the topic at hand has been closed.

Developing Social Graces in Children

When I was a child, my parents deliberately instructed me and my siblings in what they referred to as "social graces." Some might interpret this to mean we were taught to wait our turn, to say please and thank you; and my parents did the usual coaching in these courtesies, but in addition, they taught us to be good conversationalists. I only recently learned that this was a conscious goal of theirs. When I told my parents I was writing a chapter on talk, my father said, "Tell your readers to be sure to include kids in their adult parties."

As I recall, the nine of us were always present for the early hours of my parents' parties. We all usually had a job to do. Some of us would join my parents to greet guests. Our job would be to say, "Can I take your coat? I'll put it upstairs in the bedroom at the top of the stairs." Others had responsibility for passing the cheese and crackers, or for clearing away the used glasses.

My father tells me this was all deliberate. "If you give children roles to play, it helps them feel at home, and it gives the adults an opportunity to draw them into the conversation." Meanwhile, we were being coached in the importance of looking into a person's eyes while speaking with that person. Now I give my sons the same coaching.

I also encourage my boys to demonstrate an interest in other people's lives. I nurture this by telling them intriguing bits of information and wonderful stories about people they know, and prompt them to ask questions. At a family wedding, I told Miles and Evan intriguing details about two of the older relatives they were greeting. "Did you know Aunt Lucy and Uncle Bill went hiking through Scotland recently," I whispered to Miles. "Why don't you ask them about their trip?"

Then I watched from a distance as Miles approached his relatives. "Well, hello there, Miles," Aunt Lucy said. "Hi!" Miles answered. Then, without missing a beat, he said, "I hear you've been traveling through Scotland! How was your trip?" Aunt Lucy and Uncle Bill were clearly taken aback by Miles's enthusiastic interest, and they responded with fabulous tales of their adventures. Soon, three or four of the younger cousins were engaged in the conversation, listening with open-eyed wonder to their stories.

Just as we coach our kids to say, "Thank you," we can coach them to take an interest in the people around them. When someone visited our home from Oregon, I engaged the kids' interest in Oregon by showing them on a map where the state is and telling them a little about it. And when we traveled with a colleague who is a Mormon, I told my sons enough about the religion so that they were brimming with questions.

I try to help my children to be interested in their friends' lives too, not just in the lives of adults. Take again the example of coming home from a summer vacation. Imagine that your daughter's friend Lee calls. They talk for a few minutes and then hang up. "So what's Lee been doing with her summer?" you ask. "I don't know," your daughter answers. "You didn't ask her?! How surprising! I would think you'd be wondering," you might say. "Did you tell her about our vacation?"

My mother says she decided to marry Dad because *his father* was, in her eyes, a great man. And the great thing about Grandfather, apparently, was that he was interested in everyone. If Grandfather went on a train ride for example, he'd always say to the people who met his train, "Do you want to know who I met on the trip?" Then he'd tell his family about the butcher, the baker, and the candlestick maker he had met. Today, my sons and I try to travel through our lives with a similar receptivity to the stories and lives of those around us.

Improving Children's Oral Language

Frequently, I see parents deliberately trying not only to open channels of communication with their children, but to improve their child's oral language skills. At the park, I hear a mother say to her three-year-old, "Point to something green!" After praising his response, she prompts, "Point to something purple!"

We've all heard variations of this. The father says to his son, "What time is it?" The little boy looks for a long time at his watch and then says, with some tentativeness, "Two-thirty?" "Good job," the father says.

A mother points to her child's toy screwdriver and asks, "What tool is this?" The child fills in the blank with the correct answer, so the mother points to the wrench. "And this?"

Always, I want to intervene and say, "Stop!" What kind of talk is this? Talk shouldn't be used merely to display knowledge and win approval, to fill in blanks on an oral worksheet.

What's really sad is that this kind of talk is prevalent in classrooms. Teachers ask an average of 1 question every 11 seconds. It's not unusual for a teacher to speak like this: "Today, class, we're going to study what, class?" The class chimes in the correct answer, "Haikus." "Good; haikus." (The teacher begins to write on the board.) "How do you spell haikus, class? And what country originated the haiku? Japan, good. How do you spell Japan? That's right. And what book did we recently read on Japan?"

When talk is nothing more than spoken fill-in-the-blank questions, the pattern is: question, response, evaluation. When the boy's father responded by saying "Good job" to the child reporting the time as two-thirty, the interaction is revealed as a test, not a conversation.

This isn't how people talk in the course of a day. Although many researchers argue that when parents ask "known-answer questions" of their children, it prepares them for the rapid-fire short-answer questions many teachers ask in schools, I resist this kind of talk among my family members. Fill-in-the-blank questions teach children little about actual conversation. The child who plugs in a missing word isn't initiating conversation, growing ideas, analyzing a thought, elaborating on a plan, or weighing alternatives. The child isn't even speaking in sentences! The way to lift the level of our children's oral language skill is to listen to what they say and to respond thoughtfully.

Of course, the parent who holds up a wrench and asks, "What is this called?" probably is working on developing her child's vocabulary. And this is a reasonable goal, but there are far better ways to do this. First, we enrich our children's vocabulary by enriching their lives. If a child plays with plastic horses and we talk extensively with her about horse riding, the child can gain a host of new words for her vocabulary. If we are knowledgeable about horses and don't hesitate to include horse terminology, our child will soon be understanding and using words such as girth and stirrups, withers and forelock. Similarly, if our child cooks with us and we don't "dummy down" the language we use to accompany our efforts, he may come away from the experience using words like poaching, pureeing, grating, and the like.

We don't need to drill children on vocabulary words for them to learn new words. The language researcher, Frank Smith, has found that children know an average of 20,000 words by the time they get to school, which means they've learned new words at the rate of at least 20 a day.[12] How do they learn these words? Not from 20,000 flash cards. By the time our children are sixteen, they know at least 50,000 words, not from 50,000 trips to the dictionary or 50,000 word games. Children learn vocabulary from talking, reading, writing, and from playing with words.

Margaret Meek points out that one of the distinguishing features of habitual readers and writers is their curiosity about language. "They enjoy it. They use it with feeling and flair when they talk, tell jokes, invent word games, and do crossword puzzles. They are, in a sense, in control of language, as a skilled player manages a football, a versatile violinist interprets a score, or a racing driver handles a car."[13]

Ideally, children begin at a very young age to relish language play. From nursery rhymes, fairy tales, and familiar stories children discover wonderful, fun ways to say things. They stomp upstairs to bed saying, "Fee fi fo fum. I don't wanna go to my room!" They build bridges over the bathtub and make their rubber duck trip trap, trip trap across. "Don't eat me, eat my brother!" they cry in delight, over and over until onlooking adults smile, sure there must be some deep psychological significance to the refrain.

Our children play with rhyme, making silly trains of sound-alike words. "Oh no, it's time to go . . . so fee fi foe . . . and if you show, that you don't want to go. . . ." Before long, the sentence makes no sense, but the sound of the nonsense is rich.

Jokes, too, are important. "How many knees do you have?" my boys ask me over and over. "Two!" I answer, on cue, and they fall down laughing hysterically. "No!" they call out. "You have four." Pointing to their knees, they say, "One knee, two knees" and then, with tremendous delight, they move on to the joke's climax. "Wee-nie! Hi-nee!"

Adults may groan over the "silly humor," but we also delight in our children's explorations of language. We delight, too, in their pleasure over books such as the *Amelia Bedelia* books. What fun it is to watch Amelia dust the room by sprinkling dust everywhere; and to see her dress the turkey in a sweater and shoes. Readers of the *Amelia* books soon begin to play similar language games. An Evan story goes like this: "The lady said, 'I'm Hungary. I want some Turkey with Chile on top.' " True, it can be tiring to live through this silly joke phase, but this is the ultimate in language education. It is this sort of language play—not question-answer vocabulary drills—that enriches our children's oral language development.

It's equally helpful to explore with our children the way words relate to each other based on prefixes or root words. For example, Miles, Evan, and I collected words with the prefix "sub" to determine whether they all mean "below." This began with submarine. Then we were off and running with subfreezing temperatures, submerging boats in the water, subservient, subterranean. Finally, the question: "Are substitute teachers below regular teachers?"

We've had equally interesting discussions of root words. With one word—say, marine—my sons have access to so many others. On our refrigerator they have written a list of marine words. So far the list contains: marine biology, the Maritime Center, the Ancient Mariner, submarine, and marinating.

The single most effective way to support children's vocabulary is to support their reading. When Miles says words phonetically— such as when he spoke of ass-in-ating Julius Caesar (Ses-er) and of for-i-gn leg-e-ons—I take quiet pleasure in his mispronunciations because they reveal that he is saying words as he sees them in print. When I correct his pronunciation, I do so gently, never critically, because any child who feels so at home with language that he takes on the words he finds in books deserves praise, not criticism.

Evan's efforts with vocabulary at this stage, of course, are less rooted in reading, but no less idiosyncratic and charming. Both my sons use lots of words incorrectly and both of them do so fearlessly. The payoff will be that they can easily assimilate the complexities of our language.

It's a mistake to think that the only way to improve children's oral language abilities is by extending vocabulary. College entrance examinations put heavy emphasis on vocabulary simply because it is an easily measured factor that goes hand in hand with other less easily measured components, which combined, matter very much. The goal, then, should be not a strong vocabulary but a strong engagement with the world. Children who talk and listen easily are also children who know how to make insights out of observations, to make meaning out of their lives. These are children who can think more confidently about language, about their ideas, and about the ideas of others. The best way to strengthen children's learning is to let children live like richly literate people the world over.

CHAPTER 2

Reading Aloud: An Apprenticeship in the Literate Life

We're supposed to read to our kids. We're supposed to give them baths, to brush their teeth and we're supposed to read to them. That's no secret. It's educational. If we read aloud to our kids, we'll turn them into good readers. Somehow.

The U.S. Department of Education Commission on Reading, after evaluating 10,000 research findings, issued a report, *Becoming a Nation of Readers* (1985), which states that "the single most important activity for building the knowledge required for eventual success is *reading aloud* to children."[1]

The study also found "conclusive evidence" supporting reading aloud not only in the home but in the classroom. Furthermore, it claimed that *it is necessary for adults to read aloud to children not just when children can't yet read on their own, but throughout all the grades.*[2]

In his best-selling *The Read-Aloud Handbook*, Jim Trelease discussed these findings, then went farther. He summarized many of the research projects, including Delores Durkin's famous study of children who read early.[3] To no one's surprise, all of the early readers in her study turned out to be children who had been read to frequently. So it's official. Reading aloud is educational.

Reading Aloud for Educational Payoffs

Okay, so we know it's essential to read aloud to our children. But this raises other questions: "Are we reading aloud in a way that will reap

31

those educational payoffs?" As we read about Mike Mulligan and his steam shovel for the tenth time it's sometimes hard to trust that this will have a lot of educational payoffs. And we wonder how valuable it is to be reading aloud when our kids are fiddling with their hair or their teddy bears. Furthermore, many of us can't help but believe that for our reading to add up to something, we better make sure that our kids are remembering the story and learning the new vocabulary words. Finally, we feel sure that once our kids can read for themselves, it's better for *them* to read to us.

These concerns are understandable and common, but they also get us into an enormous amount of trouble. For example, just before I began this chapter, I asked Lydia Bellino, the contributing author to this book, "What's the one thing you most want to say to the parents in your school about reading aloud?" Her answer was not what I expected, which was "Tell them to do it." Instead Lydia said, "Tell them to stop making it instructional. Tell them to stop acting like teachers."

Reading aloud to our kids will have educational payoffs only if we stop worrying about those payoffs. We must stop pointing at and calling attention to each word as we read it, stop nudging our kids to read parts of the book themselves, stop instructing them on vocabulary words, stop checking that the story means the same to them as it does to us. In short, we must stop grilling them with little questions. Instead, we need to follow author Jane Yolen's advice and "fall through the words to the story."

When I read aloud to my children, my goal is not to teach them to recognize high-frequency words such as *the* and *are*, or to show them uses of the *ch* blend. I don't want to be sure they can match the title of E. B. White's *Charlotte's Web* with the characters Charlotte, Wilbur, Fern, and Mr. Avery. When I read aloud, my goal is to snuggle around the warm glow of a story. I want us to be awed by Charlotte's loyalty to her friend Wilbur, to cheer her ingenuity and wisdom in making the web that saved the pig's life; I want us to weep together when we learn of Charlotte's noble sacrifice. In *The Sign of the Beaver*, by Elizabeth G. Speare, I want us to face the hard, lonely winter together, and to worry and tromp through the deep snow with homemade bow and arrows together; to stand together, feeling small, under the vastness of the Milky Way.

I read the best of children's literature to my sons because I want them to grow up with these stories as part of the fabric of who we are. I want, in my family, to create a culture which counters that of television's. I do not want my sons' only heroes to be those portrayed on television—the tough, slick, cool guys holding drinks and cigarettes, who break laws and kill people, then swagger away. I want their heroes to include the wise and loving spider Charlotte, spinning her web to save the life of Wilbur; and Mary and Colin from *The Secret Garden* by Frances Hodgson Burnett, taming the wild animals, the rose bushes, and each other in their "secret garden."

Reading to Encourage Children to Want to Read

If there is a literacy crisis in this country, it doesn't revolve around whether children *can* read, but rather whether they *choose* to read. A U.S. Department of Education longitudinal study of almost 25,000 eighth graders found that students watched television an average 21.2 hours a week, but spent a mere 1.9 hours a week, outside school but including homework, reading.[4] And when literate fifth graders were monitored to determine how they spent their free time, 90 percent devoted less than 1 percent of their time to reading; in contrast, they spent 33 percent of their time watching television.[5]

A major purpose for reading aloud is to share and nurture a love of reading, to help our three-, four-, and five-year-olds to love reading, and to encourage our nine-, ten- and eleven-year-olds to continue to love reading. Many studies have shown that the home is the single most important factor in a child's literacy, and that being read aloud to by a parent is the characteristic most strongly associated with eventual reading ability.

Nevertheless, when my firstborn reached the reading age of six, I found it difficult to remember and to trust that I was doing something crucial when I read aloud to him. I worried about Miles's independent engagement with those little black marks on the page. "Why doesn't he love to read on his own?" I asked myself, trying to quell the frantic feeling in my stomach. "Haven't I done everything right? How can it be that I have to *lure* him to print with cookies and hugs?" It was hard, at the time, to put much trust in the fact that Miles liked *me* to read to *him*. He would lie by my side for hours listening to almost anything, but it was another matter altogether to get him to point to words, calling out what they said. I had to cajole him to read on his own. When left to his own devices, Miles would avoid reading the primer books in favor of looking at comic books or big, fat nonfiction texts on castles and submarines. With these, he'd fantasize, creating his own scenarios to accompany the books' illustrations, or worlds that were not unlike those he created to accompany his play with block and Lego structures.

Now in the third grade, Miles is the kind of child who carries books with him to the soccer game and the grocery store. While I do the shopping, Miles sits near the checkout counter reading. He keeps a stack of books beside his bed, and transfers three or four between home and school each day. He is a good reader because he reads a lot. "My hobby is reading," he says. Now I know I was nuts to worry.

Looking back, it is clear to me that Miles is the reader he is today not because of the time we spent with his finger on "Big fish. Big, big fish." Miles is an avid reader because of the times we traveled through C. S. Lewis's "wardrobe" together. Sitting over a shared book, we've pushed our way past coats and felt the rush of cold air and wet snowflakes on our faces.

Miles's experience is not unusual. Teachers throughout the world are aware that for many kids, learning to read begins as a slow, somewhat difficult process, and then suddenly children become engrossed in big fat books on their own. But there are also children for whom the "zoom!" never happens. For them, reading continues to be a ponderous, difficult process. What separates one group of children from the next? Being taught that books can take them on journeys; making them see more, feel more, live more. The love of reading and the ability to lose oneself in another world are gifts we give our children when we read aloud to them. In the end, nothing matters more than helping our children compose lives in which reading matters.

Because helping children fall in love with books is one of the biggest reasons for reading aloud, it's crucial that reading times be comfortable, intimate, warm occasions. If I'm frazzled and irritable, and I have to force myself to read aloud because I feel I must do so, if I read aloud as a chore, as a way to reform or to educate my children, then that read-aloud time can be detrimental instead of beneficial. As important as reading aloud can be, it's even more important that these episodes result in a joyful, peaceful, loving experience for all. When reading aloud to children becomes an ordeal, it's best not to do it at all. Some parents will say they feel frazzled most nights, so what are they supposed to do? They need to remember that reading aloud can mean a single poem as a goodnight gesture, a promise of more to come. Or reading aloud can be a special treat on Friday nights, or holidays, or rainy Saturdays.

Parents may also want to recruit baby-sitters or other caretakers to share in the responsibility of reading aloud. When my children were very young and had full-time child care, I suggested to their nanny that she read books *she* loved to the kids. During my busiest days, I relied on her readings to substitute for my own. It was a compromise I had to make and found I could live with at the time.

When we *do* read aloud, we may want to consider how this shared reading can truly convey our love of reading. What incredible educational payoffs there are if on a snowy Saturday morning, we say, "Doesn't this day make you want to make some hot chocolate and read our book?" What lessons we teach if we tell children we can't bear to stop reading after just one chapter. "Let's stay up late until we find out whether or not the boy reaches home safely." What a gift we give our children when they overhear us talking with our grown-up friends about the read-aloud book we're reading. What a message we send if, one night, *both* parents take the kids up to bed because neither wants to miss the story.

Choosing Texts to Read Aloud

This process becomes easier once you start reading what I call "chapter books" to your children. One-night picture books require parents to select and begin a new story every night. In our house, the kids would argue over which book to read and we'd end up having to negotiate with them before we finally settled down to read. Sometimes the picture books were too long for one night's reading and yet too short to be spread between several nights, and other times they were so short that Miles and Evan clamored for a second read-aloud.

All that changed, however, when we began to read chapter books. John and I found it easier to get ourselves involved as well as the kids when we read aloud the best, most intoxicating chapter books we could find. Of course, chapter books will not necessarily fit every family's tastes. The parent who loves reading poetry aloud should by all means read poetry. Or, if a father prefers to read picture books aloud, then that's what he should do. For John and me, it has worked best to read chapter books. If you agree, then I suggest that you read chapter books for your sake, not just for the sake of your children. It's important to me that not only Miles and Evan get caught up in the drama of these magnificent stories, but that John and I do as well. When my voice catches as I read that the hound Little Annie is trapped in the icy rivers of *Where the Red Fern Grows* (Marjorie Rawlings), I'm teaching what matters most about reading. When peals of laughter fill the room as Evan, Miles, and I rejoice in the antics of six-year-old Fudge in Judy Blume's hysterically funny *Fudge-a-mania*, I'm teaching what matters most. "Be seen to sob over books," children's author Mem Fox advises us, and when I'm reading these books, I can't do otherwise.

With chapter books, parents of course have to answer the question, "Which books are the appropriate level for my child?" Before Evan entered first grade, we read many full-length novels together, including beloved books from my own childhood: *Stuart Little* (E. B. White), *The Wizard of Oz* (Frank Baum), *Winnie-the-Pooh* (A. A. Milne), *Charlotte's Web* (E. B. White), *The Little House in the Big Woods* (Laura Ingalls Wilder), along with many favorites of youngsters today, including *James and the Giant Peach* and *Charlie and the Chocolate Factory* (Roald Dahl), *The Hundred Dresses* (Eleanor Estes), *The Best Christmas Pageant Ever* (Barbara Robinson), *The Cricket in Times Square* (George Seldon), and every book we could find by Dick King-Smith.

When choosing books to read aloud, parents need not worry

about their child's reading level but we do need to consider our child's listening and emotional level. I read aloud *The Lion, the Witch, and the Wardrobe* (C. S. Lewis) even when my sons were reading primer books themselves. Although it is a long novel, it felt more appropriate for Evan than many picture books, for picture books are often written for the adults who read them as much as for the children who hear them. Certain chapter books are very much in tune with the priorities and perceptions of young children.

Other chapter books are, of course, emotionally inappropriate for very young children. For example, some of my own favorite children's authors—Patricia MacLachlan, Gary Paulsen, Katherine Paterson, Walter Dean Myers, Jacqueline Woodson, Lois Lowry, and Paula Fox—have written books that I regard as too emotionally advanced for Miles and Evan. So before I read chapter books to my children, I either preview them, or rely on recommendations from people I trust.

Certain people may consider it a waste to read such richly layered classics as *The Lion, the Witch, and the Wardrobe* to a six-year-old. The dramatic story is of a family of children, who while exploring an old house, come upon a closet—a wardrobe—and when they reach through the coats, they are taken to the land of Narnia. In this land, the children become royalty, are given special powers, and, together with talking trees and animals, battle between good and evil. The author was a Christian theologian, and the Narnia books are regarded by some adults as allegories for the Christ story.

For many young children, these are simply beautiful, heartwarming stories about children, animals, and trees with special powers. Is it a waste for children to hear these stories while they are still quite young? I don't think so. Of course, our children will quickly learn that good books are read, reread, and reread again. It is important for us to help children know that books like *The Lion, the Witch, and the Wardrobe* are not "used up" once a five-year-old (or a fifty-year-old!) has heard them. Then, too, our children understand more than we suspect. When High King Peter, the oldest of the four children in *The Lion, the Witch, and the Wardrobe* was taken aside by the great lion Aslan, and told that this was his last visit to Narnia because he was growing older, Miles, my oldest, sobbed, "Why *can't* I go back to

Narnia?" Miles keeps the entire Narnia series separate from his other books on the top of his bookshelf, and he has already reread the volumes on his own. Like many children, Miles loves to reread the books others have read to him. I suspect that when he returns to Narnia years from now, he will remember not only the story but also the child who believed so totally in it.

Although these books give a lot to us, they also ask something of us as readers. Chapter books require that we and our children maintain our hold on the story line over the duration of the reading period. They require that a child keeps a story alive across days or even, sometimes, weeks. For children who have only been read books that are started and finished in a single setting, this can be a challenge.

It's helpful, therefore, to begin by reading short chapter books. By this, I do not mean the early reader titles such as Cynthia Rylant's *Henry and Mudge* series, William Steig's *George and Martha* series, de Meinhardt's *Little Bear* series, or Arnold Lobel's *Frog and Toad* series. These books, and others like them were written for the fledgling reader (often in late first grade or early second grade) who wants the thrill of making his or her own way through chapter books. These books contain short sentences, simple words, and repetitive phrases, designed for early readers. When I speak of reading aloud short chapter books, then, these are not the ones I have in mind.

Instead, I recommend titles such as Ted Hughes's *The Iron Man*. This is a fast-paced, heartwarming story of a huge iron man who emerges from the sea to terrify the neighborhood. The Iron Man is befriended by a young child and in the end, becomes a hero. Composed of five short chapters, it can easily be read over the course of a week. And the prose is magnificent. Hughes writes in a way that makes better readers of all of us. Other short chapter books that are particularly effective include:

Stuart Little, by E. B. White
The Dragonling, by Florence Koller
Cat Wings and *Cat Wings Returns*, by Ursula Le Guin
Mr. Fantastic Fox and *George's Marvelous Medicine*, by Roald Dahl

The Hundred Dresses, by Eleanor Estes
Harry's Mad (and others), by Dick King-Smith
Matthew and the Sea Singer, by Jill Patton Walsh
Chocolate Fever, by Robert K. Smith
A Lion to Guard Us, by Clyde Robert Bulla
Owls in the Family, by Farley Mowat
Stone Fox, by John R. Gardiner

One caution: As brief and as spellbinding as these books are, many very young children won't be able to maintain their interest in the story unless the episodes are read on a day-to-day basis. If several days go by between episodes, then it's better to stick with shorter texts that are self-contained experiences. I find that it also helps to read more than a chapter a day, especially at the beginning of a chapter book. I read at a brisk, dramatic pace so that we can quickly get past the necessary prelude and into the drama of the story.

Balance and Breadth in Our Read-Aloud Selections

In addition to reading aloud whatever books we as parents love most, it's important for us to think about whether we can have some balance and breadth in the range of texts we choose to read aloud. If I asked a group of parents to tell me their favorite read-aloud books, my hunch is that they would tend to fall into the same trap that elementary-school teachers fall into. Without realizing what we are doing, we all tend to choose as read-alouds only the books which we love the most . . . and, especially for women, surveys show these books tend to be realistic fiction.[6] There are several problems to this.

First, we need to keep in mind that reading aloud is a way to bring alive the cadence and rhythm of a kind of text. Children need to hear "the song" of a wide range of texts. To be flexible and open-minded readers and writers, our children need to have an embodied feel for how journalism, poetry, science fiction, book reviews, manuals, and nonfiction essays all sound.

It is fabulous, therefore, if parents can find times to read poems and fairy tales, historic fiction, magazine articles, reference books, riddles, letters, and comics. When we read from these and other genre, we introduce our children not only to new texts, but also to new "kinds of texts." A balanced read-aloud diet gives our children an appreciation for the sounds and shapes and purposes of many different kinds of texts. In his memoir, *Wordstruck*, Robert MacNeil suggests that when our language storehouses are filled not only with stories, but also with jokes, proverbs, verses, and prayers, this nourishes us like a placenta, giving us an ear for bookish language, in all its diversity.[7]

It is especially important to read from a variety of texts if our children don't have the same taste in books that parents do. Sometimes the texts we love most will not be the ones our children love the most. Many people who grow up to become avid readers are lured toward reading not by a love of fiction or poetry, but by a fascination with a particular subject—baseball, computers, horses— and for these readers, nonfiction is often more enthralling than fiction. Other people love science fiction or biographies.

Too often, children aren't introduced to other genre until junior high, when they are assigned a particular book for the sole purpose of writing a book report or to pass a test. How much more fulfilling it is to meet a genre by having our parents read from many different texts. It's especially important that parents read biography, science fiction, nonfiction, fantasy, and historic fiction to boys because research suggests these are the genre boys often like most. Elementary-school teachers tend to be women and they are more apt to read realistic fiction rather than science fiction or nonfiction, for example. Perhaps this is one reason why girls tend to read more than boys, and why boys constitute 70 percent of American remedial reading classes.[8]

We also need to read from a wide range of texts because this demonstrates to our children that various texts are read differently. When Evan was fascinated by caterpillars, we went to the town library to check out several books on insects. We spent a few evenings reading aloud these books. Evan and Miles learned that, instead of reading these books from cover to cover, we turned first to the index to find relevant pages. They also learned that we did not read the books one at a time, but jumped between texts, comparing the books, noticing discrepancies, and merging the information. In order to help Miles and Evan understand and participate in this process, I often voiced what I was thinking. For example, as I was looking up caterpillars in the alphabetic index, I said: "Let's see . . . caterpillars, that's a C." Then as I ran my finger down the index, I said: "A, B; here are the C words . . . cage . . . caterpillar!" Then I read aloud "page 38." And leafing through the book, I read the page numbers out loud, too. When I arrived at the page on caterpillars, again I read the bold headings. This kind of follow-through provides children with important lessons in reading strategies.

If I was a better parent, I'd ideally read aloud a wider range of genre. Someday soon I hope I'll show Miles and Evan that I love to browse through poetry books, looking for poems I love and that I often read a favorite over and over, luxuriating in the sounds and images of it. Perhaps I'll bring the Sunday *New York Times* up to their bedrooms to read at night; or perhaps we'll read it together when my sons climb into bed with me in the morning. But meanwhile, I will continue to read aloud the texts I love most, and hope that my sons' classmates have other loves and that they bring a contagious attachment to their best-loved books into the classroom.

The Importance of Talking about Books

I once listened to my contributing author Lydia Bellino read *Little Nino's Pizzeria* by Karen Barbour, to a classroom of first graders. The children listened raptly to the story of a father who owns a popular, homey, ethnic pizza shop, where his young son Nino helps out. When some men with suits persuade the father to close the shop and open a chain restaurant, Nino isn't welcome there anymore. But in the end, the father reopens his own place, and renames it Nino's Pizzeria.

As Lydia read, she paused often to look quizzically at the children. On cue, they'd respond. When Lydia paused on a certain page, a little girl with a tiny face and huge brown eyes stood up, walked to the book, and pointed to a heart, cut into the wood of a small cradle in the far corner of the family's living room. Lydia looked at the heart, the cradle, and the sleeping baby inside and said to the child,

"There's a little baby sister! You know something, as many times as I've read this book, I've never noticed that baby sister!"

"Same with me!" another child announced. "My father only talks to my brother." "Yeah," a third child added. "And in the book he names his shop after the boy, not the girl."

"He doesn't talk to the mother either."

"Same in my family. The boys try to rule."

"He should have talked to the mother. She would've told him not to buy the fancy pizza place."

"My father's the same way. He ignores me because I'm the girl and the youngest."

At this point, the teacher, who had been sitting on the side, approached Lydia. Shaking her head in dismay, she whispered, "Don't they know it's just a story!"

Later Lydia and I recalled the teacher's words. "It's *just* a story . . ." she had said, implying, "Why get so worked up talking about *a story?*" But isn't our challenge as human beings to take the moments, the stories, of our lives and to ask, "How does this fit into the whole of who I am?" "How else could this story have been told?" "Why did the story end this way?" "How will I live my story differently?"

At home with our children, it's important to pick books up, but it's also important to put them down, to talk about the deeper meaning of the story and how it relates to life. We need to talk about how we would feel had that story happened to us. We need to talk in response to books because books can help us to talk in response to our lives. So often in life we learn to guard feelings, to put on a good face. "Reading," Kafka has said, "can be the ice ax that breaks the frozen sea within us."

For me, this is true and I know it is true for my husband as well. John's father died of Alzheimer's disease and in John's last years with his father, John would often visit and realize, during the visit, that his father didn't recognize him. John doesn't talk a lot about those visits or about his father, but when he recently read a scene from *Autumn Street* aloud to Miles and Evan, he couldn't hold back the memories or the grief. He put the book aside and, that night, the shared story was the story of John's last visit with his father, the funeral, the visits to the grave. It was a story of memories and regrets and resolutions; a story of fathers and sons trying to talk together.

The reading researcher Mortimer Adler has said, "Some people think a good book is one you can't put down, but I think a good book is one you *must* put down—to muse over, to question, to reflect on." The books that have mattered most in my life and in my family's are those we have put down often, the books that have helped us to think more, feel more, question more, dream more.

Reading aloud and talking about books is part of the education of the heart, and it is best done in families and around shared stories. The psychologist Mary Pipher points out that, ideally, "Children learn from their families what to love and value. Some parents have the impression that they shouldn't impose their values on their children. But if parents don't teach their children values, the culture will. Calvin Klein and R. J. Reynolds teach values. Good parents are what Ellen Goodman called counterculture. They counter the culture with deeper, richer values."

We need to remember that television, movies, and video games teach values as clearly as any church or school. The average child is exposed to more than 4 million ads in a lifetime. The media teach our children that they are the most important people in the universe, that pain shouldn't be tolerated, that hurts can be fixed with pills, drinks, and fancy clothes.[9] I reject these messages. I want my sons to know that people have to live with pain and sadness, and to be able to find new resources within themselves and within their families to do so. I want them to understand that living through struggles can help a person discover new insights and new strengths.

And so we read aloud, then we put books down to talk. We talk to identify with new heroes, to dream new lifelines, to weave new stories into the fabric of ourselves. We talk about books because we believe in the education of the heart, but also because talking about books helps children read more thoughtfully, to speak and write more fluently.

Teachers know the value of talking about books. The reading curriculum in most elementary-school classrooms is scheduled to allow time for large- and small-group discussions about books, and for students to write their responses to books. Once children can do the printwork of reading, teaching reading in essence becomes teaching-talking-about-reading and teaching-writing-about-reading. By helping children to have conversations about texts, we help them to have conversations in their minds' eyes as they read silently. Children who pause to say aloud "I wonder what'll happen next?" will probably, when they read alone, also pause to *think*, "I wonder what will happen next?" This sort of leaning into the story makes for active, powerful reading.

Interestingly, children who have no trouble talking about TV shows or movies or their friends' lives may find it difficult to think about and around and against and off of stories in books. It's not unusual for a teacher to pause in the midst of reading aloud to ask, "What are you thinking?" No response. Students look at their hands, the floor, their desks, anything to avoid meeting their teacher's glance. What's going on? Why do our chatty children often have such difficulty talking about books?

Part of the problem is that teachers often have a battery of specific questions and answers in mind. Recently, I listened as one teacher read the heartwarming story of two friends, *Frog and Toad* by Arnold Lobel. The open-ended question "What do you think?" was soon followed by the more pointed question, "How would you describe their friendship?" Continuing, the teacher said, "Frog and Toad are friends who are . . . what, class?" A child could rightfully supply lots of answers to that question, and one child tried, "Frog and Toad are friends who are animals." Another offered, "And they are adventuresome."

The well-intended teacher, however, was working from a guidebook on multicultural education, and the directions said that the children should respond that Frog and Toad were friends who are different. And so she dismissed the children's contributions, and forced the issue by asking, "Anyone else have an idea?" Finally she simply *told* the class the answer she wanted to hear.

It doesn't take children long to realize when teachers have one "right" answer in mind. Intimidated, many children learn to be silent during book talks. Parents can change this by really listening to the sometimes zany, idiosyncratic ideas our children have about books. Oftentimes, what our child says is quirky enough that it takes a mother or a father to understand what they're trying to say at all. My son Evan recently paused in the midst of our reading of *Shiloh* by Phyllis R. Naylor. In the story, the main character had turned on his television to one of its two channels. Evan said, "Probably one was football." I was intrigued, so I pressed for an explanation. "I was thinking which channels he'd have," Evan said. "He's not the sort to have the Disney channel or history. But his father seems like he's the kind of guy who likes to sit down to watch his football game. So I guess one channel is a football channel." How lucky our children are when they can learn to talk about books in the supportive context of the home.

Helping Children Talk and Think about Literature

Parents, too, may feel intimidated at the prospect of having literary conversations about books. We are apt to keep our noses to the print, and to simply follow the trail of the story. The problem with this is that talking about books helps people to live and to read better.

Last night, for example, while reading *The Wonderful Wizard of Oz*, by Frank Baum, to Miles and Evan, we came to this passage:

> "Tell me something about yourself, and the country you came from," said the Scarecrow, when Dorothy had finished her dinner. So she told him all about Kansas, and how gray everything was there, and how the cyclone had carried her to this queer land of Oz. The Scarecrow listened carefully and said,
>
> "I cannot understand why you should wish to leave this beautiful country and go back to the dry, gray place you call Kansas."
>
> "That is because you have no brains," answered the girl. "No matter how dreary and gray our homes are, we people of flesh and blood would rather live there than in any other country, be it ever so beautiful. There is no place like home."
>
> The scarecrow sighed.
>
> "Of course I cannot understand it," he said. "If your heads were stuffed with straw, like mine, you would probably all live in the beautiful places, and then Kansas would have no people at all. It is fortunate for Kansas that you have brains."[10]

Miles, Evan, and I read this funny, quirky, rich passage twice. Then we talked and talked and talked about it.

Evan thought that even though the Scarecrow was supposedly brainless, he seemed very smart indeed to be asking these questions (which, of course, becomes an essential point in the story, for in the end the Wizard can only help the Scarecrow celebrate the brains he already has). Miles wondered whether his cousin Matt, who had lived for years in Kansas, found it to be gray there. We wondered together whether a land could really *be* dreary and gray or that it could only *seem* dreary and gray. And then why would a place you love *seem* dreary and gray?

Of course, we could have read those paragraphs without doing any of this talking. We could have bypassed the "There's no place like home" line, which becomes such a unifying thread in the story, and we could have taken the Scarecrow's brainlessness at face value. But what a different story it would have been, if we had missed all the nuances in this section and in others like it.

Teaching reading has everything to do with helping our children read with as much alertness as possible; to think more, feel more, question more, notice more. Reading includes talking and writing about reading.

But how can we adults feel confident that our book talks will be wise? My suggestion is that we need to trust what we do as readers. If we pay close attention to our thinking as we read aloud and make this thinking public to our children, we'll be doing something valuable. If we find, as we read a particular part of a book, that it draws us in, we will want to voice this by saying, for example: "I love this part. I keep wanting to go back to it!" And in fact good readers often return to sections of a text just as people return to favorite sections of a park. When children hear us thinking in front of them, this works to prime their thoughts more efficiently than any series of questions. They join our line of thought, and soon are chiming in with what they think the author may have meant. These moments of lingering over a well-crafted section can make a world of difference when our children try to create their own effects in the stories they write or tell.

I sometimes nudge Miles and Evan to join me in wondering what will happen next in a story. After a recent read-aloud session, I shooed them off. "You guys, go brush your teeth," I said. Then, knowing full well they were watching me, I snuck back to the bed, picked up the book, muttering to myself, "I can't bear it . . . I'm just going to peek ahead for one minute . . ." Not surprisingly, the room was soon resounding with a chorus of "No fairs!" and Miles and Evan both hopped back into the bed with me. Soon we were all peeking ahead at the chapter titles and the tiny illustrations, trying to imagine what was next.

I want children to know that good readers do lean forward into a story. When a character slips a knife into his pocket, fingering the blade for a moment, we're all in suspense, aware that the knife must be significant. When a story fills me with foreboding, I voice this, too. "Something gives me a scary feeling," I'll say. If I find in the midst of reading, I'm voicing words without really attending to them, I'll pause to say, "You know something, my mouth has been saying the words, but I've lost track of the story. Can we reread for a second?"

Book talks, obviously, needn't be long detours. Many small book talks can be woven into the ongoing pace of our read-alouds. When I skipped a day of reading aloud, or when, for other reasons, I sense that my sons have lost their grip on the story, I'm apt to spend a few minutes before we launch into our reading, looking over the book, recalling what's been going on. For me, it is important to do this without turning it into a comprehension quiz. And so rather than drilling Miles and Evan with a battery of questions such as "Who are the people in the story?" or "What happened first?" I instead just scan over the pages of the book, talking aloud as I do so. "Let me see, the boys' names are Jerome and um, (I look over the page) . . . um, ah yes, Harry." As I do this, Miles and Evan often chime in, so we work together to recreate the story. Meanwhile, I'm demonstrating something that readers often do. I take the time to name what I'm doing. I may say, for example, "I like to do this before I continue reading. It helps to look over the book and recall what's going on. Do you do that in *your* reading?"

When a family reads a book together, the people in the book become family friends. It's only natural to wonder whether Laura, from the *Little House in the Big Woods*, by Laura Ingalls Wilder, would like the way your family celebrates Thanksgiving; or to speculate whether she fights with her sister Mary as much as your daughter does with her little brother.

Children will also distinguish themselves from the characters in a book, saying, "I'm *nothing* like that boy." When this happens, we can help our children empathize with the characters in their books, which will teach them to empathize with people in their lives who may seem, at first glance, to be very different from them. I want my children to understand that in books, as in life, bullies usually aren't all bad, grouchy people have gentle sides, and silent, distant people often long to feel connected.

When we join our children in talks about the characters, in musing over what might happen next, or in noticing the craft of the author, it is crucial to remember that these conversations are not detours *around* reading, but are instead, the essence of what it means to be thoughtful readers. To read well is to think well.

How Does Reading Aloud Support Emergent Readers?

When children are preemergent, emergent, or early readers (which tends to be when they are three to seven years old), it is vitally important to read not only *to* them, but *with* them. The question is only whether this happens during "bedtime storytime," if we call it that, or whether this happens on a separate occasion. In Chapters 4 and 7, I suggest ways to read with, as well as to our children.

For now I want to recommend that parents try to avoid a "figuring out the words" agenda during read-aloud time. Ideally, this is a time to go under the spell of beautiful literature; a time to weep and laugh and hope in the context of a story; to inquire and marvel and learn with a book; to chant and dance and feel with a poem.

Ideally, when our children are learning to read, we will set aside time to read to our children and also, at another time, to read *with* our children. This is a tall order for busy parents. In any case, however, I think it's best not to expect children to perform as readers during read-aloud time; otherwise these precious moments can turn into ordeals. I've heard parents quizzing their children, "What's that word?" And I've seen them pointing to words and telling children, "Sound it out," or "Break it apart." I understand the rationale for doing these things, but we reduce the potential value of reading aloud with our children when we turn these occasions into quizzes, exercises, and assignments. This doesn't mean that our reading aloud *won't* support our young children's own independent reading. Far from it!

When we read poems, picture books, and early series books aloud to preemergent and emergent readers, we are introducing them to the texts that fill the shelves in our children's classrooms and libraries. These are the books our young children are most apt to encounter when they read on their own. When our children stand in their classroom or their library scanning the crowd of books, each book filled with those unsettling little black marks, what a joy it is for them to spot a familiar book! As grown-ups, we know what it is to stand on the edge of an unfamiliar crowd, searching for a familiar face ... and to spot, suddenly, the face of a friend. The crowded room changes, and we change too. We are called out from behind our mask of indifference, called out of hiding, and become ourselves. This is the gift we give when we read picture books aloud.

When we and our children have stood together, hushed, at the edge of the clearing in Jane Yolen's forest, straining to hear the "who who who" of an owl, then our children will never again see *Owl Moon* without thinking of the intimacy and adventure it's given us. And so when we read Jane Yolen's beautiful *Owl Moon*, we take the time to feel the quiet of the forest in winter. We peer into the beautiful pictures as if we're peering into the shadows of the forest. The children beside us on the couch will spot the eyes of an animal, peering out from behind a tree, and in this way, they will enter into the world of the story. This, then, is a big reason for reading picture books aloud to emergent readers.

It makes sense that we sometimes deliberately read aloud the books which our children are most apt to find in their classrooms, the books which are most apt to come home in their backpacks, the books which their teachers regard as special favorites. If we aren't able to research these titles and authors, then it's safe to guess, in the meanwhile, that most K-2 classrooms will contain a variety of picture books by these well-regarded authors, among many others:

Frank Asch	James Marshall
Byron Barton	Bill Martin
Byrd Baylor	Else Minarik
Marc Brown	Robert Munsh
Margaret Wise Brown	Felice Numeroff
Eve Bunting	Bill Peet
Eric Carle	Patricia Polacco
Donald Carrick	Cynthia Rylant
Joy Cowley	Maurice Sendak
Donald Crews	William Steig
Tomie de Paola	James Stevenson
Mem Fox	Cynthia Voight
Paul Galdone	Bernard Waber
Eloise Greenfield	Rosemary Wells
Pat Hutchins	Vera Williams
Ezra Jack Keats	Jane Yolen
Steven Kellogg	Charlotte Zolotow

I've listed authors, rather than titles, for efficiency. Once we've read a few Charlotte Zolotow books aloud to our children, they quickly get a sense for Zolotow, and can approach her books as friends. As we pick up another Zolotow book, we will probably ask, "Will this Zolotow book, like so many of hers, be shaped like a list with a twist?" And even before we open a Bill Peet book, we begin to tap our feet to the anticipated rhythm of his verse. We and our children can construct our own knowledge of authors merely by poring over books, or we can use educators around us as resources. Most elementary-school teachers and librarians are great fans of children's authors and would love to introduce us to the authors who play important roles in our children's school lives.

Of course, I've now made a case for reading aloud every different genre and author imaginable. And there are, indeed, wise reasons for reading almost *anything* aloud to our kids. Given that life is finite,

that we can never do it all, we'll have to make choices and compro-
mises. In the end, my advice is, "Read what feels right, in the way
that feels right." In an ideal world, our children will travel to school
carrying with them the love of particular authors, genres, and ways
of reading. One child will spot *Owl Moon* on the shelf and rush to it,
embracing it, quoting a favorite line aloud. Another child will spot
an anthology of fairy tales and, with awe, announce, "*These* stories
have lived longer than *anyone* in this classroom!" In this way, the gifts
parents and grandparents give to one child become gifts to classrooms full of children.

CHAPTER 3

Early Writing: Growing Young Authors

Over the last 10 or 15 years, there has been a revolution in the teaching of writing, and nowhere is this more obvious than in kindergarten, first-, and second-grade classrooms, where writing has become a major part of the curriculum. Teachers are realizing that growth in writing precedes and supports growth in reading. Marie Clay, past president of the International Reading Association, has said the single greatest predictor of success in reading at age eight is the child's breadth of experience with writing at age five. Today, in hundreds of thousands of schools, writing is a major component of the language arts curriculum, even for kindergarten children.

How different this is from my experience as a child. When I was six years old, the only writing I did was to copy my teachers' words off chalkboards or worksheets and to occasionally dictate stories to teachers who transcribed my words. Now, in schools throughout the world, even very young children independently compose signs and letters, poems, and research reports. In first grade classrooms, children write to share their lives, plan the school assembly, announce the arrival of a new class pet, record observations of their polliwogs, and to make an audiotape of lullabies for their teacher's new baby. At home, Evan uses writing to "make the world go 'round." Case in point: When a telephone call interrupted our bedtime read-aloud session, Evan resorted to writing to lure me back to our story. His effort is shown in Figure 3.1.

The four- or five-year-old writes rules, recipes, traffic tickets, wish lists, and stories, such as the one in Figure 3.2 about a monster named One-Eye (1i).

Figure 3.1

Figure 3.2

In big purple and pink magic-marker letters, Katie Allyn plans the shared literacy events of her life, as shown in Figure 3.3. She writes signs and tapes them to her bedroom door. She drafts official proclamations and reads them with great ceremony. Other six-year-olds solve math problems for make-believe school, as illustrated in Figure 3.4.

As parents, we are wise to respond to our very young children's writing by worrying over how to pay for the traffic tickets they give us, order from the menus in their restaurants, acknowledge the rules inscribed on their bedroom doors, and shudder at One-Eye's menacing appearance.

Encouraging Children to Learn to Write As They Learned to Talk

"But why hurry kids? Shouldn't we let children be children?" a friend asked after hearing me talk about early writing development. "Shouldn't they learn through natural childhood activities?" I nodded in agreement. Yes, children should learn through natural childhood activities; through playing with blocks and painting, through song and dance. But writing, too, is a natural childhood activity. Long before they go to school, many children are writing. With marks that may look like chicken footprints, they write on their big sister's schoolwork, on their father's financial reports, on misty mirrors, and wet beaches. "I was here," their marks say. We, as parents should support our child's growth as a writer in the same ways that we support our child's growth in oral language.

Learning to talk is a stunning achievement. More and more, educators are asking, "What do parents do in their homes that results in almost every baby, in every culture, painlessly accomplishing the enormous intellectual task of learning to talk?" Educators are realizing that it is wise to follow the parental example, to support children's relationship to written language as parents have supported children's relationship to spoken language.

As I pointed out in Chapter 1, the first thing we as parents do to support children's oral language development is to talk with and

Book Grip
At rovr
HAWS
Love KAte

Figure 3.3

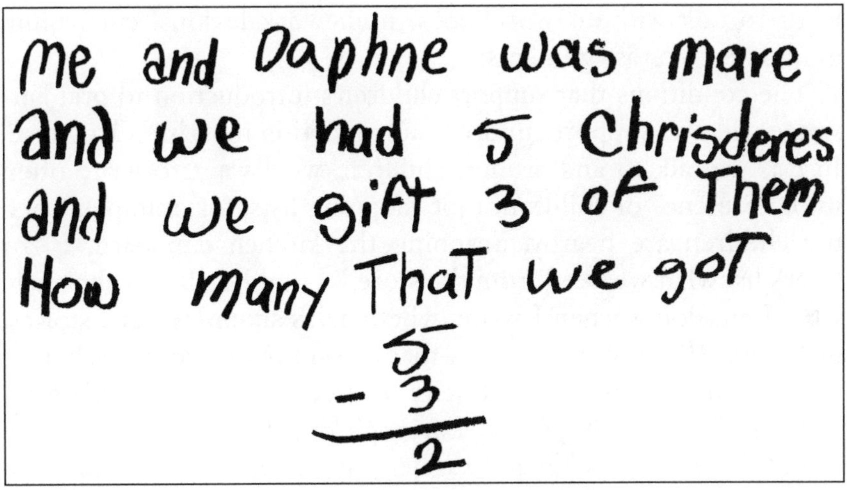

me and Daphne was mare
and we had 5 Chrisderes
and we gift 3 of Them
How many That we goT

$$\begin{array}{r} 5 \\ -\ 3 \\ \hline 2 \end{array}$$

Figure 3.4

within range of children, to tell stories, share ideas, make plans, and swap secrets. Brian Cambourne, an Australian literacy educator, describes what we do for children when we speak around them as "immersion." We saturate babies in the cadences, sounds, rhythms, and purposes of spoken language.

We also invite our children to participate fully in conversation. We act as if babies understand what we are saying, and we encourage them to talk for all the reasons that people the world over talk: to entertain, to form relationships, to protest, and so forth.

We expect babies to join in by approximating conversation. When babies "talk," we respond as if whatever they say makes sense. "Baa baa," our child says, reaching with outstretched arms toward the bananas on top of the refrigerator." We don't worry that the child will fixate on bad habits, that she'll say "baa baa" instead of banana for the rest of her life. We don't say, "Shhh. Don't talk until you know the right word." We don't say, "Wait. First you must learn all the component sounds. You've mastered the /b/ sound, now let's work on /n/ /n/. Can you say nan?" Instead, when our child says, "Baa baa," we see through her error to what she is trying to say, and we produce the fruit for her. "Banana? You want a banana?" we say cheerfully. "Here you go." And so our children learn to talk. They learn to talk without workbooks, homework lessons, curriculum guides, tests, or assignments.

The conditions that support children's introduction to oral language will also support children's introduction to written language. Just as we talk to and around children, we'll want to write often in the presence of children. I jot shopping lists, for example, when my children are nearby. Scanning the kitchen cupboard, I say, "Let's list what we need from the store." I find it helps to chronicle what I am doing when I write, whether it's shopping lists, stories, or letters. "I'm going to send a thank-you note to your teacher," I say. "Hmmm, how should I start it? Let's see . . . Dear Cathy. I wonder . . . No, I hope . . ." Later, picking up a blank envelope, I say, "We better put her address here, so the mail carrier will know where to take the letter."

In these ways, we demonstrate more than we could ever dream possible about writing. Watching us, our children learn that people write to keep in touch, and that letters are usually answered. They learn that thoughts can be encoded into black marks on the page, that a person pauses to ask, "What should I say?" and that we sometimes think of one thing to write and then choose something better. Watching us, children learn that letters begin with "Dear," and that addresses begin with a person's name; they learn that we read and write from left to right, and that there are spaces in between words. They learn about purposes, occasions, and materials for writing.

But children will learn from these demonstrations only if they believe that what we're doing they can do, too. And so we want to include our children in the writing we do. "What else do we want at the store?" we ask. And if the child suggests ice cream, we can respond, "Great idea" and then, modeling and inviting the child into the act of writing, we can repeat "Ice, ice," highlighting the sounds in conjunction with the letters. Then, pen in hand, we can begin to write an I.

Alternatively, when the child suggests ice cream, we can pass the shopping list and say, with all the faith in the world, "Add that, okay?" The child is apt to look at us for direction, but if we encourage her to just write ice cream any ole way at the bottom of the shopping list, there may soon be a bit of scrawl that will signal an attempt at writing. If children are invited to write the best they can from a very early age, they'll learn to write as they learned to talk. They'll use whatever they know to construct an approximation of writing.

When we take our children's writing seriously and listen to their intended message, we are supporting writing development. If the child has written diamonds and stars at the bottom of our shopping list to represent ice cream, the best way to respond is to read "ice cream" off the list and then to get some! It's far better to support a child's writing by responding to its intended message than by exclaiming, "What a good job you did!" When the baby says, "Baa baa," we don't respond by saying, "Good talking!" Instead, we reach for the banana.

Jerry Harste, a language arts researcher from Indiana, has often said, "I see education as creating in our classrooms the kind of world we believe in, and then inviting children to role-play their way into being the learners we want them to be." These are brilliant words. When I first researched children, I felt like I'd dressed up in a researcher's outfit and was merely playing someone else's part. I said words that weren't my own, and acted in the ways of others. Gradually I grew into the role. In the same way, I want youngsters to grow as readers and writers. Therefore, when I see a little girl pretending to be a writer, I go along with her role play just as I go along when my children act the part of airplane pilot, train conductor, parent, or teacher.

A parent may worry, "If my child has only pretended to write, how does it help to act as if I can read the message?" Yet when a child learns to speak and to walk, we are so trustful. When a toddler says, "Dah dah," we phone all the relatives around the country to celebrate that our brilliant child has said "Daddy," when the truth may be that our youngster was merely playing with sounds, and not saying anything at all. And when a child arranges a line of chairs and asks us if we'd like a ride on the train, we buy a ticket and climb aboard. When a child sweeps by pushing dust back and forth across the floor, we say, "What a great help you are!" Yet when it comes to a child's early efforts to read and write, we are so afraid. Our stomach tightens at the thought that our child may develop "bad habits," may not succeed, may look stupid . . . and so we lose perspective.

Helping Children Become Authors

Parents and teachers alike often ask me, "How can we teach our children to write?" This is a question not only about writing but also about teaching. Teaching is always a mystery. It is never exactly clear how one person can teach another. Randy Bomer, my colleague at Teachers College, points out that this is especially true if we are teaching someone to do something. We cannot really "give" a child the ability to talk, swim, sing, or to write because ultimately it is the other person (in this instance, the child) who must do the talking, swimming, singing, or writing. In the end, our influence will inevitably be indirect. So it is with writing; all we can do is to create the conditions in which children can learn to write.

The single most important element children need to grow as writers is the belief that they are writers. When children regard themselves as writers, they will learn about written language from the texts all around them.

When parents suggest to their three-year-old daughter that she add her signature to the bottom of her drawing, they are giving her a start in the formation of her identity, which puts her on a learning path as a writer. Once our children regard themselves as writers, as the kind of people who need to know and to use the little marks on books and signs, they will see the letters on their parents' briefcases; they will notice the golden "M" arches which beckon them to McDonald's; and they will see the G on the door of the girls' bathroom, and the snake-like S on the STOP sign.

The first time we nudge our child to write, we may suggest she add a signature to her artwork. Another day, we suggest, "Do you want to label things so everyone will know what they are?" Perhaps Jesse, who has drawn an airplane, will label it with the only two letters she knows, "JS." If Jesse labels her picture of an airplane with the letters JS, this will look irrational and incorrect to most parents, but Jesse is wisely using the letters she knows (the letters from her name). This is progress from the squiggles she once used to label her work.

Children will not all follow Jesse's example. Sometimes a child in the early stages of writing development will blithely and briskly fill a whole page with a jumble of letters so that her paper looks at a glance like a grown-up's story. The "author" may never have had an intended message at all. I am interested when such a child "reads" her writing out loud. Does she produce a totally different story each time she reads her piece? Does she have a sense that the text should be read from the top left corner, across the page and down? Does she read as if she knows that each spoken word is represented by a clump of letters?

Often when very young writers fill up pages with what appear to be random marks, it may be helpful to rein in the length of the text so as to strengthen the link between the letters and their meaning. To accomplish this, I usually suggest that children *draw* a story and then label or perhaps caption the picture. Often, when a child sets out to label a drawing, his hand will hover uncertainly, for example, near the sun, and the child will look up at us for instructions. I'm delighted that the child knows enough to pause at this moment; he knows there is a correct way of proceeding. In such a circumstance, I don't like to simply dictate the correct letters (s-u-n); I prefer to give the youngster strategies that allow him to write independently. I might say, "sssuuunnn," emphasizing the initial /s/ sound in such a way as to invite the child to join me in saying "sssuuunnn," to demonstrate that writers stretch words out, listening for the sounds in them.

One teacher asked a little girl to say Santa, slowly, with her. "What sounds do you hear?" the teacher asked. The little girl repeated, "Ssssanta, Santa, Ssss-anta," listening intently. Then, brightening up, she said to her teacher, "I hear 'Ho! Ho! Ho!' " Of course, many times a child might respond, "I hear /sssss/," in which case, the child may be stymied over what letter matches the /s/ sound. Then it might help to prompt, for example, "Do you remember that ssss-stop sign?" Alternatively, after finding the child is stymied even after she has isolated the /s/ sound, I might tell her the letter. "It's an S." Then I might also draw the letter in the air or on a nearby scrap of paper to remind the child of its shape.

With our help, children will proceed in this manner to record initial and perhaps final consonants. My rule of thumb is to try and help the child do today what she will be able to do independently tomorrow. I don't want my assistance to be too far beyond the child's independent abilities or she will be put in a dependent position, always waiting for and wanting assistance. I am, therefore, pleased when an emergent writer writes a B or a BT to represent boat. I know that if I want a child to be an independent and confident speller, my expectations need to be within grasp.

In the early stages of writing, it's impossible for children to be both independent *and* correct spellers. If my goal were for my four-, five-, or six-year-old to spell *correctly*, the price would be my doing all the work; my child would merely transcribe the correct letters as I dictated them. The problem with this is that the only person who would get practice at the work of spelling—at saying a word slowly, listening to the sounds, searching for a letter or combination of letters that will carry that sound—would be me, and presumably I am the least in need of this practice!

After a few days of joining a child, and stretching some words out while listening to them, I expect the child to attempt this part of writing independently. When a child wants to spell tree, then, I won't dictate the correct letters, nor will I make /t/ sounds over and over. I want the child to do this. And so I'll simply say, "Can you give it a go?" then wait and watch, determining my next move based on how the child responds. If the child still seems to have no idea of how to start, I'll move in to help. "Can you say tree slowly with me?" I'll ask; and then, together, with my voice a little lower than the child's, we'll say "trrrrreeee." Some teachers describe what we are doing as "stretching a word out like a rubber band, listening to its sounds." What I *do not do* is divide the word tree into separate staccato sounds, /tah/ /tah/ /ra/ /ra/ /ee/ /ee/, because this creates spelling problems. When words are sounded out in this fashion, children hear and will reproduce the extra vowels.

When children listen to the sounds in a word and try to record the appropriate letters, they make common errors (we prefer to call them approximations). The word tree is often spelled jre or chre. This may look bewildering but young writers who have listened with some care to the /tr/ sound often match it with a /j/ or a /ch/ or an /h/ (hait*ch*). The word went is often spelled yet. Children use the *name*—not the sound—of the letter y to provide the /w/ sound. Thus window may be spelled yndo. For a similar reason, children may begin daddy with a w. This may seem illogical to adults unless we realize that the *name* "double-u" begins with the /d/ sound. Similarly, young children are apt to represent the /ch/ sound as ait*ch* (H).

Before long, our children will come to us, bearing bits of paper on which they've written their hieroglyphics. Even if their strings of letters do not really represent words, the best response is to act as if they are meaningful, and with all the faith in the world, ask, "Will you read it to me?" Often the young writer will have forgotten what it was he originally "wrote." Like the child I described earlier, he may nevertheless proceed to pretend-read the piece. When this happens, I respond to whatever the youngster says is written on the paper. "Is that right!" I might say, knowing full well he's pretending that he's written this. "I had *no idea* you went on that trip! Wow!"

On the other hand, if a child seems stymied by the request to read aloud what he wrote, it's tempting to dismiss his paper, assuming he's written just strings of random letters. The problem is this doesn't encourage the child to attempt to write more letters, or give more clues and assistance to readers the next time he writes. Instead of giving up on his text, I try to join him in peering at the letters, trying to piece them into the caption, label, or sentence that accompanied the drawing. Our attention to his print, our reliance on the clues he's given us, our trust that there *must* be meaning on his page all convey so much!

Once a child has written a bit of text, we can officially declare him an author. If the story consists of only two pages of pictures, each with a few labels, we can nevertheless suggest he may want to add a cover to his "book." Together, we can look at the books of other published authors and notice that they have titles and authors' names on the covers, and dedication pages and About the Author sections. Soon our young author will be putting call numbers and library cards on the back cover of a six-word book! These trappings of literacy are important. They help build a child's identity as an author.

It's even more important to give children audiences for their writing. "You should read this to the whole class!" we suggest. Or, "Why not let this be your little brother's goodnight story?" we say. "Let's give this to Grandma for her birthday!" we prompt. Once a child believes that she is an author, she will live differently. Even if she only knows a handful of consonant sounds, we can help her to live like an author. Her writing and her learning about writing will skyrocket as a result. Meanwhile, we can also help to improve her ability to spell. Later in this chapter I will return to the issue of spelling, but for now it is important to move on to the purposes and processes of writing, because once a child has drawn a picture of a boat and labeled it BT, that child is ready to live and write like a writer.

Inviting Children to Write and Revise for Real Purposes

Once we have inducted our children into the role of author, we will want to help them experience all the reasons why people the world over write. As we observe our children during their work and play, there will be lots of opportunities to nudge them to write. When they construct block highways, we can suggest they write road signs, billboards, and "Don't Wreck It" signs. When they build make-believe stores, they can use writing to advertise their sale items, for instance. Children who love to play chanting games against each other's hands and knees can write down their chants. Christmas and birthday lists can be mailed to family members. Children can use writing to plan the schedule for a weekend, the itinerary for a trip, the agenda for a playdate, the menu for a feast, or to get a specific point across. When Lydia's daughter Michelle was seven years old, she yearned for a room of her own and finally resorted to writing her mother the letter shown in Figure 3.5.

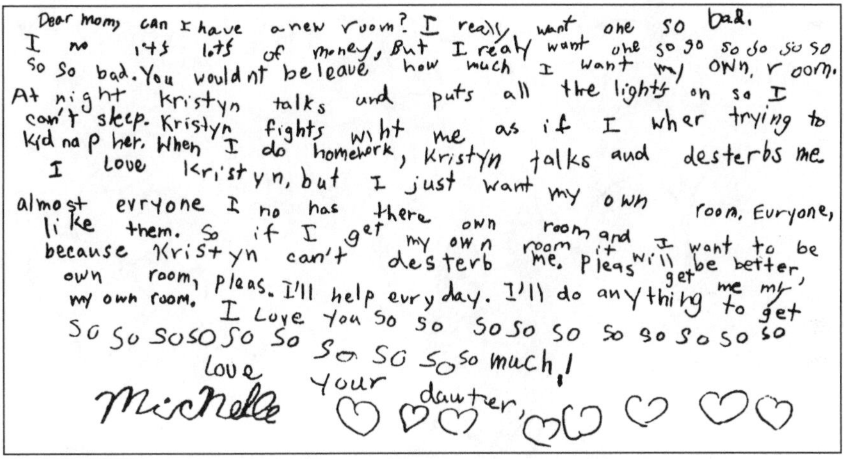

Dear mom, can I have a new room? I really want one so bad. I no it's lots of money, But I really want one so so so so so so so so bad. You wouldnt beleave how much I want my own room. At night Kristyn talks and puts all the lights on so I can't sleep. Kristyn fights wiht me as if I wher trying to Kidnap her. When I do homework, Kristyn talks and desterbs me. I love Kristyn, but I just want my own room. Euryone, almost evryone I no has there own room and I want to be like them. So if I get my own room it will be better, because Kristyn can't desterb me. Pleas get me my own room. Pleas. I'll help evry day. I'll do anything to get my own room. I Love you so so so so so so so so so so so so so so so so so much! love your dauter, Michelle

Figure 3.5

The best time to nudge children toward functional writing is when they are in the midst of doing purposeful work. If a child is preparing a fancy feast, for example, it's easy to say, "You know what you might want to do? You could write a menu, just like they have at fancy restaurants!" Part of teaching writing is to watch for those times when a child's purpose could lead her to write, and then suggest, "Why don't you write that?"

Another way to encourage children to write for real-world purposes is to equip them with appropriate paper and writing tools. If we give children beautiful stationery and perhaps sealing-wax stamps, they'll probably want to write letters. If we give them clipboards, they'll be more likely to record observations. If we give them graph paper, perhaps they'll draw blueprints for forts and redesigned bedrooms. If we make little blank books, perhaps they'll fill them with stories. If we give them poster board, billboards may result, such as the one in Figure 3.6, which a first grader hung from her make-believe store.

Figure 3.6

Encouraging Children to Write and Draw

Writers, no matter how young, also write to craft literature, to make words sing, to capture something lovely, to think through an idea, to make literature.

Teachers often provide time each day in school for children to draft and revise their own literature, and these endeavors will naturally spill over into the home. But for those parents whose children are not in a classroom that encourages writing, the parents will need to go to extra lengths to entice their children to draft and revise stories, poems, and lullabies at home. Children of five, six, and seven years of age usually love this sort of writing.

Often the easiest way to help children write literature is to first encourage them to draw. Five-year-old Tony's drawing began as a picture of a spaceship blasting off, then the spaceship erupted into scrawled flames which soon consumed the vehicle.

"What's happening?" I ask, pulling up alongside Tony.

"It's blowin' up," Tony says, and begins to draw a rescue plane which zooms into the scene.

"You should write that! What a great book this will be!" I exclaim, and with all the trust in the world, I point to the empty space at the bottom of Tony's page. Then I might prompt further: "How will you start your book? Do you want it to begin with the spaceship taking off? Or with it blowing up?"

After Tony has written a line of 11 letters, which supposedly reads: "The spaceship went up. It blew up," I encourage, "You need more paper." In a flash, I staple six sheets of paper onto his first page. Now the stack of papers begins with a blank page, followed by Tony's captioned picture. Pointing to the initial blank page, I ask Tony what the title for his book will be.

My goal is to help Tony become an avid and independent author of literature, and to help him to write more. I look forward to the day when Tony writes a story without my intervention. I help him to grow toward this by demonstrating that I expect his story to continue, by turning the page and asking "What will happen next?" and by recognizing that Tony needs to draw before he writes in order to develop his ideas. Somewhere in the midst of drawing, the next episode in his ongoing drama will occur to Tony.

It is not difficult to lure children to write books. Then the challenge becomes helping them to write better books. One way to do this is to encourage children to reread and revise their initial drafts. Parents and teachers can reread with them and guide them to realize that, perhaps, the story isn't clear. With our help, a five-year-old author, for example, can add clarifying information at the end of a caption. Or we can help him to understand that the story needs a resolution. "What happened after this?" we can ask. "Did it turn out okay in the end?" Typically, the child will reveal the missing conclusion, and we can simply say, "Add that!"

Children grow as writers by coming to understand and to participate in the process of writing. Like poets, novelists, and journalists throughout the world, young children find seed ideas in what they draw, see, wonder, notice, say, remember, feel, and experience. They take these ideas and consider, "How shall I write this?" Even young writers decide on form and genre; they write and revise for clarity and for grace.

This rhythm of writing—writing, taking a breather, and then adding more—is common among young writers. Melissa, for example, brought me a page on which she had written, in hieroglyphic spellings, "Dear Daddy. I love you. Love, Melissa." Reading her letter aloud, I said, "You really love him, don't you?" "Yes," she answered. Then with great solemnity she added in her high, sweet voice, "I love him because he lives with me."

Turning her paper over, searching the back and the margins, I asked, "Where did you put that?" as if it must be there somewhere. "I didn't have enough room!" Melissa said. I responded, "Come on, Melissa, I'll show you where you can get some more paper." While standing beside the paper supply, I asked Melissa if she wanted to write a long scroll-like letter or a book? She chose the latter, and soon was back at work, industriously and happily filling up a six-page "book" with all the reasons she loves her father.

Similarly, Jane wrote a little book about what she saw in her backyard. Each page contained an elaborate drawing and a brief label. When Jane finished her book, I asked her to reread it and tell me all about it. Soon, on the page that had read simply "And cuotcambrs" (and cucumbers), Jane added a large Post-it. Now the page looked as shown in Figure 3.7.

Revision comes easily to young children. It usually doesn't take much encouragement for parents to tap into a child's strengths as an observer, a chronicler, or a poet. If a child brings us a page on which she has written "I went to the beach," usually all a parent has to say is, "Did you?! You went to the beach! What was it like?" Generally, the child will respond with charming, fresh images.

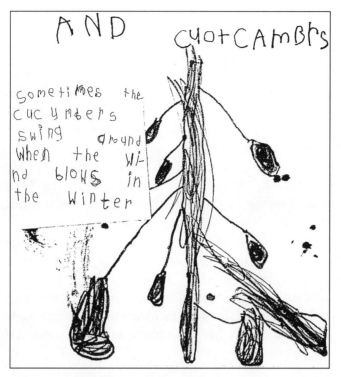

AND   CYOtCAMBrs

Sometimes the
cucunders
swing around
when the wi-
nd blows in
the winter

Figure 3.7

When a child is more reticent, however, and responds with only, "I don't know," a parent can go further, asking, "Can you close your eyes and picture that beach? What's it like there? Help me to picture it." If the response is still minimal—let's say she murmurs "There's waves"—rather than becoming discouraged, it's best to value even the smallest detail because ironically, this is the best way to encourage expansion. "Waves!" we can say, fascinated, "Waves . . ."

"The waves came in, and wooshed around my feet," the child might add, realizing we are picturing it, too. "I can picture it," we respond. "Yes! The waves came in and whooshed around your feet. . . ?"

"And then went away."

"Did they?! They whooshed around your feet, and then they went away? What was that like when the waves slipped away?"

"They pulled the sand out from under my toes!"

This is one way to help a child create a story in her mind.

Alternatively, we could suggest the child draw the beach as she remembers it, and then use the drawing as an invitation to talk further. While drawing, a child might add a passing boat, then write, "A boat went by." In this way, drawing can function as an interested adult, eliciting more language and more detail from the child.

Drawing, like writing, can be a vehicle for thinking. Ideally, when a child draws a scene at the beach, she will notice more and question more and feel more and elaborate more. While she draws, then, we may ask, "What are you wondering?" or "What's the picture you're seeing in your mind?" or "How did you feel, standing there?"

Whether we encourage children to draw or to mentally envision a subject, we will be helping them to notice and to record small details.

In Figure 3.8, five-year-old Charlotte initially drew a picture of her Cowl duck. Later, Charlotte returned to the picture to add more details. Then she redrew her picture and wrote the caption shown in Figure 3.9.

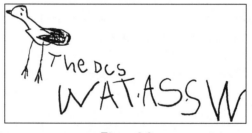

Figure 3.8

Once a child such as Charlotte has learned to carefully describe something that is literally before her eyes, it's not a big stretch for her to *imagine* something in front of her, and then to describe what she sees in her mind's eye, as she has done in Figure 3.10.

When Charlotte wrote, "I am on the back of the canoe," she was not actually sitting in the stern of a canoe with pen and paper. She

Figure 3.9

The ducks white as snow
Water trickling down their back

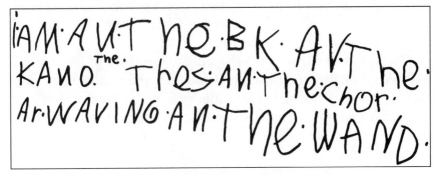

Figure 3.10

I am on the back of the
canoe. The trees on the shore
are waving in the wind.

imagined herself in that place, re-creating a moment in order to put it on the page.

Charlotte has done this writing with coaching. She and six of my nieces and nephews are part of a little writer's workshop I hold during our shared summer vacations. Every morning, the cousins, ages three to ten, gather with writer's notebooks in hand. Often, we begin by thinking through how we'll position ourselves as writers that day.

One day, we decided we would try to write about something from our everyday world. Because it was breakfast time and the aroma of freshly baked cinnamon rolls filled the room, we put one cinnamon roll on the table, with the goal being to write about it in two ways: first using "just the facts"; then putting down whatever the roll made us think about. Miles, who was seven at the time, wrote what is shown in Figure 3.11.

A month later, after the start of the school year, I picked up Charlotte and Peter from school. "So, Charlotte," I asked once they had settled down in the car, "What have you been writing about in school lately?" "Well," she replied, "Today I wrote about a bugle."

I was intrigued. How had this kindergarten girl come upon the idea of writing about a bugle, of all things? "How'd you think of that?" I asked. "I just had it in front of me, so . . ." she mused. "Where'd you get the bugle?" I asked, curious as to why the instrument was in the classroom in the first place and how Charlotte came to have it in front of her. "From my lunchbox!" she said. "Like when we wrote about the cinnamon roll."

Charlotte had taken a chip shaped like the Horn of Plenty from her snack bag, set it on the table before her, and written about how that little one-inch long bugle reminded her of horses gathering for a day of fox hunting. A homespun writing workshop had given her a new way to approach writing, which stood her in good stead during the school year.

Today it is common practice to encourage children as young as five years old to choose their own writing topics and audiences. Kindergartners write in every genre imaginable. Writers of all ages see particulars of their lives as grist for the mill, as resources for writing. Naturally, most draw on their personal experiences. They

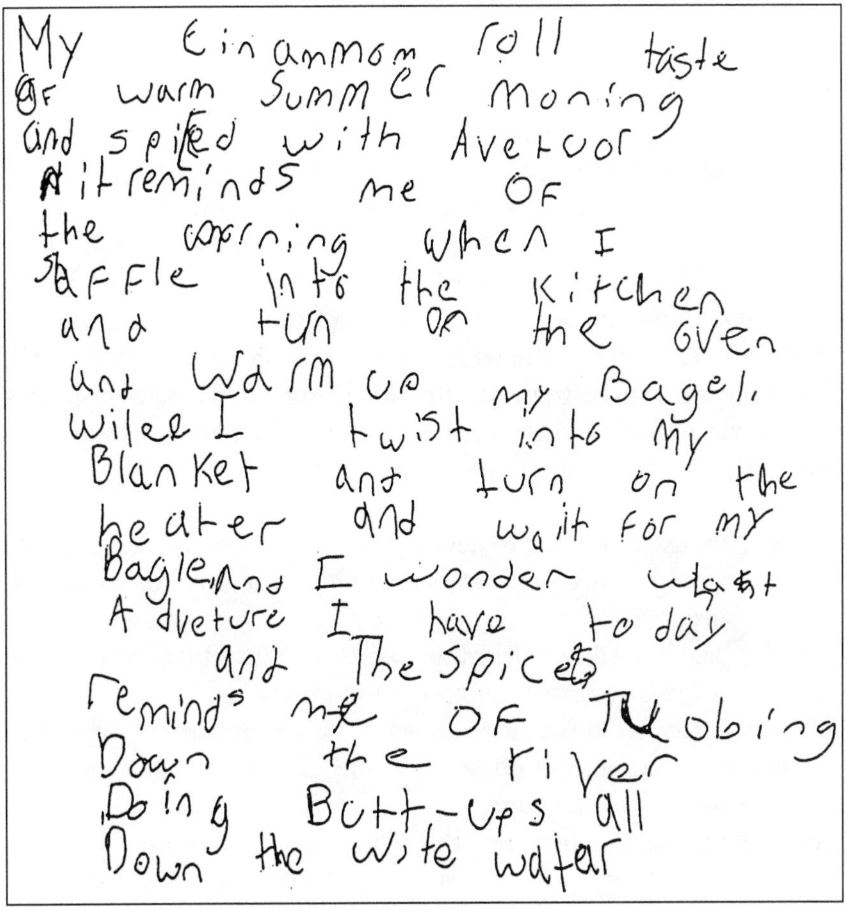

My Cinammom roll taste
Of warm Summer moning
and spied with Ave koor
A it reminds me OF
the morning when I
Saffle into the kitchen
and tun on the oven
and warm up my Bagel.
wilee I twist into my
Blanket and turn on the
heater and wait for my
Bagle, and I wonder what
Adveture I have to day
and The spice
reminds me OF The obing
Down the river
Doing Butt-ups all
Down the wite water

Figure 3.11

write, add details, clarify questions, and expand important parts. For young children, these revisions also often involve stapling, taping, or inserting carets and arrows. Thus, for them, writing is not unlike carpentry.

Extending Spelling and Other Language Skills

If children are to become independent, confident, resourceful writers, we need to give them permission to spell the best they can as they're learning, then give them strategies for improving. Parents often ask me, "Once my child is writing fluently and independently, how can I help her become a more skillful speller?" My first response is that in order to help children to go farther as spellers, we first need to recognize what they already know.

Let's assume a little girl draws a man, then pauses to announce, "This is Dad," adding his telltale bushy hair onto her primitive drawing. Then she adds a big fist onto the figure, saying, "He's fighting." Then she says, slowly, "Hesss, Hessss, Heessss" as she writes EZ. Now she says, "fighting, fighting, /f/ /f/ /f/" and she writes a V. Looking at the page, we see that she has written: EZV. How easy it would be to think, "It's all wrong," to list all that she has done wrong. But to support this young writer, we must see and celebrate all that she has done right:

- She has used drawing to develop an idea, just as she'll eventually use writing as a vehicle for growing her thoughts, for coming to new insights.
- She has revised her drawing to convey particulars, just as she will eventually revise her text, adding details.
- She has isolated the text she wants to write, and held it still in her mind long enough so that she can do the slow work of putting it onto the page.
- She has moved between the whole of her intended message "He's fighting" and the small parts of encoding particular sounds.
- She has stretched out the sounds of her words and listened to them, putting quite appropriate letters onto the page to match the sounds.

During a child's first year as an independent speller (which may be when a child is four, five, six, or seven depending mostly on the instruction the child receives), it can be difficult to decipher what her "words" say. Some teachers will record the child's intended message (or a translation of what the child has written) in tiny adult cursive letters on a remote corner of the page. This is a very satisfying arrangement, I find, because an adult can glance covertly at the translation and then, pointing to the child's letters, join the child in decoding the intended meaning. When a classroom full of young-sters are all writing simultaneously, however, there will be times when a teacher cannot translate what every child tried to write and their papers will be brought home bearing gobbledygook.

Parents need to understand that just because we can't uncover the thought process in a child's piece, this doesn't mean the thought didn't happen. And a teacher should not be regarded as irresponsible if she has encouraged a class to write grand, important masterpieces that are often unintelligible to the rest of us.

In every community, there are those parents who, unrealistically, expect every kindergarten, first- and second-grade child's writing to always be corrected by the teacher. These parents can be so vocal in their concerns that "kids will have no standards" that they end up pressuring teachers to limit the amount of writing children do, essentially to have children write only when the teacher is present to help sound out words and supply letters (thus, doing all the work) for the child. These writing efforts do go home correct and legible—but, then, parents already knew the teacher could spell, so I wonder why this impresses them!

In short, parents need to support our children's growth in writing. Once we get the hang of it, it's not hard for us to see through kids' hieroglyphics to their intended messages, nor is it hard to regard their early spelling as approximations rather than as errors. In all likeli-hood, we will find ourselves savoring the idiosyncratic, intelligent, and original ways our children think on the page. The researcher, Denny Taylor, has said, "There is never a time when I sit beside a child and a miracle doesn't happen." Children do miraculous things in Tay-lor's presence because she expects them to do so and because she rec-ognizes the intelligence and creativity beneath their attempts.

Our delighted interest in our children's early writing efforts is an extraordinary gift. This alone will give our children a place in which to grow as writers and spellers. But more can be done in support of our children's early understanding of the conventions of written language. The wise adult will see and support the intelligence be-hind errors. We can also ask, "What's the one new thing I could show this writer about the conventions of writing? What might help the most?"

If a child has written IWTTUBH and reads it as, "I went to the beach," it might help the child to add dashes, dots, or slashes between the letters as he or she rereads the sentence, to look like this: I/WT/T/U/BH. Soon the child will add dots, dashes (and eventually spaces) *as* she writes, rather than afterward.

Alternatively, we can help our children add more letters to their words. We can teach them to stretch words out slowly, encouraging, "Watch me, watch my mouth. . . ." "Can you say it with me?" When we sound out words in order to spell them, it's important that children take part, and even that their voices are the dominant ones. As I said earlier, it's also important to say the entire word or syllable and not break it into tiny component sounds.

Within a very short time, children usually are well on the road to being independent spellers. We can also help youngsters by encouraging them to rely on the look as well as the sound of words. To assist in this aspect of the process, when a child writes "the," for example, we may want to say, " 'The.' You know how to spell 'the.' Can you picture how it looks?" A researcher once found that half the words children write are the same 36 words. Obviously, over time, these 36 words should become automatic for children.

After Evan had become a confident and independent speller, I didn't hesitate to show him how to spell words such as these:

the	went
a	said
you	yes
we	no
he	say
she	of
they	are
then	where
who	once
one	were

I also listed the words that I hoped were becoming automatic to Evan. "Go ahead and guess," I've told him. "Then use this (the list) to check your guesses." After a while, he loses the list, which is fine since I want it to become a mental list.

I have also shown Evan how to spell certain components of words. If I am nearby when Evan tries to write the -ing ending and I see him sounding it out, I might intercede and say, "ing—you know 'ing,' Evan. It's i-n-g." I've also explained to Evan that the /e/ sound at the end of many words, such as happy, is often spelled with a /y/, and that the /r/ sound is often spelled with /er/. The fact that I *tell* Evan these things doesn't mean that they are part of his repertoire. I must have told him 75 times about the /e/ sound at the end of words, yet he will still often write happe instead of happy. Eventually, this will become automatic to him, but meanwhile if Evan doesn't spell something correctly, I don't jump to the conclusion that his teacher must not have taught him properly.

When Evan is tentative about a spelling, I encourage him to try. I also explain to him that by reading what he's written, he can check his own spellings. "Check it," I say routinely. "Read it with your finger." Then Evan points to the letters as he moves through them, turning his print into meaning. This method of self-monitoring doesn't necessarily expose all his errors, but it's a good way to support a child's growth in reading as well as writing.

When Evan has finished writing a page or a story or sometimes when I just want him to spend a few minutes practicing his editing skills. I might say to him, "Reread this and find 10 things you can fix." At the very least, I routinely encourage him to reread what he has written. Knowing I'll do this helps *me* to be relaxed about his tendency to ignore spelling altogether when he first composes something. My goal for Evan's writing certainly isn't correctness, but I do want Evan to know that spelling is part of writing, and I want him to take a few extra moments to reconsider his spelling. I also try to keep the work on spelling unpressured. Last night, for example, he wrote on a get-well card to his father who was in the hospital, "I mis you woching fat-bol," and then came to me laughing merrily over how he had written fat-bol for football.

As we guide children gradually toward mastering the conventions of written language, we must expect that children will overuse and misuse this information initially; nevertheless we should delight in their efforts. For example, if we teach a child quotation marks, the child will sprinkle them liberally throughout every story. We should also anticipate that if we give children too much information at one time, they will give us very clear signals that we must back off. One definite sign is when children begin to ask constantly, "Is this right?" or "How do you spell——?" It is crucial to indicate in word and deed, "Just put it down any way . . . just have a go," and stop, for a week or a month, coaching conventions, bearing in mind that this does not suggest they will stop growing in their ability to use them.

My goals for young children as spellers include:

- That they are comfortable focusing more on content and language than on spelling during first drafts.
- That they become fearless and independent spellers, using precisely the words they want without detouring around those that pose spelling difficulties.
- That they become fluent writers, learning that it's okay to just "give spelling a go" during rough drafts, but that they tend to reread to correct the spelling.
- That they develop a growing repertoire of sight words; and that as their reading develops, it provides greater support for their spelling.
- That they develop strategies for improving their spelling, such as checking a spelling by rereading the word "with their fingers," pausing in the midst of spelling to think about similar or rhyming words, and envisioning the words in their mind's eye.
- That they write and read frequently.
- That they find the way that words are spelled to be intriguing, and that they go through life noticing surprising spellings.

The Lifework of Writing

Writing is not only a little thing we do with black marks on the page, it is also a big thing we do with our whole lives. Children who write well do so, above all, because they live with honesty, insight, originality, and reverence. Parents have a special role to play in helping our children write well, because we are uniquely positioned to help our children live writers' lives.

In discussing the ways in which writing changes how we live, Newbery Award-winning author Katherine Paterson tells the story of her son David, out in the backyard, calling, "Mom, come quickly! He's about to shed his skin!" Together, Paterson and her son watched closely as a tiny slit in a cicada's back gradually extended, as though the bug had a waist-length zipper. Then they saw hints of color through the slit: first green, then yellow, aqua, cream, and flecks of gold, appearing like jewelry on its head. Next the wings emerged, first crumpled ribbons, then glossy and smooth. As they watched, the cicada swung like an acrobat onto a twig and eventually flew off, "oblivious to the wake of wonder it left behind." Paterson wrote, "As I let that wonder wash over me, I realized that this was the gift I really wanted to give my children, for what good are straight teeth and trumpet lessons to a person who cannot see the grandeur that the world is charged with?"[1]

When Katherine Paterson says "*This* is the real gift I want to give my children . . . ," I can't help but ask, "*What* is the gift?" She's referring not to the gift of a cicada, but to the gift of being moved by the everyday miracles in one's own backyard.

That story is a metaphor for what matters most to me as I help children to write and to live like writers. In the end, our days are filled mostly with ordinary little things: with waking up and brushing teeth, eating breakfast and packing our stuff, and heading out into the day. We could say our lives are boring, that nothing ever happens. Or we can live full of reverence, respect, and wonder. Writing helps us to do that. As the author Byrd Baylor says, "We human beings are in charge of celebration."[2]

It is no accident that it was Paterson's *child* who called his mother out into the world to watch a cicada tumble off like a circus acrobat and to stand, letting the wake of wonder wash over her. Children can do this for us.

The important point to realize is that children aged four to seven are—or can easily be—the best writers in the world, in all but the actual writing part of it. Although very young children's spellings will be underdeveloped, these children often live and see and think and talk like gifted poets and storytellers.

Seven-year-old Luke can teach us something about what it means to live like a writer. When he asked his little brother, "Why are you so happy?" his brother answered only, "Jacob 1992." Luke could have dismissed his brother's words, but instead he cupped his hands around them and declared them to be poetry, shown in Figure 3.12.

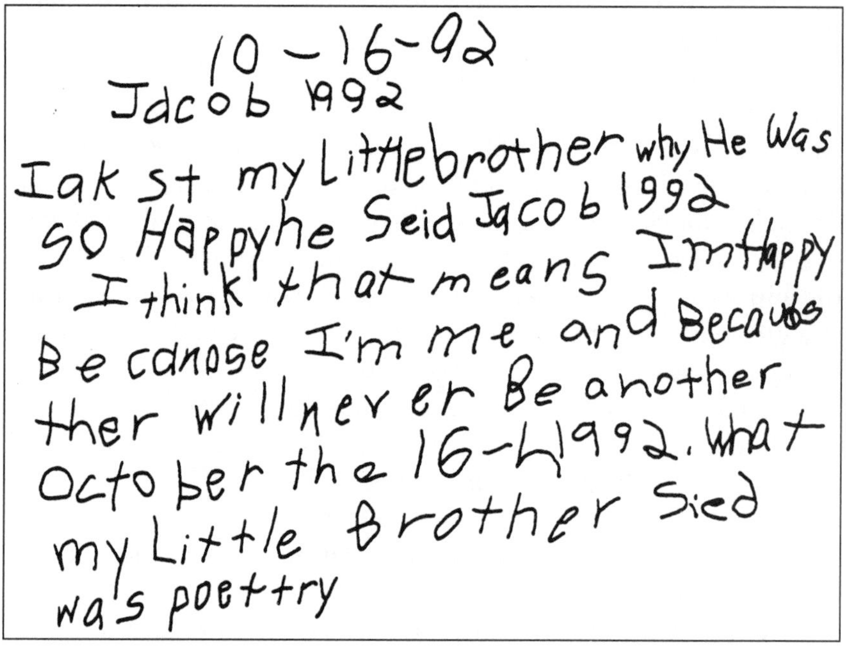
10-16-92
Jacob 1992
Iak st my Littlebrother why He Was
so Happyhe Seid Jacob 1992
I think that means ImHappy
Be canose I'm me and Becaus
ther willnever Be another
Octo ber the 16-1992. what
my Little Brother Sied
was poettry

Figure 3.12

Luke's reverence and respect for an ordinary thing in his life suggests that he knows how to live like a writer. All youngsters can learn to live in this way.

Pulitzer-prize-winning writer Donald Murray describes the writing life by saying that by writing, we see more, hear more, think more, feel more. We can help our children write well by supporting all the ways in which they live like writers. Even if our children don't have paper and pencils in hand, we can teach them to think like writers. I teach writing when my sons and I push aside the schoolwork on a winter's evening and go outside, to stand under the spell of the full moon. "The moon makes the snow look . . . um . . . ," I say. "Glowing," Evan answers, and his voice turns smooth, soft. In his best imitation of the poets he admires, he adds "glowing with a soft light." "Like there's a night-light in the world," Miles adds.

Returning to the warm kitchen, I yearn for us to capture these words onto the page; and perhaps we will, but probably we won't. In the end, it doesn't matter. What matters is that we lived like writers, and that I told them so.

Likewise, I let my children know that when they lag behind to peer closely at a little flower growing between the cracks in the sidewalk, they are living like poets. "You are such observers!" I tell my boys. "It's what gives you your writing talent!" How proud I was when Evan's teacher told me that as the class walked across a school lawn together, Evan looked up at the willow tree and said, "I could write about that tree. It looks like a girl with long hair falling all over her face."

Sometimes Miles, Evan, and I take "writer's walks," and we often do this without pencils or paper. This began when Miles was in kindergarten. His teacher would take the class outside for walks. Upon their return, she would write down what she called "a language experience story," recording what members of the class saw on their walk.

Miles saw a flag pole.
Thatcher saw a library.
Pam saw a parking lot.

"It wasn't a very good writer's walk," Miles confided after his first class walk as we hiked along a little trail later that day. "We didn't notice anything good." "So let's take a *great* writer's walk!" I announced. "You notice something first." Miles stooped to pick up a crinkled old leaf. "Miles sees an old leaf," he announced. "No, Miles, see it like a writer!" I responded. I demonstrated by picking up an acorn and said, "Lucy sees an acorn with its cap pulled low over it's ears." Responding, Miles said, with great tenderness, "Miles sees a leaf turned into a little cup, a place where squirrels can drink."

My real goal, of course, is for my sons to walk the trail of their whole lives, seeing small particulars which are worth lingering over.

I help them to do this by keeping my eyes and ears open for the potential poems and stories that are there in their lives.

The day after Evan slept over at Gregg's house I asked if he had been lonely. "Weeell, no," he said, his voice full of ambivalence. Then, his tone changed. With confidence he said, "When we ate spaghetti, I wasn't lonely. When we played 'race you to the bottom of the sleeping bag,' I wasn't lonely." He let those comments hang in the air for a moment, and we drove on quietly. Then, in a tiny voice, he added, "Only one inch lonely." "Evan," I responded, "What you just said is a poem." Before long, Evan had published the poem shown in Figure 3.13.

Later, Evan and I talked about the power of this poem. I wanted him to know what he had accidentally done so that he could do it again, deliberately. And so I named for him what worked in his piece. "I love the rhythm of it. I could read it over and over, just for the song of it." We named the form of his poem, "a list with a twist," and called it "a gathering of 'I wasn't lonelies' with one 'I was lonely.'" I also talked a lot about the honesty and courage in Evan's poem, how he was brave and smart to put down his true feelings. I pointed out that he reached for the right words, and that's why his poem rang true for those who read it.

It is much easier to help a six- or seven-year-old to speak and write truthfully, to put their true selves on the page, than it is to teach these same lessons to older writers.

When I am with young children, I'm often reminded of William Faulkner's thought that his little postage stamp of native soil was worth writing about, and that he would never live long enough to exhaust it." Young children are eager to believe that "their little postage stamps of native soil" are worth writing about.

At night, when I put my sons' blue jeans in the laundry hamper, and find their pockets filled with sparkley stones and sprouted acorns, I smile and say to myself and to them, "What writers!"

My sons aren't unique. Most very young children are fascinated by the world around them. Sadly this awareness dissipates by the time they are in second grade. I meet youngsters in upper elementary classrooms who tell me, "Nothing important happens in my life," or "My life is boring." Older students say this not only in words

Sleep over
when we slerped up hot spagety

I wasin't lonly

When me and gregg had a pilow fight

I wasin't lonly

Whe We decerated christmas doow

I wasin't lonly

only one inch lonly

Figure 3.13

but in deed, as well, when they write only about Power Rangers, Ninjas, and bridal gowns studded with jewels; or when they retell the story of a long-ago trip to Disneyland.

But very young children find the world full of wonder. It is important for us to support this reverence and respect. Recently, I found a roll of undeveloped film in a kitchen drawer. I couldn't, for the life of me, recall the origins of the film. With some mixed feelings, I dropped off the film at the photo shop. A day later, I opened the envelope to find 36 color prints of Miles's bleary, distorted face. "Miles," I called. "What are these pictures from?" He ran to the kitchen, alarmed by the tone in my voice. "Oh," he said, glancing at the photos, "Those are my pictures from sleep-away camp." "From *camp?*" I asked, astounded. There wasn't a single shot of cabins, docks, boats, or of anything except Miles's blurry face.

"When I was homesick, I took them," he explained. "I just wanted to remember how bad I felt."

"Miles," I responded. "You are such a writer, wanting to capture how sad you truly felt. I'm that way, too. Somehow I feel better if I can put the true sadness onto the page." I hadn't planned to teach my sons to treasure even their own sadness, but it occurred to me later that this, too, is part of living as a writer.

We need to make the writing life accessible to our children. They shouldn't grow up imagining that writers use feather quills, wear velvet jackets, are geniuses, and lead famous lives. Writers do not live more significantly than nonwriters; writers just know how to find the significance in the backyards of their lives. I try to make the writer's identity accessible to children, helping them feel as if they are writers already because I believe all of us can grow like sunflowers toward the wonderful things people see in us.

As the children's author Cynthia Rylant said when she was asked about her writing process: "We are talking about being an artist every single day of one's life. It's about going fishing as an artist and having relatives over for supper as an artist and walking the aisles of Woolworth's like an artist." We, as parents, are with our children when they walk the aisles of Woolworth's and have relatives over for supper. We are uniquely able to help our children live their lives with the alertness of writers.

CHAPTER 4

Early Reading: First Things First

I have a photocopier in my office that automatically sorts sheets of paper into different bins. Watching it, I sometimes think, "Our world is like this machine. Our children are slotted into different bins just like those pieces of paper." And I know it's our children's reading abilities that make the difference.

I remember well the reading groups from my childhood; there was a Bluebirds reading group and a Buzzards reading group. I also remember that on those little S.R.A. score cards, some children whizzed along the top rows of colors, and others plugged along the bottom rows. The reading groups of my elementary school became a feeder system for the "basic," "regular," and "honors" tracks in my secondary school, which then became feeders for colleges and careers.

No wonder those of you reading this book may have been tempted to bypass the chapters on talk, reading aloud, and writing in order to make a beeline for this chapter. Sure, we are pleased when our children pursue projects and hobbies, when they love the bedtime read-alouds, or write us funny little notes, but in the end, we're certain that it's reading that *really counts*.

And it's true. On the whole, children who read a lot will tend to write and spell better, will be familiar with more vocabulary words, and will know more than children who rarely read. Reading opens possibilities to become involved in history, biology, geography, and politics. Reading invites grand conversations and can engender a depth of feeling and thinking. Yes, reading matters.

But it is absolutely *not* true that children develop as readers separately from how they develop as block-builders, story-tellers, geologists, or writers. I am supporting Evan's ability to make meaning from print when I help him create a machine out of a broken propeller dragged from our garbage, or when I join him in building worlds made of blocks and Legos. Once, after I agreed to play Legos with him, he scampered off to the playroom, calling "I'll set up the story." Similarly, I am supporting Miles's ability to lose himself in imagined worlds when I drag the hose over to the sandbox and help him flood the moat around his castle. I am also supporting his ability to think about his own thoughts when I record his idea that Evan is like Thomas Jefferson because he is good at many things. In all of these and countless other big and small ways, I help my boys see that print holds ideas and observations, stories, and plans. I help them to realize that literacy gives them ways to pay attention to their lives, to make something of their lives. We support our child's growth in reading, then, not only when we read with our child but also when we work, play, talk, create, and write with our child.

To me, the tragedy in reading education is that in hundreds and thousands of schools and classrooms, reading is turned into just a little thing children do with black marks on the page, when it can be so much more. When we parents, intent on doing everything possible to support our children's reading, focus only on the "small parts" of reading, we may end up doing more harm than good. Reading matters, but children's mastery of reading is part and parcel of their growth as writers, listeners, creators, and learners. If we make our children believe that reading has more to do with matching letters and sounds than with developing relationships with characters like Babar, Madeline, Charlotte, and Ramona, we do more harm than good. If we help our children break apart words, but don't give them special shelves for beloved books, bedside lamps, and a ritual for poring over books before they go to sleep, we do more harm than good. If we drill our children to ensure that they instantly recognize vocabulary words, but don't notice and celebrate when they have the confidence to try reading the print they find on grocery store shelves and roadside signs, we do our children more harm than good.

In reading, as in writing, we need to think about both the close-in work with spellings, word endings, and quotation marks, along with the larger-scale work that encompasses children's concept of reading and their life habits as readers.

In Chapter 3, I made the point that even before a child has a good grasp of sound-letter correspondences and spelling, that child can live with a writer's alertness, noticing and responding to the details of the world. A child who spells with only initial and final consonants can nevertheless revise a draft in order to clarify the sequence of events or to respond to predictable questions readers may ask. Most important, a child who knows only a handful of consonants still can have the sense of "I am an author," and it is this self-concept that will help that child form the habits and knowledge an author needs. We can learn to accept our young children's early approximations at writing, because we find it easy to be dazzled by that quirky, funny intelligence that shines through when our children begin to write.

But for many of us, reading is another thing altogether. We say, "So you've written a story!" when our daughter shows us her hieroglyphics; and we proudly hang our child's primitive picture of a tree onto our refrigerator; and we eagerly encourage our child to ride a two-wheeler with training wheels. But when this same child holds a favorite book upside down and backward, turning the pages and reciting words, we're quick to say, "She can't *really* read. She has just memorized it." But it's a great moment when a child reads a story by heart, so don't worry, or ask, "Why let her delude herself? Why not teach her, step by step? Why not start with the sounds and then progress from there?"

Our children need us to have the same confidence in them as readers that we have in them as bike-riders, writers, and illustrators. If we feel anxious and messed up about our children's reading, they will know it, and they, too, will feel tight, anxious, and messed up about their reading. I often encourage parents to begin helping their child read when the child is just four or five years old, because whatever a four- or five-year-old does toward reading, we think the child is brilliant. By the time a child is six, and makes the same progress, we look to the right and the left to see if our child is keeping up with the neighbors. We fret, "Is this really reading?" No learner can thrive when surrounded by such anxiety.

And so my first wish for the parents who read this chapter is: try to believe in your child, and in whatever you do as a parent to support your child. It is far more important for you to be trusting and confident and cheerful and full of admiration for your child than it is to use a particular approach in supporting your childs reading. The Australian children's author Mem Fox once told me that when she was a new parent, not knowing any better, she made giant poster-size word flash cards and laid them all over the lawn. Then, with her toddler daughter, she would run from flash card to flash card, as if they were bases on a baseball field. At each flash card, Mem's little girl would call out the word, and Mem, dazzled, would take her "brilliant" daughter in her arms, hug and kiss her, before they raced to the next flash card. No doubt Chloe learned more from Mem's lavish loving than from the flash cards themselves, but what a lesson this is for us all. We need to feel confident and glad with however we support our children's reading.

Coaching Very Early Readers

Parents often describe a child's growth in reading as a miraculous and sudden metamorphosis, announcing, "For the longest time she wasn't reading at all. Then suddenly, out of nowhere, she began to read."

For many youngsters there is a definable phase in which the different strategies for reading come together almost like the teeth of a zipper joining together. When this happens, youngsters often zoom forward as readers. But this phase does not occur suddenly, "out of nowhere." Too often, uninformed adults discount and dismiss all the crucial steps children take en route to becoming independent readers. Children, therefore, make all sorts of marvelous and important breakthroughs right before our eyes, but we don't see these as significant. Instead, we keep shaking our heads in dismay and saying, "She's *still* not reading."

Frequently, we have our eyes set on one goal only: We're waiting for our child to encounter some totally unfamiliar print and be able to read it correctly. Until the child does this, we brush away the child's approximating, saying "She has just memorized it," or "She just pretends," as if there is no value to anything other than the Real Thing.

To support children's early progress toward reading, it is helpful to anticipate, watch for, and celebrate the progress they make en route to being independent readers. To do this, we must realize from the start that children often "pretend" their way toward being readers. The child who holds a book upside down and "reads" an elaborate fairy tale is on his way toward reading. He may not know all his upper- and lowercase letters, yet clearly he has many of the building blocks for successful reading. Reading researcher Margaret Meek says, "The child who plays at reading by imitating what readers seem to do is in a better position to begin to read than those whose first step is instruction in the alphabet."[1] Of course, it is important that children learn sound-letter correspondences, and I'll discuss this and the role of phonics later. But meanwhile it's crucial to understand that children can make tremendous progress as readers while being in what the uninformed adult might think of as "the nowhere land of 'just pretending.'" Let's examine two scenarios as examples.

One boy pretend-reads by flipping aimlessly through a book, beginning at the back, his eyes jumping hither-skither over the pictures on the pages, in no particular sequence. Three pages show a dog, and then a cat appears on the fourth page. This child "reads" as if there were separate parts in the book about dogs and about cats. Another child picks up the same book, turns to the cover, and pretend-reads the title of the book, adding with perfect intonation, her interpretation of the author's name. Turning to the title page, she might repeat the title and author's name. Then, looking through the entire book, studying the pictures and making guesses about the story line, she announces, "I got it! It's a chase book." Then she turns back to the first page, puts her finger on the first word in the upper left-hand corner and proceeds to point and read word by word down the page. Although she is pretend-reading and she guesses what the print probably says rather than decoding the print, her story sounds plausible. Her tone changes in response to quotation marks, and her spacing matches the length of pages, sentences, and words. How much farther along this child is than the first.

So how can we help our children develop as readers even before they can independently decode a page of letters? What can we do if our child is like that little boy who opened the book back to front and whose eyes darted about the page in no logical order?

First, as always, we need to acknowledge what our child *can* do. Although we could look at the boy and focus on what he was doing wrong, it is far more beneficial to talk about what he was doing right:

- He self-initiated reading. He saw a book as worth his time, as potentially interesting.
- He knew that the pages of the book contained characters and ideas.
- He knew that readers open books up to find interesting things on the pages inside.
- He knew that readers turn pages and speak aloud what is on the pages.

In the case of this little boy, of course, the best way to help is to read along with him. When he picks up a book and begins to read it from the back to the front, we can say, "Let's read the cover first." Then we can either read the title aloud or let him pretend-read it. Either way, we want to pause to think together about the real or imagined title. Repeating the title, we muse over what the book will probably be about. This is early reading education at its best.

Even when we say, "Let's study the pictures first, that's what I like to do," we're being marvelous reading teachers. If the child studies the pictures intently, we notice this and say, "What a reader you are! I love the way you really study the pictures. You get so much out of them!"

In this fashion, we read with our very young children, highlighting some of the basic strategies that effective readers use. Over time, it's a good idea to get into the pattern of using these (and other) strategies:

- Look over a book before actually reading a page from it. From the title and cover, begin to surmise ideas about the book, including information about the topic of the book, how the book connects to our lives, and how this book connects with others by the same author or in the same genre.

- "Read the pictures," surmising from them how the text will develop.
- Turn to the starting page, look again at the pictures, then put a finger on the first word and begin to read with the child, moving your finger across words left to right, down the page. On each succeeding page, look first at the picture, encourage the child to guess at what the words say and, if possible, help the child to look at initial letters and the length of the word to see if the guess seems reasonable.
- Pause frequently to make brief connections to our lives, to comment on the characters ("He looks mad, mad, mad!"), to wonder what might happen next, to notice obvious print conventions ("They made these words darker than the others, didn't they?").
- Most important, watch and respond to the child doing any of these things, and join him in the process of reading.

Early in a child's growth as a reader, a great deal of reading instruction happens as we cuddle with our child while reading simple, predictable books together. Reading *with* a child in this way is different than reading *to* a child. The goal is not to sweep the child up onto the magic carpet of reading and carry that child off to other lands, other lives as I described in Chapter 2; it is to open up the process of reading, to slow down and make apparent our strategies for reading, so that a young reader can join in this activity easily and comfortably.

When I read with a youngster, I like to stay one tiny step behind, to let the child turn the pages of the book, then wait to see if the child initiates the move to study the picture. If not, if perhaps she reaches for the next page and the page after that, I gracefully become the reader this child will soon be. "Wait," I say. "I love to look at the pictures, don't you?" I let that process happen in slow motion, then I voice what I am thinking. Perhaps I will muse, "Hmm . . . I wonder what he's doing?" Then add, "I think he's . . ." Ideally, at this point, the child will interject: "He's chasing the cat. The cat'll run up the tree," or whatever the case may be.

We do this for a while. Then I might say, "Should we read the words?" Again, I hold back for a second to give the child the chance to lead the way in pointing to the first word. If he or she still makes no move to do this, I might say, "Let's put our fingers on the first word." Soon our hands are together, perhaps one on top of the other, pointing to the words.

During these early times of reading with this child, I'll probably be the one to say the words. I don't ask the child to break words down or sound them out during this early demonstration of reading. I'm trying to highlight the bigger, more elemental, concepts of reading and I'm trying to get the book at hand "under the reader's belt" so at another time, she will be able to approximate reading it alone. For now, I want the child to get a sense for book language, to grow toward an understanding that some texts contain stories, others are lists, some are how-to directions, and still others have patterns. I want the child to grasp the big picture of reading, cover to cover, left to right; to see how illustrations support words and how the words of one page lead to the words of the next page. I want the reader to begin to learn what constitutes a story, a page, a sentence, a word, a letter, even to begin to understand the purpose of punctuation marks.

Before long, a child usually begins to approximate reading. The following illustrates this process with Becky, who was involved in a Dr. Seuss book. Becky approximated the story like this:

See what you've done! He went out and got a big box. He carried it in. And the fish said, "What are you doing here? What's that big box you have got?" And Thing One and Thing Two ran out of the box. And the box shaked Thing One and the girl shaked Thing Two and they were friends.

After listening to Becky's version of the story, I admired the intellectual work she was doing, then extended it. This begins with seeing and valuing what the child can already do. When children are in the early stages of reading, they are not yet able to open an unfamiliar book and say aloud the words that are written on the page. Instead, early readers may sing through a memorized text, such as Bill Martin's *Brown Bear, Brown Bear.* "Brown Bear, Brown Bear, What do you see? I see a redbird looking at me. Redbird, Redbird, What do you see? I see a . . ." When my sons were emergent readers (a kinder and more accurate term than the common "nonreaders"), I was glad if either of them approximated reading those books they knew by heart. I was equally satisfied when they read, for example, *The Cat in the Hat* as Becky did, constructing a version of the story from all they knew about books in general and about that book and that author, in particular.

I'd tell Becky that she really captured "the song" of Dr. Seuss's writing. Then we might talk about how different books have different voices, different tunes. I might tell her she was wise to not make the Dr. Seuss book begin with the typical "Once upon a time" line, but with a more jazzy tune in keeping with Dr. Seuss's style. Perhaps we'd notice how other books sound very different. I'd also compliment Becky on "reading" the pictures, and matching the words with what was happening in them. I might also comment that she seemed to know what the quotation marks represented on the page.

But I'd also want to draw Becky's attention to the print on the pages. Sometimes I do this with young readers simply by asking, "Are you reading the pictures or the words?" and by suggesting we try reading the words together. With Becky, we turned to page 1 of *The Cat in the Hat* and I asked her to point to and read the words.

When Becky read, "The sun did not come up" instead of "The sun did not shine," I did not correct her because her approximation made sense. Even very fluent readers make substitutions.

It wasn't surprising that Becky was so proficient in dealing with print, but if she had been reticent about trying to read the actual words, I might have prompted: "What might it say? Let's look at the picture and think." Then if she guessed, "The sun wasn't out. It was too rainy to go out," I'd ask, "Can we find any of those words here?" I might even say, "Sun? Let's see if we can find that word on the page. What letter would sun start with, do you think?"

In these ways, we can help a child go from approximating to finding some of the words on a page. Of course, Becky's choice of a text—*The Cat in the Hat*—isn't an easy book for an early emergent reader. I would try to guide a child to work with texts in which the pictures more closely match the words. If Becky had been stymied by "The sun did not shine. It was too wet to play," we could have chosen a book that offered more support.

Once a child is discerning the genre of the text, and reading the pictures in order to guess how a text might go and then looking at the print to see if in fact the little black marks on the page hold the expected message, this child has progressed a long way from the child who simply pointed to items on a page and labeled them "dog," "dog's head."

Children who are learning to read will tap into many support systems. They might look over a book before tackling any one line of words, trying to gain a sense for how the book goes, for "the trick of the book," before attempting to do the printwork of reading. Sometimes children essentially memorize the story. The child will read in a word-by-word way as if she is following the print even when she isn't. (Teachers would say "The child isn't doing one-to-one.") The child may, for example, look at a page which says, "Where is my father?" and read, "I - can't - find - where - my - father - is."

I'll prompt, "Will you point to the words as you read them?" If the child points to "Where is my father?" but reads "I can't find where my father is," and if the child doesn't know enough about sounds and letters to notice the mismatch between what she's saying and what's printed on the page, the child will run into difficulty with her one-to-one correspondence. She'll either run her hand along the line of print as if unaware that the white spaces create separate words; or she'll begin the sentence matching a spoken and written word. Pointing to "where" in the printed line "Where is my father," she'll read "I" . . . pointing to "is," she'll read "can't," and this will continue for awhile. But then she'll find her version—"I can't find where my father is"—has too many words and so her finger will probably just hover over the last word on the page while she blurts out "where my father is" without attaching it to any print at all. When this happens, it's important to help the child realize: "Wait a minute, this isn't matching like it should," and to encourage her to return to the beginning of the sentence, to try again to match the spoken words to the written ones. Experts in the field of early reading often stress "one-to-one" pointing. They cite the importance of children developing the realization that each spoken word must match a written word and that long words have more letters than short ones. When children recite memorized texts, a good deal of the work of reading happens around the challenge of matching the spoken words to the written ones.

It is a golden instructional moment for our child to run into a mismatch between what she's saying and what she's touching. It's not a good idea to step in at the first sign of a problem. We need to let the problem become apparent and then help the child to later self-correct. If the child tries to self-correct, even if her second effort is no more successful than the first, I say, "Great self-correcting!" At this phase of reading development, one of the major goals is for the child to learn self-correction. That is, my goal is for the black marks on the page to give her enough feedback that she adjusts her approximation. This marks a huge step in the process of learning to read. Thereafter, children have what researcher Marie Clay calls a "self-improving system," meaning that texts themselves can provide the necessary feedback.

When children still haven't mastered this capability, I watch for confusion as they struggle with the print, and then try to voice and support the confusion. "Hmm . . . it's not working, is it?" I pause to see if they back up to reread on their own. If not, then I'll say, "Let's back up and try it again; that's what I usually do." That is, rather than correcting their errors, I model the strategies readers use when they encounter these problems. I'm with her, doing the same reading work she's doing. I almost become six again as we sit side by side, reading together.

In these ways, we teach our children these effective strategies for reading including:

- Orienting themselves to a book as a whole.
- Studying the pictures to heighten their sense of what the words say.
- Guessing at what the print probably says.

- Checking to confirm or disprove their guesses.
- Pointing. (Note that pointing with the finger should be done for only a short period—perhaps six months. Then it's a good idea to switch to a bookmark aligned underneath a line of words. This leads to what's called "eye-pointing.")

Other strategies include monitoring for when one-to-one correspondence isn't working or for when a guess isn't making sense (as when a child reads, "I jumped on my bit and rode away."), and rereading to self-correct.

With all these strategies in mind, however, it's essential to know that what is a solution at one stage in reading development can become a hindrance later. Thus, while it is critical to support many five-year-olds in pointing to each word as they read it, it may be just as critical to coach seven- or eight-year-olds to do less of this one-to-one pointing. "Let your eye take in bigger chunks of the sentence," we say to them, or "Why not use a bookmark to keep track of the line you're on in a book rather than pointing to each word?" Eventually, we should say, "You don't seem to need that bookmark under the sentences; you'll read faster and smoother without it."

Furthermore, although some children are happy to do a lot of pointing to the words in memorized texts, and take pleasure in performing like readers, others, including my sons, find this process holds few rewards. Both my boys resisted pointing to words or even working with words that they already knew by heart. After all, reading a text you know by heart means there are no surprises in the story, no adventures, no new thoughts. Many kindergarten and first-grade classrooms probably overuse memorized texts. These texts allow children to perform like readers, but when children don't need the text at all in order to "read" a book, this book isn't ideal for teaching children to read. Paying attention to print has few payoffs for these texts.

The opposite is also true. When texts are completely unfamiliar to emergent readers, children will often find that paying attention to print in those texts also doesn't have a lot of payoff. Ideally, for emergent readers, it's best to learn to read using somewhat familiar texts that are simple and in which the pictures match the words.

Books such as Kraus's *The Carrot Seed*, Shaw's *It Looked Like Spilt Milk*, Barton's *Building a House*, Christelow's *Five Little Monkeys Jumping on a Bed*, Hutchins's *Rosie's Walk*, and dePaola's *The Knight and the Dragon* are among the many books that are ideal for these early readers.

Helping Early Readers Tackle Unfamiliar Texts

Emergent readers, of course, face new obstacles when they attempt to read texts that are totally unfamiliar to them. Parents need to consider, "What if they don't know what any of the words say, and yet very much want to know? How can we help?"

The first answer lies in the choice of books. Repetitive, patterned texts give emergent readers extra support while they are reading. Many books for emergent readers repeat a jazzy, rhythmic phrase on every page, changing just a word or two. Consequently, after hearing even just a few pages of these books, children usually are able to successfully read the book independently. But choose such books carefully, because some of these texts are nothing more than meaningless, silly little ditties. In addition, when children read too many rhyming books with repetitive structures, they may begin to think that this is how all literature is written. Thus it's important to find additional ways to support very early readers.

One solution is to give them stories to read in which the words are predictable and logical, yet interesting and tailored to a child, and are about the child's life. In our family, for example, the children hang on every word of our Trouble Stories, hearing them so often that they correct our oral renditions. Therefore, it'd make a lot of sense for us to write these stories down. If we did, these texts would give our youngsters a lot of reading support because they already know how these stories go. Similarly, if I wrote about a shared adventure between my sons and me, even the first time my boys saw the text, they'd be supported in their reading by the fact that they had experienced the adventure. Although the text itself would be new to my boys, they'd be able to recall the adventure and therefore anticipate what might come next in a sentence. This would help them with the printwork of reading. It is ideal, therefore, for parents to write simple books about family adventures and to use these as primer readers. This, of course, is no small project for a family to undertake and few of us actually get around to doing it.

I do try to find books in which both the topic of the story and the connection between the pictures and the words combine to make it easy for young readers to approximate what the print says on each page. If I want to provide children with extra help, I join them in looking at a picture before we look at the words. As I look at the picture I say, in a conversational tone, exactly what appears in the print (and nothing more). That is, if there is a black-and-white photo of a kitten crawling into a brown paper bag, while the mother cat watches over the scene and the print says, "The kitten hides in the bag," then I might look at the picture and say, as if I'm just noticing this for the first time, "Look—the kitten hides in the bag!" And then turning to the print, I'd say, "Let's read this," and I'd help the child point to the words, "The kitten-hides-in-the-bag." I might even prompt the reading by saying, "The kitten . . ." as we point to the first words. I hope I've made it clear that we help young readers "read the words" by the broader ways in which we shape the reading event, as well as by what we do when the child struggles beside us, getting stuck on a particular word.

If, after looking at the picture together, the child still seems stymied when she looks at the printed "The kitten hides in the bag," I'm apt to say quietly, "Take a guess. What might it say?" because I know that effective readers must guess at what a book says. I might say, "Let's look at the picture again, sometimes that helps me." I might—if I wanted to give the reader extra support—also say, "Would you like me to read the page first and then you echo read?" or "Would you like to read it with me, both of us reading together?" (and then I'd try to keep my voice one beat behind the child's, whenever possible).

It's also reasonable to say to the child, "When you get stuck, what do you want me to do? Should I read a little bit for you? Should I let you read and then help when you get stuck? Give you time on your own to work on it? Or what?"

If the child is trying to read the word "kitten," I'm more apt to say, "What would make sense?" or to simply provide the needed word by saying "kitten" rather than give hints such as, "What is a young cat?" Asking "What would make sense?" is a strategy a child can use on her own another day. My hints won't be there on another day, on another word, but the strategy of asking "What might make sense?" *will* be there. Similarly, if the child is stuck on the word "bag," I won't give a clue such as, "What's that thing you carry to school? A lunch———? It's a lunch———, a lunch *bag?*" I might conceivably say, "sound it out," but I'm far more likely to do this once the child has already made a guess based on the meaning and the lilt of the sentence. But let's turn to the issue of phonics for a fuller exploration of this.

The Debate about Phonics

Some people think that there are two camps of reading educators, the "phonics camp" and the "literature-based (or whole-language) camp." Unfortunately, different people mean very different things when they say "I'm a whole-language educator" or "I believe in phonics." And both whole-language educators and phonics-based educators can teach in ways that are problematic. No labels describing a person's teaching philosophy can guarantee that children will flourish under it.

When I find whole-language or literature-based classrooms to be problematic, it is usually because the teachers, intent on supporting children's reading and their love of reading, fill their classrooms with so many literature-based arts and crafts projects and easy-to-memorize books that have little meaning, that children don't have enough time to read real books with rigor and thoughtfulness. Once in a while I find teachers who are so dedicated to encouraging children to love reading and writing that they are reluctant to hold each child accountable for doing their best work.

Phonics-based classrooms are problematic for different reasons. Often in these rooms, children devote most of their reading time to filling out worksheets and doing exercises. And, typically, only one skill is developed in an exercise, making this work much less challenging than actual reading, which requires children to draw on an array of skills. Children who interpret reading as filling out worksheets tend not to grow to love reading, nor to understand why other people like to read. Children in phonics-based classrooms also may develop an overreliance on sounding out words, and subsequently read in a belabored, staccato fashion.

Dividing reading educators into these two camps is misleading because people then conclude that literature-based educators do not believe in phonics or that phonics educators never allow children to read real books. Neither is true. Most reading educators in both camps value phonics and whole stories.

Neither Lydia nor I would call ourselves members of the phonics-only camp, but the idea that we don't believe in phonics is fallacious. The word phonics refers to the relationship between the letters on pages and the sounds and meanings of those words, between an M and a "mmmm" sound. Obviously, when a six-year-old child draws a cat and says, "Cat, cat, ccccaaaatttt," and then writes CAT (or KAT), the child has used phonics. And when a child reads, phonics is one of the clues she relies on in order to bring meaning to the words on a page. When the child reads, "I jumped on my——" and then pauses over the next word, the fact that it begins with a "b" will *of course* be one of the clues she uses to guess "bike." The issue has never been whether phonics is a part of reading, only whether phonics is the *only* key to achieving success in reading. It's probably more accurate to call these camps "phonics-only" and "phonics and meaning."

Phonics-based educators are apt to direct the child who is stymied over the word bike to "sound it out" or "break it down." They might also cover part of the word with a thumb so that the child moves sequentially from saying "/b/ /b/" to "/i/ /i/" to "/k/ /k/." Then they might say, "Blend it together."

With a child who had just hesitated after reading, "I jumped on my——" I might say, "Sound it out." But I am more apt to say any one of these comments:

- "Hmmm . . . what could that be?" Rereading the line, I'd muse, "I jumped on my——."
- "Can you give it a go? Try it." and I'd watch whether the child rereads and tries again, looks at the picture, or sounds it out; and I'd talk about the strategies she tends to use when she's stuck.

- "Let's look at the picture and see if that helps. 'I jumped on my——.' "
- "Let's read on for a minute. I do that a lot, don't you? 'I jumped on my *something* and rode away.' Hmm . . ."
- "Let's back up and try that sentence again and see if we can figure out what the word *could* be."

I'd help the child in these ways rather than simply saying "sound it out" because I regard phonics as only one of several resources or cueing systems available to readers. In general, though, I find it more efficient to rely first on meaning and on the sound of the sentence. Phonics, in my experience, is most useful when a reader already has some general notion of what a word should be. In the sentence, "I jumped on my b—," it becomes clear that the missing word is probably a thing, and although words such as bit or but might be phonetically reasonable, they wouldn't sound right. Children who rely on the meaning (semantics) and sound (syntax) of a sentence first, would make different errors, perhaps guessing "horse." Although there are ways in which this is an incorrect guess, it is also half-right, and so I'd support the right aspect of the answer. Then I would point out that the word starts with a "b," and encourage a second guess. The "b" in bike is very helpful to the child who doesn't know whether the character has jumped on a horse, a motorcycle, or a bike.

Phonics is even more necessary to children who are writing their own stories, for they need to provide not just the initial letters, but all of the letters in the words. I do my most intensive instruction in phonics, then, when children are writing. (For more on this, review my discussions of spelling in Chapters 3 and 8.)

It's easy to understand why learning to read is often regarded first and foremost as being about learning to sound out and blend words. Frank Smith, one of the world's foremost reading researchers, suggests that many adults hold onto the idea that reading is, above all, about unlocking strings of sounds, then adding them together to make a word, *because phonics works once you know what a word says.* He explains that adults, looking on while a child reads the word hotel, know just from word recognition what he is trying to read. Therefore, when we urge that child to sound it out, we fully expect that he will begin by making the ho sound, as in Santa's "ho, ho, ho." But as Smith explains in *Reading without Nonsense*, the child who doesn't yet know the word adds up to be hotel has no way of differentiating among the fifteen sounds the letters ho can represent (hot, holy, hoot, horse, house, home, and hoist). That child is not likely to articulate correctly the first syllable in hotel. He may, for example, read "hot." Similarly, when adults read the word father and urge a child to sound it out, we, already knowing what the word says, expect the child to begin with "fa" and then move to "ther." And we expect that a child sounding out fathead will see the "th" differently.

An overreliance on phonics can cause reading problems, because in the English language, letters don't stand for just one or two possible sounds. As Smith explains, the letter "o" alone can be pronounced more than a dozen ways (consider the difference between brook and blood.) For this reason, Smith says, "The spelling to sound correspondences of English are so confusing that, in my judgment, children who believe they can read unfamiliar words just by 'blending' or 'sounding them out' are likely to develop into disabled readers."[2]

When Lydia and I encounter struggling readers in third-, fourth-, and fifth-grade classrooms, almost inevitably these children think that reading is all about sounding out words, not trying to make sense of a story. They struggle in part because they have learned misguided ideas about reading.

Alphabet Work

Children's immersion in sound-letter correspondences should occur in connection with, not before, other aspects of literary development. Although both Miles and Evan entered first grade as reasonably strong readers and writers, neither of them knew how to print, identify, and sound out all the letters of the alphabet. To this day, Evan doesn't know the proper way to make a "q," but that hasn't kept him from being an avid reader and writer. Growth in reading doesn't proceed in a step-by-step fashion beginning with mastery of the alphabet. However, in our house, we did incorporate some instruction in the alphabet. This instruction tended *not* to feel like schoolwork. For example, I sometimes drew letters on my sons' soapy backs while they sat in the bathtub together, and inevitably I made the letters they love most, E-V-A-N or M-I-L-E-S, or an "L" for love, a "B" for butt. . . . Sometimes I'd trace letters on their backs in order to send secret codes as part of our goodnight back rubs. Often John made pancakes in the shapes of letters. Or we'd play "I spy" using letters, in this way: "I spy something yellow that begins with a "B." Sometimes we'd bend our bodies into letters, and "spell" words to each other. I'd climb onto my hands and feet, hump up my back, and do all I could to become an "M." We had our own names for the letters of the alphabet, too: "M" was mountains, the upper-case "B," big belly.

We also found letters everywhere. We talked about letters when we stopped at stop signs and when we followed the blue H signs to the hospital. We identified the letters that indicated which restroom was for them and which was for me. We noticed letters on signs at the beach (No Diving), in their bowl of alphabet soup, on the ice cream truck, and on Lego boxes and milk cartons. Of course we noticed letters in books, too, as when they'd poke their heads under my arm to peer at the pages of my novels, interrupting me to say, "I can read your book. It says U-N-T . . ." Mostly, however, my sons' introduction to the alphabet came as we talked about sound-letter correspondence while they wrote.

Writing time has always been a forum for working with sound-letter correspondences. Once my boys became independent spellers, I welcomed their questions about spelling. Recently Evan asked me for the spelling of "talk." Usually, when he asks me how to spell something, I respond by asking him what he thinks would be a good guess. This time, however, I just rattled off the letters. Copying them onto his page, he paused to say, "Wow. That is weird." Then he added, "I'd only have gotten two of them [the letters] right." He whispered "talk" to himself, and looked again at the letters. "Weird," he muttered again. Then, turning to me, he asked, "Which of these letters has the /w/ sound?" That evening, Evan and I began a list on the refrigerator of words that rhyme with talk.

My point is I don't recommend giving children a great many

workbooks or computer programs by which to drill them on letters of the alphabet. In and of themselves, such drills are fine, as long as they're not the main literary event in a home. If a child spends 10 minutes several times a week playing with a fun, lighthearted computer program in which letters sing and dance, this certainly is fine. But when I find homes or schools in which literary work primarily involves worksheets and computer programs, I do object. A computer program that instructs "Circle the pictures that start with an 'S' " isolates phonics from meaning. Worksheets on sounds are no better. Also, this work is unambitious. It is easy and dull. Such exercises don't ask as much of a child as does actual reading or writing. I want children to understand what reading is, why we read, and how we read.

Supporting a Child's Self-Concept As a Reader and the Child's Concept of Reading

Sadly, as early as kindergarten and first grade, many children already associate reading with schoolwork and with failure. Parents of such children hear me talk about youngsters who self-initiate reading and wonder if I'm joking. They are especially frustrated that their children avoid reading even though they vigilantly supported their children's reading habits. They wonder what went wrong.

Often these parents have made a big effort to ensure that their children took reading *seriously*. In the hope of teaching their children to be industrious and hardworking, these parents have said things like, "You must do your reading before you can play." They've set their children up to read alone at the kitchen table, or they've sat stiffly beside their children on the sofa in order "to check on" their children's reading. They've referred to reading as "homework" and they've asked their children, "Did you do your homework? *All* of it?" These parents watched vigilantly to be sure their children didn't cheat and do less than the expected "work."

Sometimes these parents chose books for their children based on levels written on the book covers. And they have tried to ensure that the reading level continually advances. They've kept an eye on their children to be sure they weren't ever "just looking at the book." And if they suspected that their children had memorized a book, they were quick to say "They're not really reading. They've just memorized it."

Is the answer to promise pizzas or money to lure children to read? I don't think so. I suggest that these parents look long and hard at the messages they have been inadvertently conveying about reading. With the best intentions in the world, these parents have often conveyed messages such as:

- Reading is onerous, hard work and I know you'll try to invent any way possible to avoid doing it.
- Reading is like medicine. It tastes bad but in the end it is good for you. We have to force you to read, but 20 years from now, you'll be grateful.
- The goal of reading is to be done with it, to be able to close the book and play.

Throughout this chapter, I have demonstrated a different set of values and attitudes about reading. I want to convey to children that reading is one of life's greatest treats. When my sons ask what I want for my birthday, I say, "A great book would be the best thing, of course." When we light a fire on a winter night, I'm apt to say, "Don't you feel like getting a book and snuggling down in front of the fire?" When one of my sons reaches the end of a book, I say, "Aren't you sad sometimes to reach the last page of a book?" When my kids ask what college is like, I tell them it's lovely. "You get to spend whole days in the library reading book after book," I say. When they ask what we'll do for our vacation, I tell them, "Don't worry. We won't sightsee *too* much. We'll still have time for just hanging around together, for reading, and talking, and playing."

I want children to know that the opportunity to read is reward in itself, that reading draws people together, that it is exciting and relaxing. I want children to grow up expecting to weave reading into all aspects of their lives. I also acknowledge when children have particular strengths as readers. This hasn't been hard to do for Miles because he has always adored reading. But Evan has sometimes felt compelled to construct a sense of himself that is in direct opposition to his brother's identity. "Miles will read his whole life away," Evan says. "I'm not like that." To which I counter: "Miles likes to go away and read, all alone, and you like reading with people. Miles doesn't ever want to talk about what he reads, whereas you're an amazing book-talker. You're both great readers, you are just different from each other." Often, I try to hook Evan's other strengths into his reading. "You remember that day you were skiing between Dad's legs, and then—zoom—in a flash, you were going over ski jumps?" I remind him. "I have a feeling you're doing the same thing in reading! You are zooming . . ." I say this whether or not it is entirely true because I suspect my words can become a self-fulfilling prophecy. I tell Evan, "You are such a brave reader, too, just like you're a brave skier, aren't you?" and my words become true.

I also try to weave reading into Evan's projects. When he had an aquarium full of moths and watched in delight as they spun cocoons, we set up a basket of related books. When he began taking piano lessons and identifying himself as a musician, I bought song sheets and music books for him.

Creating a Literate Environment in the Home

We help our children to compose literate lives first by filling our homes with books. Although it's common for well-intentioned parents to put a child's books in a single corner of the house that has been set up like a little classroom, I wonder if this gives the wrong message. Do we want our children to regard reading as part of their job as students or as one of life's rewards? My hunch is that we all want children to regard reading as one of life's greatest pleasures, and as part and parcel of everything they do.

When my sons get up in the morning, they each spend a few minutes nesting with a pillow, soft blanket, and a heater. Of course, we keep a basket of books beside each child's nest. We refer to our guest room as the boys' "study" and keep a larger collection of children's literature there. Every month or so, Evan and I raid this collection for the special books he'll keep on the bookshelf in his bedroom. We divide these books into three categories: "look-at books," "I-can-read books," and "read-alouds." Miles likes to set up his books alphabetically, with favorites on the top shelf and special baskets for series books. He has also rigged up a special bookshelf—a table turned upside down—for his top-bunk bed where he keeps his current books.

When Miles and Evan were younger, we kept baskets of books in different rooms of the house. The how-to books that accompanied their art and science projects were kept in a basket near the kitchen table. When Evan began poring over submarine books, we put them in a special basket near the living room sofa. When Miles loved the Waldo books, they, too, were given a special box, a special place.

One way to create an environment that supports reading is to make sure it's impossible to avoid books. Like many families, we always bring a backpack full of books along on long car rides, and we keep books in the pockets on the backs of our car seats. Although I generally select the chapter books I read to them, Miles and Evan are involved in choosing the other books in their lives. I give them this choice not so much because I believe they have an inalienable right to freedom-of-book-choice, but rather because I want to help them to become purposeful, planful, deliberate readers. By asking them "What kind of books do you want to pack for this trip?" I hope to encourage them to have their own agendas as readers. And sorting books into baskets also helps youngsters realize that they can, as readers, be "on or about" something.

Some parents may ask, "But what about the child who can't read yet?" My answer is that all children can read, to the best of their abilities. A two-year-old can pore over a backpack full of books even if she can't read a word. Children can make plans for their reading long before they can make sense of the letters on the page. "Independence in reading isn't an end state to be achieved," Margaret Mooney says, "but an assumption to be assumed."

When Miles and Evan were very young, I not only gave them books and opportunities to choose among books, I also surrounded them with the trappings of literacy. They had bedside reading lamps, bookshelves, bookends, bookmarks, book nameplates, bookbags, book jackets, and library cards. My sister Joan once phoned me just before the start of a new school year to ask whether I had bought new pens and so on for the children, or did I think it was enough to round up the pens already all over the house, and divide them up. I told her, "If you can swing it, by all means buy them new stuff. Buy them the pencil cases, the fancy pens and rulers, the bookmarks with silk tassels." In the great drama of life, we outfit our child to look like pro soccer players and ballerinas, so why not outfit them to assume the roles of great scholars and avid readers?

Supporting the Reading Habit

As important as it is to give children a love of reading—providing books, magazines, and poems—and identities as great readers, it's equally important that we help children make time for reading. When Miles and Evan were little, John and I were very consistent in putting them down for an hour-long afternoon nap. When Miles outgrew the need for sleeping each afternoon, I gave him a choice: he could sleep or he could read during his rest period. Miles began to gleefully spend an hour each afternoon sitting among his books. He felt like he was getting away with something because he was able to read during rest time. (Meanwhile, John and I got our own time to read.) To this day, on weekends and summer vacations, it goes without saying that if we are around the house, we always take some time off for rest and reading. When we vacation with the extended family, everyone knows that reading time is scheduled into every day; and we try to coordinate the time so that all over the house, folks are snuggled down with their books. This has become such a ritual that my sons wouldn't think of questioning it. I don't know how long this will last, but for now I suspect they believe everyone in every family has a midafternoon reading time.

I also put Miles and Evan to bed early enough so that they can stay awake for a half-hour or 45 minutes, reading in bed. They know not to get out of bed to play; the options are to read or to sleep. This works for all of us. They feel lucky to be able to keep their lights on and read, and I have much-needed time for my own projects.

I'm fully aware that often during these afternoon and nighttime reading sessions, Evan spends a great deal of his time looking at books rather than really reading them. When I have the energy, I intervene to ensure that he will read. Just before I head downstairs for the night, we'll lie down together with a book that he can read easily, and he reads some of it to me. At an interesting point, I slip away. I also sometimes suggest that if he wants I'll read nearby in case he gets mixed up. Then I read my book beside him and am "on call."

These and other strategies encourage Evan to read the words on the page. Nevertheless, it is crucial that we recognize that time spent poring over books is also important reading work. Usually, when Evan ponders the pictures in a book, he is constructing a sense of what the story is about, which is a major part of what effective readers do when they read. Or he examines a book in order to answer particular questions he has about the story. Recently, for example, I saw him flipping back and forth between pages of a picture book, and when I inquired what he was doing, he explained, "I'm figuring out which kid goes with which Mom." This is exactly the sort of conceptual work effective readers engage in.

Because everyone in our family regards Evan's time alone with books as "reading," this means Evan spends a great deal more time reading than would be feasible if he needed to wait for the presence of a supportive adult. If I had waited for when Evan could read print fluently and only then tried to instill in him the habit of reading before sleep, I might well have found that I was left trying to influence my son just when he was into countering my every wish. It's far easier, I think, to help a child grow up with the habit of reading often, even though in fact much of their reading may be little more, at first, than looking at puzzle books, studying cartoons, or counting guns on submarines. The important thing is that our children grow up thinking of themselves as the kind of people who read often during a day—that they see themselves as avid readers, right from the start.

CHAPTER 5

Playing Well: Building Cities Out of Blocks and Finding Worlds in the Backyard

As parents, we are wise to shake our heads over the toys of today. We are wise to feel uncomfortable over the games which fill the shelves and birthday lists of today's children, for when toys come with scripts attached and children merely follow someone else's plans for how their play will proceed, something is lost. When I was young, I made doll clothes from scraps of fabric, turned shoe boxes into cradles, and wove my dreams and fears into story lines for my dolls and teddy bears. Now dolls come with birth certificates, wedding gowns, mansions, and boyfriends. When the characters are already named, worlds already created, and plot lines already imagined, children are less able to be the authors of their play.

When I was young, I rolled playdough to make snakes with tiny pink tongues, and stretched it to make Indian bowls. Now playdough comes with a machine. Children simply crank the lever, and out pop perfectly formed hearts and stars. When I was young, I used toothpicks to stick raisins and marshmallows onto potatoes, making potato people and a potato zoo. My hands smelled of potato juice, but I didn't mind. Now potatoes come made out of plastic, with premade holes waiting for premade eyes and ears.

The problem is that when we think fondly of the Red Flyer wagons from our own childhoods, what we remember are not the wagons themselves, but what we made of them, what we brought to them. At one moment, they held our lumberyards, at another, they became our baby carriages or our shopping carts. The difference between those red wagons and many of the toys of today is the difference between drawing on a white sheet of paper and drawing inside the design of a coloring book picture.

"My greatest worry for children today," children's author James Howe writes, "is that they are losing the capacity to play; to create a city out of blocks, to find a world in a backyard, to dream an adventure on a rainy afternoon. My greatest fear for children today is that they are losing the capacity to play."[1] Of course, this capacity has not been lost altogether. I think of the child who enters her plastic horses in a horse show, complete with miniature trophies and ribbons; of the child who weaves small dramas around three dolls, a tea set, and a dish of Cheerios-cakes. What a joy it is to watch the energy and expressiveness of such play. This is play at its best because it bears the imprint of the child.

My work as a teacher, researcher, and writer all centers around literacy. But I am also a parent and although it is easy to become consumed with anxiety over whether our children will "break the code" of print, the truth is that they will probably learn to read words and to write words. But will they explore texts and the world with energy, ingenuity, and resourcefulness? Will they welcome opportunities to think collaboratively with friends and authors, to affect and be changed by the ideas of others? Will they be enterprising, tenacious, curious, and confident? These are the qualities which ultimately matter most in our children's lives—*and in their literacy.* These qualities of mind cannot easily be taught in school, nor can they be taught during homework sessions at the kitchen table. These qualities of mind, instead, are nurtured first and most efficiently through our children's play.

We are wise to take our children's play seriously, because how children play has everything to do with how children work. The five-year-old who often drifts around waiting for someone or something to entertain her could easily become the ten-year-old who sighs deeply as she looks at a bookshelf and says, "These books are dull." And this child could easily become the twenty-year-old who gets out of college and then drifts around waiting for the Right Job to come along. This same person could, years later, look at a spouse and think, "This marriage is dull. I need something *new* to be happy." It's easier to nurture qualities such as initiative, resourcefulness, tenacity, imagination, optimism, and enthusiasm in a five-year-old than it is in a twenty-year-old.

The qualities that matter most in a child's education and life are nurtured first and most efficiently through play. It is important to pause and consider, "Am I doing all I can to support my child's play?" It's a rare parent indeed who questions ways in which we can support our child's play.

We're used to the notion that we need to support our children's reading and math. We're accustomed to the idea that we'll teach our children to have good manners. But we've tended to think of our children's play as "their time." We speak of "sending our kids off to play." When we're busy we tell them, "I'm busy; why don't you go play?"

For many of us, it's new to consider that we might actively, thoughtfully support the quality of our children's play. But just as some children struggle with reading, or writing, or sports, other children have sustained, ongoing difficulties involving play. "She never knows what to do with herself," we say of such a child. "She's always bored; she's looking for me to entertain her."

Children who struggle with play tell us "There's nothing to do in this house," or "I need some new toys." And instead of initiating their own playful projects, they become almost addicted to the computer, the game board, and the television. More and more children are restless and out of sorts unless they're plugged in to the television, the video game, the computer, or the telephone. Many children "strip-mine" the toys in their environment; they race around, making one toy talk, another walk, and yet another transform itself. Click, bang, boom, done.

How, then, can we teach our kids the importance of play? There is nothing we can say or do that will, poof, like magic, give our children the ability to read well, to swim well, to sing well, or to play well. In the end, our influence is inevitably indirect.

One of the most efficient ways we have for teaching a child to do something, then, is to create the conditions in which the learning is likely to happen. It is this understanding of teaching that leads knowledgeable teachers of young children and school principals such as Lydia Bellino to take very seriously the need to create "rich learning environments." We need to learn from this. To start, we can influence our children's play by thinking carefully and wisely about helping our children to be resourceful when they play.

Helping Children to Be Resourceful

Fifteen years ago, when my husband John and I were married, a friend—and one of the leading educators in the world today—Donald Graves, traveled to my childhood home in order to perform the wedding ceremony. Don had been Director of Christian Education in the same church when I was a child, and now he resumed his former place at the front of the sanctuary.

Looking out before the group of family and friends that had amassed from all corners of the world, Don began to speak. "We've come from Phoenix, Arizona and from Traverse City, Michigan; from Portland, Oregon and Guilford, Connecticut. We've come also from the birth of Baby Rachel (my niece, born the day of the wedding) and from the death of Ed Cook (my uncle, killed in a car accident en route to the wedding). For everything there is a season, a time to be born and a time to die, a time to laugh and a time to weep. And now is the time for the wedding of Lucy and John."

Turning to my husband-to-be, Don used little vignettes to introduce John to the congregation. Then Don turned to me. I remember thinking, "I wonder what he'll say?" I'd known Don all my life, and I was at the time working as a research associate with him. Surely this was a moment for a compliment. Would he mention my energy? My ideas? My hard work?

Don didn't mention any of these fine features. Instead, he took my breath away by saying the oddest thing. "Lucy," he said, looking out at the wedding crowd. "Lucy. Who knows so well how to live off the land." I stood there in my wedding dress thinking, "What? Who knows how to live off the land??" Don continued. "Lucy. Who knows how to live off the land," he repeated. "To turn sticks and stones into toys and stories for little children."

At the time I was deflated, but I have since realized that Don was giving me a star to steer by. For I am at my best as a mother, a teacher, a writer, a lover, when I truly can "live off the land." I am at my best when I can take what is available in my life and make something of it; when my sons and I christen the rock on the top of our hill as Story Rock, and make a tradition out of leaning against that rock, looking up at the lacework of leaves, and spinning stories together. I'm at my best as a parent when we pretend an English muffin is a cake and have a celebration in honor of the season's first snowfall. And my children, too, are at their best when they can take the everydayness of their world and fill it with significance. Theodore Roethke wrote, "Sometimes, if your life doesn't seem significant enough, it's not your life that isn't significant enough . . . it's your response to your life."

When Miles was in nursery school, I enrolled him in two different schools (in my perennial search for The Perfect School). Midyear, I moved him to a new school, and so didn't know that Fridays there were show-and-tell days. Apparently, Miles's first Friday at the school came, and one by one each of the children took his or her place at the front of the room, proudly displaying toys that beeped and bopped. Miles's turn came, and he'd brought nothing. Nevertheless, he took his place on the chair of honor. The class looked at him expectantly. "Ummm . . ." Miles said slowly, looking out at the circle. Then he fished around in his pocket, and with great seriousness, produced a little yellow thread that had come from his blanket. "I brought this thread," he said, turning ceremoniously so everyone could see it. Then he began rolling the thread on his hand like a miniature snowball. "If you roll it like this and like this," he said, "you can make a love ball." And Miles gave the love ball to Jonathan, who was becoming his friend.

When the next Friday came, Miles's companions again brought flashy bright toys, and again, Miles was empty-handed. This time when he reached into his pocket, he produced a small white stone. "In my family, we save memory rocks," he said. "You save a special rock from the top of the mountain, or from the beach, and when you hold it and close your eyes, you can remember the mountaintop and the sea." Then he added, "I didn't even know this was a memory rock! I found it in my pocket today. I got it when I went to the big church, and it was very boring, so I picked it up from the floor."

Miles added, "Now when I close my eyes, I can remember just how boring that church really was."

When our children turn threads into love balls, socks into dragon puppets, and blankets into curtains for a stage, when they create palaces and railroads out of the stuff of their lives, they are authoring worlds of meaning. This is fundamental to all that they will do and become in their lives.

If we want our children to be able to "live off the land," then it's not only the playthings we give them that matter; it's the playthings we *do not* give them that matter, too. My sister Ellen has always made a point of not giving her children all their fondest desires, and I respect her enormously for this. By virtue of the fact that Ellen and her husband Joe know how to say no to their children, they help Peter and Charlotte to "live off the land."

One of the things we should give less of is the television. Almost half of American children between the ages of six and seventeen have a television in their bedrooms. Children between the ages of four and fourteen watch an average of four hours *a day* of television. Imagine what a child misses, spending approximately 18,000 hours from birth to age seventeen in front of a TV screen! As Bill Moyers puts it, "Our children are being raised by appliances." There are even televisions in birthing rooms. Before they are four, children are inundated with scenes of prepubescent children in underwear embracing each other. Video games flood them with images of buxom, bikini-clad women. Psychologist Mary Pipher, author of *Reviving Ophelia*, says "We must remember all television is educational."[2] Children watch up to 4 million ads in a lifetime, and learn from these that the cure for any woe is a purchase; that happiness comes from owning things.

As Jim Trelease points out in *The Read-Aloud Handbook*, "If the bulk of your free time is spent watching other people do things, and little or no time is spent doing things yourself, it is impossible to grow smarter." When the Trelease family decided to outlaw television on school nights, everything changed in their home. "Suddenly we had the time each night as a family to read aloud, to read to ourselves, to do homework at an unhurried pace, to learn how to play chess and checkers and Scrabble, to make plastic models that had been collecting dust in the closet for 100 years, to bake cakes and cookies . . . to play on all the parish sports teams, to draw and paint and color, and best of all, to talk to one another, ask questions, and answer questions."[3]

Our family limits television to half an hour a day, and we do not own video games. John and I also try to resist scheduling too many activities in advance. "The days of most middle-class children are filled with scheduled activities," child psychologist Bruno Bettelheim said. "Boy or Girl Scout meetings, music and dance lessons, organized sports all leave them hardly any time to be themselves." He went on to argue that children need "free scope, plenty of room." For John and me, this has meant curtailing even something as productive as organized sports involvement. Although my sons participate in the sports programs sponsored by our town, when John and I start to spend too many hours carting our sons to and from games or sitting on the sidelines cheering for them, we try to remember that although organized sports have lots of advantages, the choice in favor of Little League is a choice against other things. It's no accident that suburban "Soccer Moms" aren't "Reading Moms," or "Free-Play Moms." We need to be conscious of our choices and we need to make these choices with care.

It's not only organized sports that can consume an extraordinary amount of our children's playtime. *My* plans and intentions for my sons can limit their opportunities to be resourceful and inventive.

When I was a child, I recall complaining to my mother, "I'm bored." "That's because *you* are boring," she always responded. "It's not life that is boring; it's the person who makes a life that can be boring." My mother resisted the temptation to fill all my time with beneficial, highly educational activities. She didn't take me or my eight siblings from one class to another, from camp to tutorials, from this project to that project. So sometimes, now, when I'm tempted to sign Miles and Evan up for a new sport, a new club, or a new series of lessons, I remember my parents' philosophy—one held by a great many educators—that less is more.

Yesterday I smiled as I watched Evan laboring to dig a broken fan from some roadside garbage. "We can invent with it," he said. Just a few days earlier Miles and Evan had found wonderful coils inside our old waffle iron and now I knew Evan had his eye on the fan's propeller. Then, last night, on the way home from getting an ice cream cone, Miles and Evan played "Rabbit" in the backseat of the car. Miles laid down on the seat, snuffling a bit, while Evan scratched the base of his neck and cooed, "Nice rabbit." John and I, overhearing this new game, looked across at each other and smiled. "It doesn't take much," John said, and I agreed.

Playthings: Materials Carry Messages

When my sons were toddlers, I pored over the published lists of recommended toys. But once Miles and Evan became old enough to tell me what they wanted, I found myself taking a less active role in choosing their toys. I guess I assumed they had the right to choose their own toys.

But at some point, I realized that what I'd done was not to give Miles and Evan control of their toys, but to give advertisers and toy manufacturers control of them. When my children want something, their desires grow not out of their genes, but out of the people around them. I am one of those people, and I, too, can have a role in shaping my children's hopes. I, too, can advertise. I can demonstrate and promote the things I want my kids to want, and it is worth doing this because things are not valueless or neutral. Some things encourage a more thoughtful, inventive kind of play than others. Some things ask children to bring more to—and therefore get more from—their play than other things.

I next recognized that I needed to educate myself in the possibilities for children's play. So I began to read, and to talk with other parents, asking "Which toys do you recommend?" Of course, there is no one list of universally "good" toys. The toys that work well for one child won't with another. My nephew and godson Peter loves board games and sports, so these are more prevalent in his home than in mine. Peter's five-year-old sister Charlotte loves little things, and she loves putting things away. Thus containers are an important part of her play; she loves little suitcases, tiny treasure chests, and little boxes that can become stalls for horses, crates for her dogs, beds for her babies. Charlotte uses bits of fabric, cardboard, and popsicle sticks to make her bowls, dog or horse jumps, leashes, red ribbons, and—most important—babies.

Although children's toys of choice will always be idiosyncratic, it is nevertheless helpful to browse through other people's toy shelves, just as it is helpful to browse through their bookshelves. If you were to browse through our toy shelves, you'd notice first the blocks. We have the big cardboard blocks and plastic waffle blocks of various sizes, but we especially value a classroom-sized set of wooden blocks, including the arches and floorboards. My sons love Legos, too. For similar reasons, they enjoy playing with sand and cardboard boxes. With all these materials, they create worlds and then bring little characters of one kind or another to life, enacting small dramas inside castles, boats, islands, stores, and homes.

And so the world building supplies matter and so, too, the *little guys* matter. I don't care if they are Lego or playmobile guys, stuffed or rubber, or if they are people or horses or squirrels. I do care if my children's characters come with manufacturer-assigned names and story lines; if they do, my children embellish the story lines they've been given, or create their own.

We also love tables. My sons have several card tables, which when combined with blankets and pillows, function as human-sized blocks. My sons become the villains, victims, or heroes inside stained-glass cathedrals and shadowy forts. The tables also enable Miles and Evan to move their play into other rooms of the house. Of course, it's even more thrilling for them to move to an outdoor location. Recently, Miles and Evan took their one-inch micromachine vehicles outside and created bases for them in the clay walls of a gully. Their cousin Charlotte joined their play, claiming the patch of moss above their tiny cliff as her magical forest, in which she lodged little animals. The knobby jagged clay cliff became as grand and exotic as the Grand Canyon to them. New energy and resolve erupted from the simple act of moving their tiny toys out of doors! When a bit of play begins to feel commonplace and mundane, one way to bring new dimension to it is to move its location. Legos become interesting all over again if they are moved to a sunny table in the dining room.

I value the art supplies that invite children to be inventive and intentional. I think sharp scissors are well worth the risk, and I think marker pens and reams of white copy machine paper are well worth the cost. When my children draw, as when they build with Legos or blocks, they are usually devising worlds and stories. Dramatic sounds accompany their drawing: "This is a new kind of spaceship. Aliens live here. They're taking over!! Psheww!!" Sometimes, instead of using their drawing as a forum for dramatic play, Miles, Evan, and their cousins try to create something artistic. "What's your favorite color?" they ask me, then return to their work, filling a page with blue flowers. As I watch them alter their drawings, birthday cards, necklaces, posters, and decorations to please the recipient, I'm reminded again of the link between art and literacy.

My children have gone through the stage of loving the watercolor paints that come in tubes, "the ones real artists use." Woodworking materials also seem to me to be worth the risk—and the mess. John made Miles and Evan workbenches, complete with pegboards for hanging their tools. We make periodic trips to the lumberyard to raid the trash cans full of scrap lumber, which come in shapes and sizes perfect for hulls for ships, floors for rabbit hotels, and motors for all sorts of machines. My boys stretch heavy-duty colored rubber bands between nails and hooks to make railings and gears. They save their money to buy pulleys, ropes, electric drills and screwdrivers, and buckets; and for their birthdays, they often request replacement hammers and saws for the ones they've lost.

We also value equipment for dramatic play. When my children were very young, we had a rack from which hung 15 hats, ranging from astronaut helmets and pilot's caps to crowns and sombreros. We save our Halloween costumes, as well as old scarves, bridesmaid outfits, and the like.

Of course, if my children were girls, our list would be somewhat different. But I also know that if I had daughters, I would still resist shopping only in the pink and purple aisles of toy stores, just as I now resist much of what stores market for boys. And I know I'd wrestle with questions about whether to supply my daughters with purses, jewelry, and Barbie dolls with matching pink convertibles. I worry that Barbie dolls idealize an image of women—thin-waisted, big-breasted glamorous women—that doesn't match my hopes for women. But one of my closest colleagues insists that Barbies soon lose their glamour, that young girls like these wild-haired friends not because of their waist sizes or their fashions but because they are the perfect size for dramatic play. Perhaps I'd feel as she does if I was the mother of daughters. Or perhaps I'd resist buying lots of Barbie dolls for daughters just as I resist supplying my sons with machine guns and heavy artillery.

Clearly, playthings matter. The best playthings teach kids that *anything* can become a source of adventure and inquiry.

Storing Playthings

Children's play is influenced not only by the toys we do or do not provide for them, but also by our systems for storing and using those things. An early childhood educator once told me, "You can judge a primary school by its system for storage." It's easy to laugh at this idea. Surely our closets and cupboards needn't be clean in order for our children to play and learn well! But after teaching in a world-renowned British primary school, I realized that storage systems *do* matter. When I returned to the United States, one of my colleagues asked, "What'd you learn?" I answered by describing the grace and dignity with which those schools stored and displayed classroom equipment and children's work. "You're not saying the biggest lesson was that they store and display stuff better than we do?" my colleague responded. I nodded. "Yes, that's what I'm saying," sharing her amazement.

In my family, my brothers, sisters, and I threw most of our toys into two central toy boxes. And probably I would never have considered any other option. But in England, I saw classrooms in which everything was kept in its own drawer, its own bin. As a result, I asked John to hang those pegboards I described over the small workbenches he built in our garage; I insist that my kids' paints are in one box, their chalk in another, their markers in a third; I use five clear plastic frames to rotate my sons' latest artwork. Over the years, I've come to believe that the lessons I learned from the British primary school were entirely logical. Storage systems do matter.

When tools are kept in a jumble, we tend to treat them with less respect. Why wouldn't the same be true for toys?

The first priority for storing things is to be sure kids have easy access to their tools and materials. When kids rely on adults to dole out whatever they need, they won't think beyond our plans for what they should do. For example, if a child who is coloring must wait for me to hand out paper and crayons, then she is dependent on my vision of what is needed, and probably won't devise her own wonderful extensions of her original work. If she limits herself to the materials I dole out, then she will not even consider taping a cardboard tube or bits of fabric onto the drawing. If I lay out six crayons and one piece of paper on the table, chances are that child won't cut and fold the paper, or explore what happens when paint is sponged over paper. Creativity is all about taking an idea farther, about letting new plans emerge out of the project at hand; and children need independent access to new materials throughout the course of their play.

Conversely, it is also a problem when children have access to too many things. If everything is always readily available, kids tend to race through their things, strip-mining their environment, using everything fleetingly and incompletely. Thus, some monitoring is called for, but not so much that it inhibits creativity.

In our home, we use big plastic tubs or crates for storing toys. Two, which hold wooden blocks, are on rolling coasters, and they are permanently available. The other tubs are labeled: "playmobiles," "soldiers" and "rubber animals." With coaxing, supervision, and help, Miles and Evan sort their stuff into the appropriate bins when they put things away.

In addition, I generally keep a few bins in "deep storage." This means for about three months the rubber animals, the little cars, and the playmobiles may be unavailable to the boys. When the toys re-emerge, they have some of the appeal of brand-new ones.

Deepening and Extending Children's Play

The idea of keeping some playthings tucked away so that children play longer and deeper with other playthings may sound like a small trick-of-the-trade, but in fact, this gestures toward one of the ideas that is at the core of what education is all about.

Whether teaching children to write well, to talk wisely about books, to explore hunches in science, or to play inventively, one of the central moves educators make is to extend and deepen children's efforts. We see this, for example, when a third grader mentions in her book report that a book was sort of boring. The teacher responds, "What made the book boring?" and "If *you'd* been the author, how might *you* have written the book differently?" Throughout these questions, the teacher is trying to say to the child, "Build on your idea, stay with it longer."

To the young artist who has painted a single white cloud in the blue sky, the teacher says, "I love the way you added white against the blue. Can you look again, and try to capture all the colors of that sky? Can you look with equal care at the grass?" Or a young mathematician can be prompted to list different combinations of numbers that, when added, total the number 10. The teacher can go farther still, by asking the student to arrive at the number 10 through subtraction, division, or multiplication. In all of these examples, the message is, "Can you stay with this? Can you take what you've done even farther?"

Similarly, this is one of the most powerful ways that parents can make children's play as educational as possible. When my children were babies, they both attended a Lab School at Teachers College, Columbia University. One day as I sat in the rocking chair with Evan, I watched Miles, who was then two years old, pick up two blocks and begin walking around the room, absentmindedly banging the blocks together. One of the teachers at the center looked at Miles for a moment and then exclaimed to the toddlers around her, "Oh look, Miles is making a parade!" When Miles heard this, initially he seemed surprised, caught off guard. But quickly he began banging his blocks like cymbals and lifting his knees in a proud, parade-master fashion. Soon a line of toddlers and caretakers holding infants joined Miles's parade, weaving their way throughout the room.

That day, hearing the teacher announce, "Oh, look, Miles is making a parade," I thought, "What a lesson!" So often as parents, we see our children gesturing towards doing something. How important it can be for us to get behind our children, turning their half-hearted bangings into parades! This is important emotionally as well as intellectually.

On the other hand, it can be just as important *not* to intervene, and usually we can tell by the signals our children send us. Sometimes when I try to interject, I sense I've broken a spell, thwarted an intention. At such moments, I remind myself to watch more closely, to be more tentative, to give children lots of time to spin the story of their play.

The best way to "get behind" our children's play is to do as those caretakers did when Miles gestured toward making a parade. They picked up instruments and joined in, lifting up their knees with spirit. What a gift we give our children when we take on a role in their dramatic play: become the bad guy, the parent, the third child; build our own little cabin, not far from their fort; or become one of the players around the Monopoly board. Joseph Pearce writes in *Magical Child*, "The child can never learn to play without the parent playing with the child. Play . . . is a huge creative potential built within the child which never develops unless it is stimulated by the adult model, the parent."[4]

My husband is far better than I am at playing with Miles and Evan. They love it when he becomes a kid, crawling on his stomach through the "woods" in order to launch a sneak attack on their fort. After an attack—which may take only 10 minutes of John's time—Miles and Evan will spend the entire next week strengthening their defense system against any future attacks. They love having an opponent who brings such excitement and drama to their game.

In my sister's home, Peter and Charlotte each are given 20 minutes of "Play" every evening. The ritual is that each child can choose his or her play, in which Joe, their father, will join. In this way, the three of them go to Charlotte's house for a tea party, enter her horses in a show, or spin a story around her dolls. And then the three of them join Peter in a makeshift game of baseball, hockey, or soccer. These children feel as if they are the luckiest kids in the world to have a wand with which they can turn their own dad into a playmate.

Joe's contribution is particularly precious because his children can count on this time; they can anticipate it. Charlotte will get her dolls dressed and ready for the party. Peter will practice throwing and catching a baseball for an hour, knowing he'll soon have a chance to use and display the skills he develops. Peter and Charlotte are in control of this time; they are the producers of their "play."

Unfortunately, well-intended parents can make play more difficult for children. This can happen when we throw ourselves into our children's play, wildly and enthusiastically, but only *fleetingly*, then pull away, leaving children feeling deflated. The value of our involvement lies in part in what happens for children *after* we've retreated to our own activities. If our involvement helps them to be more invested and resourceful, more full of initiative, then we've been helpful indeed, but if we only stimulate momentarily then abandon them, we aren't helpful.

We can help our children play by listening carefully to their plans and intentions and then talking with them to extend these plans. When Evan piles blocks on top of each other, I ask, "What are you making?" By asking such a simple question, I am suggesting that I expect him to have a plan, an image of what he's working to achieve. Thinking quickly, Evan announces, "I'm making a castle." To this I might inquire, "Do you want that book by David MacCauley on castles? The one we were looking at the other day? I think I could find it." Soon Evan and I are leafing through the intricate drawings in the book, and Evan is deciding whether his castle will be built on a table-top hill or surrounded by a moat.

As Evan builds the castle, we, of course, have other conversations. "Where do the people sleep, do you suppose?" "Where do they eat?" "How, I wonder, do they get their food if they are under attack?" Out of conversations such as this can grow an entire inquiry into medieval life. Needless to say, there are countless other ways I could have gotten behind Evan's first efforts. I could have asked, "Will this be a really big block project, bigger than the everyday ones?" I could have queried whether the castle was going to be part of an entire medieval town. I could have said, "You've got so many blocks beside you. Are you going to use every single block in this castle?" I could have mused, "You know Ev', you make such amazing castles, but we never keep them up long. This time we should take a photograph or draw what you make; we should do something so we can hold onto it forever!" In each of these instances, I am extending Evan's play by extending his intentions, his planfulness.

Many kindergarten and first-grade teachers rely on Elizabeth S. Hirsch's *The Block Book* for ideas on extending children's block play. Hirsch tells stories of children who study the city block on which their school stands, then re-create the story of that city block using their wooden blocks. She also recounts examples of children who study their school, making scale drawings of the hallways, classrooms, and bathrooms, then re-creating them on the floor of their classroom.

Reading this book, I am struck by how much intellectual work can revolve around playing with blocks. The strategy for doing this is to inquire about how life really proceeds in and around the child's structure and in this way bring out the world around the child's creation. "Where is the hay kept in this barn? How does it get up to the loft? Where does it come from? Do the horses ever get sick? Where does the vet come from? Do the foals stay with the mares or are they kept separately? What about the stallions?"

We can, in similar ways, lift the level of anything our children do. Earlier I suggested that if we often ask our children, "What are your plans?" they will eventually anticipate these questions by asking *themselves*, "What do I want to do here?" We can also ask questions that create a context around our children's play with teddy bears, dolls, little guys, or blocks. If a child has lined horses up in a row, we can ask, "Why are they in a row like this? Will this be a horse show?" Alternatively, we can ask, "Who owns these horses? What's their story?" If a child seems to be aimlessly tossing a Frisbee into the air and catching it, we can help that child devise plans and projects. We might, for example, ask, "What game are you playing with the Frisbee? Do you make up games with it?" Alternatively, we could ask, "What are you trying to do? Are you working to master new tricks with this Frisbee?" Questions such as these contain assumptions, and those assumptions can lift the level of what children do.

We extend children's play by helping them to return to, elaborate on, and extend their initial efforts. But this can happen only if their block castles or cardboard dollhouses are allowed to remain out and visible over the course of several days or even weeks. One of the problems with the play children engage in at school is that in the name of fairness, of "giving everyone a turn," children are often cycled quickly through the block area, the art corner, the dramatic play center. In Lydia's school, teachers have come to realize that more elaborate, complex thinking emerges out of children's play when groups of children spend at least a week in a particular play area. Then a great deal of planning, conceptualizing, collaboration, revision, reading, and research can be incorporated into any one of these play centers. Children are encouraged to have and pursue their own wonderful ideas.

It is worth noting that when I enter into my son's play in order to extend it, my primary role *is not to help my son avoid difficulty*. If anything, I am more interested in creating difficulty than in lessening it.

When Miles and Evan were very young, they had a warm-hearted baby-sitter who had endless patience for playing board games. But she was so intent on pleasing my sons that in every game she played with them, she maneuvered things to ensure one of my youngsters would beat her. Then she would make a big fuss, and play-act the sad-faced loser to extol my son's prowess. When I realized this, I told her, "Marion! Miles and Evan need practice in losing as well as in winning! Go ahead and win, fair and square!"

Some children never learn how to lose. When it becomes clear that they will lose a game, these children either quit, perhaps messing everything up before they go, or suddenly announce, "Let's start over again." Or else they cheat in order to win. Bruno Bettelheim points out that the child who cheats is really not different from the child who quits early. Cheating in a board game, he says, is not about a lack of morals, but about a child having too much at stake in a game and feeling threatened. If we accost such a child for cheating, he may never play the game again. And so we need, instead, to help children lose with their self-confidence intact.

It's no small challenge to help children learn to lose gracefully.

When I was ten, my father was demoted from his position as chairman of the Department of Medicine. His leadership role was taken from him and he resumed his role as physician. Thirty years later, I am in academia myself and realize now that people are moved out of Department Chair positions regularly. My parents could have downplayed the significance of the entire event. Instead, I distinctly recall a Christmas holiday filled with talk about Dad "being fired." Partly in jest, we wrapped gifts in newspaper that Christmas instead of in wrapping paper. "We've got to watch the budget, Dad's been fired," my mother said.

In one-to-one talks with me and the other kids, I remember Dad telling me about how he'd made mistakes, and that he had angered some people, and as a result, lost the job he wanted. He was very candid. At the time, I didn't realize that Dad was giving us a lesson in failing: "I knew every one of you would meet with stone walls in your lives, that you'd encounter obstacles, that you'd fail. It happens to us all. A lot of what counts is what a person *does* in the face of defeat." It's important, then, to mentor our children in the act of losing well. It's also important to help them learn to live with difficulty.

For example, Andrea had planned to create a dress for her puppet out of a piece of fabric, but the fabric was too small to completely circle her puppet. She looked in dismay at her half-clothed puppet. Watching her, I realized this was a potentially rich educational moment. The occasion challenged her to either alter her vision or to imagine new ways of achieving it. She needed to search for new materials or to adapt what she had to meet the challenge. I would have done her a disservice had I immediately jumped in to help. Children must learn to persist at projects that matter to them, to have the determination of that little train that tried again and again to make it over the mountain, chanting, "I think I can, I think I can, I think I can."

Over the past few years, creativity kits for making moccasins, wallets, birdhouses, and the like have become increasingly popular. These kits make things easy for kids. That's their purpose. The materials are all provided, and everything is already cut to size.

Children can be sure they won't encounter major snags. Where, then, does the impetus for creativity come from? I sometimes think that the kits would do a better job of supporting creativity if they contained only half the necessary materials.

Of course, there is such a thing as too much difficulty, and there are times when we need to ease our children's way. But I always try to ease the technical rather than the intellectual problems. That is, I'm more apt to finish cutting the cardboard box according to Evan's quirky specifications than I am to warn him that once the box is cut according to his design, it won't stand up. I don't think it is particularly important that Evan's hands become strong enough to cut through a lot of thick cardboard, but I do think it is important that he not let a collapsed cardboard box foil his plans. I want him to hold on to his vision in the face of difficulty, to imagine a host of alternatives for reaching his goals. These habits can be nourished when he plays, and then transferred into other areas of his life.

There is no doubt that children's play can be a foundation for their schoolwork—without us finding little ways to insert reading, writing, or arithmetic into their games. I used to be the kind of parent who would find my child making a high block tower and, in an effort to coax him to make the building "intellectually valuable," I'd maneuver things so that he'd estimate and then count the numbers of blocks he'd used, or he'd write about his creation. Now I've finally come to realize that it is equally powerful for us to simply watch for the habits of thought the child uses to build his high tower, for example, and then make those habits of thought part of the child's self-concept. "It was amazing to watch you *plan* that tower!" we might say. "When you write, do you also take a moment to plan, to think, 'How shall I do this?' "

In order to extend and support our children's play, we need to be able to sit on the side and observe our children's play. This alone is a radical idea. So often in schools, teachers will tell us that they value young children's play, but don't act in accordance. It's rare for teachers to observe and record what they see children doing during playtime, intervening to nudge children to be more resourceful and purposeful, tenacious, and collaborative in their play. Instead, if you and I were to peek in on a classroom or a school playground during

play time, we'd usually see teachers standing above children, survey-
ing them to be sure everything is proceeding smoothly.

Someday, perhaps, schools will change, but for now, it is usually us
as parents who can truly take our children's play seriously. We do
this by observing our children's intentions and supporting their
grand ideas. We do this by joining behind our children's parades,
letting *them* be the parade masters.

CHAPTER 6

Helping Children Develop Good Work Habits: Hobbies, Projects, Chores, and the Lessons They Teach

Like every parent, I want my children to have high standards for their work, and I worry when they don't. I forgive Evan's haphazard efforts to clean up his toys, telling myself he's still young, but I grow exasperated when I see Miles put his clean clothes away by dumping them on top of his bureau; and I am frustrated when he leaves a trail of scraps behind when he picks up his artwork. I grumble to my husband, "As soon as I look the other way, he does a lousy job." But then I watch Miles in the sandbox, building a tiny village, working with enormous intelligence, care, and discipline, and I know that it will be this miniature village that teaches him the joy of working hard, that turns him into the kind of person who reaches toward excellence.

Helping Children Develop a Work Ethic

When we try to teach children to work hard, frequently we do so only by supervising their chores and stressing the importance of self-discipline. We tell our kids that if they do their work well, if they keep their noses to the grindstone, they'll someday end up with a good job, a good house, a good life. Our message is that hard work pays off in the long run; it isn't *fun*, but it's *worth it*. Throughout, we assume and teach that work and play are the opposite of each other. But are they?

When my father was ten, he spent the summer at an old-fashioned sleep-away camp. One of the rituals at Camp Merrywater was that every day after lunch all of the boys would lie on their cots, and the wife of the camp director would read aloud. Dad reminisces: "I remember lying there on my cot, with one of those green Army-Navy blankets over me, looking up at the rafters and listening as she read *The Microbe Hunters*. I remember being filled with such excitement I could hardly bear it. My father's job was a job, 9:00 to 5:00, and when it was over, he had his fun. Lying on that cot, I realized it didn't have to be that way. For those microbiologists—for Marie Curie and Louis Pasteur and the others—*their work was their fun*. Lying there on that cot I vowed that when I grew up, I'd know what it was to have passion, teamwork, drama in my *work* like those microbe hunters had in their work."

Our children are growing up in a culture that values leisure and self-indulgence. They are surrounded by people who regard "the good life" as a life of beautiful clothes, whirlpool bathtubs, and after-dinner drinks. They live in a culture in which the heroes are actresses and football players rather than teachers and physicians. They hear people talk about retirement as "getting out of the rat race." John and I want to surround our children with a counterculture that values hard work.

I want all children to learn that it is a privilege to work hard on projects you deem significant. I want them to understand there can be a thin line between work and play. I want my sons to notice that their father wakes up early in the morning to weed and water his precious garden before he leaves for work. I hope they notice him crouching alongside the plants, peering at the undersides of the leaves, watching over them tenderly, ready to ward off disease, bugs, and deer. I hope they see their father bringing home a stack of books from the local library, intent on finding a way to keep the deer from defoliating our shrubs. Is this work, or is it play? For me, there's little difference between the two.

I think of the effort we all pour into the biggest project of our lives—our kids. When we take the training wheels off our kids' bikes, and run along behind as they wobble down the lane, is this work or is it play? I don't think we, as parents, work hard on the project of our children because we have good work habits, or because we believe it will "pay off in the end." That sort of motivation simply isn't enough to account for the work we do so willingly.

Likewise, if we want our children to have high standards for their work, if we want them to invest themselves heart and soul into the work of their lives, then we need to help our kids understand that love as well as discipline can lead them to work hard. If we want our children to have high standards for their work, the best thing we can do is to help them see that there can be a thin line between work and play.

Finding the Joy in Work

I used to believe I was doing my kids a favor when I pretended that I didn't want to spend a morning writing in my attic office or working at Teachers College. I'd say, "I'd rather be home with you. But I have no choice; I have to go to work." Then I heard my sons begin to moan when it was time for them to do their schoolwork, and I realized what I'd done. If I had been honest, I would have told them that few things delight me more than the chance to spend a morning at my desk, and that I head off to Teachers College feeling as if I'm on my way to a clubhouse filled with friends. Now my sons know this, and they know I wish for them to approach their work with equal delight.

My youngest adores school, and I take advantage of this: "Who wouldn't love school?" I say. "You get a chance to work alongside your friends; what a treat!" Miles loves school, too, but he sometimes sounds as if he has mixed feelings about it, so I make it a point to seem perplexed when he complains about having to go to school. "I can't imagine why you don't love it," I say. "I mean, would you rather spend the day hanging around doing *nothing?* That'd be so dull!"

I try to forestall complaints about homework, too. "Do you have any interesting math homework tonight?" I ask, anticipating that one of my sons might have been given a challenge that we could all think about together. I don't tend to have the belief that the kids need to do everything themselves. Although the assignment to make a poster *could* be done on a single sheet of construction paper, I'm happy to buy the boys sheets of heavy poster paper in brilliant colors and to lend my hand at cutting straight margins for double-mounting their maps, drawings, or word-processed reports.

If I hear their baby-sitter say, "Why not get your homework done so you can have some fun," I try to coach her to encourage a positive approach, to say instead, "Let's save time for writing." "Let's do the homework first and do a great job of it!"

Of course, sometimes all children will dread doing certain work. Perhaps they have a piano teacher who insists that they reach a certain level of achievement in one song before allowing them to work on another. Practicing the same song week after week can be drudgery. Likewise, children are sometimes assigned schoolwork they find distasteful. When this happens, I try to help them figure out why, in such a case, their work has lost its appeal. I want them to know that this isn't the norm, that something must be very wrong indeed if they can't approach their work with enthusiasm.

Learning Good Work Habits from Projects and Hobbies

Children can learn good work habits from involving themselves deeply in collections, hobbies, pets, and projects. People often ask my parents how they managed to raise nine kids, all of whom can be described as hard working. My mother insists that it wasn't she who taught us, but the musical instruments, the younger kids, the flock of chickens, and the stamp collections. Her point is that every project can lead to an unbelievable sequence of work. When one of my sisters found a catalog advertising 40 varieties of two-day old baby chicks to purchase by mail, we made countless trips to the local library, the 4-H center, and nearby breeders to resolve the question of which breeds to get. In the end, we ordered two chicks from each of 20 different breeds, and soon we were carpenters' assistants, helping my father; lugging, sawing, hammering, and nailing boards to make a chicken coop. Later, we carried steaming hot water through the Buffalo snowdrifts to thaw our chickens' water bucket. Each day we collected and washed eggs, then delivered them to the neighbors on that day's egg route. Eventually, we joined the 4-H, after which our efforts included researching our chickens in order to prepare for oral presentations at 4-H conferences, and to select the best chickens to show at the county fair.

Our projects could just as easily have been photography or folk-dancing, coin collecting, or jazz. The important point is that raising chickens could have been a childhood whimsy; instead, it became the project of our young lives. My parents made the difference, and I try to follow their example when I work with my own children.

This past July, Miles and Evan both asked for a rabbit, guinea pig, or hamster for their birthday. I cajoled John into agreeing then set off to the pet store to select the appropriate creature. What fun I had interviewing the pet shop personnel, paging through the booklets, peering into the cages trying to select the perfect pet! Fortunately, I realized before it was too late that I was having all the fun—and doing all the work. So when their birthdays came, Miles and Evan were each given certificates promising them the animal of their choice, to be selected with great care.

It was a wonderful process: We checked out 20 rabbit books from the local library, visited area feed stores and pored through news-papers in search of rabbit breeders to visit. We spent several long afternoons listening to the breeders we visited. Miles and Evan learned how to inspect the jaws of rabbits, and they understood the differences between Holland Lop, Mini-Lop, and Mini-Rex breeds. They knew how to read a rabbit's pedigree, and could begin to determine when a rabbit might be a good prospect for showing.

But equally important, learning about rabbits taught Miles, Evan, *and* me more about people. We became fascinated by the realization that the world is full of people who are obsessed about one thing or another. We met people famous for their work with rabbits, and we were intrigued by how each little circle of interest in life promotes its own heroes, stars—and bad guys, too. We've seen that there are magazines and stores and clubs designed just for rabbit owners. There is even a Holland Lop Rabbit Club, separate from the Mini-

Lop Rabbit Club. We've seen that the books and experts on rabbits contradict each other and that seemingly simple subjects such as "What snacks are good for a rabbit?" can lead to complicated and controversial discussions.

All of this involves a lot of work, and not just for the children! My mother's advice regarding projects is: "Warn people that it's a mistake to cling to the old adage, 'Be sure the children do it themselves.' " Whether children are delivering newspapers, selling eggs, building a model, or learning a musical instrument, they benefit from adult support in these efforts.

I recently learned of a ten-year-old girl whose parents bought a black Labrador retriever, and assigned it as her responsibility. The dog is too wild to keep in the house, so he spends his nights in the garage, and the young girl is expected to wake up at six o'clock every morning to clean up the dog's messes and walk the bounding creature. The girl probably resents the dog and the job, but her parents don't want to help for fear that "she may never learn responsibility!" But responsibility involves not just duty, it also involves response–ability, the ability to care. It's probably best to teach responsibility when the child is as invested in a project as possible, and adults should monitor carefully the amount of responsibility they put on a child's shoulders if that child is to thrive in her new role.

Certainly, parental support can come indirectly, such as by fueling a child's interest by taking the child to a concert, a play, or museum. David Feldman, professor of psychology at Tufts University, suggests that any one of these visits can become, for a child, a "crystallizing experience" that sets in motion the decision to follow a particular life course. For the great violinist Yehudi Menuhin, the crystallizing experience was a trip to the San Francisco Symphony when he was three. For Albert Einstein, the crystallizing experience came when he was five and his father gave him a compass.

And parents don't have to carry the burden alone. My parents rallied behind my brother's interest in tennis by giving him a first-class racket, then enrolled him in a tennis clinic. In order for most of us to become self-motivated learners, we need to reach a certain level of success. Lessons can carry learners through the early stages, and this is especially true if the lessons are part of a fairly disciplined practice regimen.

On the other hand, sending a child off to a series of lessons cannot replace parental involvement. For example, I've been giving a lot of thought lately to the issue of music lessons. My advice is that parents need to refrain from enrolling a child in music lessons unless the child *and* especially the parents are ready to commit to the regimen of daily practice. I hear parents say, with surprise in their voices, "My child doesn't practice much," or "It turns out she's not *that* interested. She only gets around to practicing once or twice a week." The difference between the child who practices and the child who doesn't are the parents. And the problem is, if parents start a child on music lessons and they aren't ready to support a consistent schedule of daily practicing, then the momentum of having begun music lessons is wasted. If the child gets into the habit of taking lessons and not practicing, it's almost impossible to reverse this. It would have been far better for a child in such a situation to wait a year or two before beginning the instrument.

Continuity matters, too. It's not a good idea for parents to sign up with the first available teacher, taking the attitude, "When my child is older and better, I'll find the perfect teacher; for now, it doesn't really matter." Each teacher has her own values, and it's best for a learner to grow up under a certain teacher's tutelage. Of course, selecting the right teacher is another time-consuming and complicated task in and of itself . . . and it's far more complicated still to shepherd a child through the years of practicing and lessons, that are necessary.

There is also the question of when to start lessons. For most children, first grade is not a good time to begin something like music lessons because of its accompanying regimen of practice. Many children find bridging the gap between kindergarten and first grade to be stressful. Suddenly they're asked to do a great deal of paper and pencil work, of desk work, of following someone else's directions. Meanwhile, the academic stakes are especially high in first grade. This is the year when many children "take off" as readers and writers, while others lag noticeably behind. Consequently, first graders need to spend time each night reading to and with their parents. Therefore, it's a lot to expect of children to also take on something as intensive as music lessons.

Even with other kinds of lessons that don't require daily practicing, I question whether first grade is the best time to begin. Sara, the woman who cuts my hair, learned that her first-grade son was struggling in school. He was tested for reading disabilities, but no specific problem emerged. "Thomas is just not catching on as quickly as we'd like," his teacher told Sara. When she and I talked about the way she and her husband could support Thomas's reading at home, Sara became agitated. "You don't understand our schedule," she told me. "There is *no time*. We take him to karate class three times a week. He spends an hour just getting dressed and undressed, because we tell him he's old enough to be independent; but he's still so slow."

The last time Sara cut my hair she told me they had dropped karate for now, and she is supporting Thomas's morning routines so that each day begins on a smooth note. They are also weaving shared reading throughout the day.

These are difficult decisions. For another child, it might have been more important to continue the karate lessons because it was that child's greatest joy. The many children who arrive late to school each morning because they've already had an hour of hockey practice or gymnastics may conceivably gain so much from their extracurricular activities that it's worth the trade-off of their being exhausted before the school day begins. The important point is that parents need to be aware that when we add to a child's schedule, something is *taken away* as well. We therefore must consider what is gained and what is lost, and when is the best time in a child's life to launch a new project. We also need to watch our children to see how they juggle the various aspects of their lives. If a child doesn't particularly like hockey, if he's on the team mostly because his big brother adores hockey, *and* he's struggling in school, the loss is clearly greater than the gain. This is an entirely different issue than the child who, for example, entered first grade already reading well and is a gifted pianist, yet still sometimes resists her Saturday morning music lessons.

When we think about what is gained and lost by involving children in a sport or a hobby, it's important to realize that whether our children are involved with Little League, pottery classes, Hebrew studies, or Girl or Boy Scouts, they learn far more than music, art, language, or sports from these endeavors. This past summer, Miles and I played a lot of tennis together. I used our matches as a time to coach Miles in social skills as well as in tennis. Once, for example, I looked up from an informal volley to see five tennis balls lying on *my* side of the net. My son's court was, for the first time ever, totally clear of balls. "My goodness," I said, pointing to the field of failed balls on my side of the net. "I'm not doing too well! It's five to nothing!"

Miles laughed loudly. "Yep," he said. "Look how many balls you've got!! And I don't have any."

"Miles," I said. "That's not the polite thing to do. Your role in this conversation is to say 'Oh, Mom, this is the first time ever that I don't have any balls.'" Then I added, "Miles, did you see how I waited till I was *doing badly* and then, in a joking way, put myself down? That's what you need to do. Wait until you're losing and then point out your limitations!"

Tennis has given Miles and me a new forum for working out our relationship, and brought Miles in touch with new people. At tennis camp, he met a new group of children and found it challenging to negotiate relationships with them. This was far more difficult than any of the tennis skills he was being taught. One day, he came home upset about an older boy who had taunted him, called him a girl, and threw tennis balls at his crotch. Hearing his distress, it was all I could do to keep from storming into the tennis camp, and shaking some sense into the bully who was upsetting my son. But I stopped myself because I knew that Miles needed to work out the problem on his own, and that my role should be only to support and advise from behind the scenes. Meanwhile, Miles also made a new friend at tennis camp, and I hope that he learned that working with people can be part of any hobby or project.

Choosing Projects and Hobbies

When children become involved in the hobbies and projects that are popular among their peers, these can be great sources of new connections and new status. But there are also advantages to choosing projects on "the road less traveled."

My oldest sister Sally played the clarinet for a long time, and was modestly successful. Then, when she switched to the contra-bass clarinet, a huge and unwieldy instrument, she quickly became the first chair contra-bass clarinet player in her band. Subsequently, she was invited to join New York State's All-State band, which was a marvelous opportunity for her. Later she was invited to join with young musicians from 46 countries at the world-renowned Interlochen Music Camp and was awarded a scholarship. My point is, these opportunities might not have come her way had she played a more typical instrument. My cousin Barbie was similarly rewarded because she played the bassoon, another unusual instrument. Thus when the time came for my younger brother Geoff to select an instrument, he chose the tuba, and soon became one of the best tuba players around. At first this was because he was one of the only tuba players around, but success begets success.

Just as we need to question the adage, "Children need to do the project *themselves*," then, we also need to question whether kids need to *select* projects themselves. The great poet Lucille Clifton once said, "We cannot create what we cannot imagine." We needn't just wait for our kids to choose their own projects, hobbies, and interests; we can help them imagine possibilities for themselves. If we don't help our kids imagine possibilities, they are apt to follow only the well-traveled roads.

My godchild Peter asked for a parakeet for his birthday, but he was perfectly amenable to his mother's suggestion of buying, instead, a pair of unusual, very small Cowl ducks. Since no one else in their suburban town had ducks, Peter's project became a wonderful subject for his creative writing. His classmates were all intrigued to learn about and see his ducks. The local newspaper even wrote a story about them. Peter and his sister entered their ducks in a local fair and won several rosette ribbons and a two-foot-high trophy for having the best bird and best junior entry.

The child who is committed to saving a historic building, raising sea horses, or growing orchids, will find these interests lead very quickly to working shoulder-to-shoulder with adults who share this interest. My eight-year-old nephew Milo takes puppetry very seriously, and I believe he is the only child who belongs to the Bay Area Puppetry Guild. My brother Ben raised Dorset sheep when he was a child, and soon he became best friends with a sheep farmer, and traveled with him to sheep-farming activities across the state. Now his daughter Sarah attends swine-judging camp each summer and competes in statewide contests. Twelve-year-old Sarah can stand in front of a pen filled with pigs and quickly assess the relative merits of each. After organizing her thoughts and amassing her data, she can argue her case to a swine judge. She is learning skills that trial lawyers and literary critics, alike, use.

Sometimes we will misjudge our kids, and the seeds we plant will fall on rocky soil. If our child's newspaper route or pet turns out to be a burden, creating constant hard feelings, then rather than thinking this is the perfect opportunity to teach responsibility, it's probably best to find a graceful way out. And so I think it's useful to help our children construct an excuse that leaves their sense of self intact. Just as we do all we can to prevent our kids from seeing themselves as failures as readers, so, too, we will probably do what we can to prevent our kids from seeing themselves as failures at raising rabbits or delivering newspapers. It was easier for my nephew to say, "My mother made me get rid of my dog," rather than to admit to himself and everyone else, "I lost interest in my dog." Deep down he probably knew that his mother wasn't the culprit, but I admired my sister for refraining from correcting her son. And it may have been sensible for my young neighbor to say, "I can't mow the lawn anymore; I have too much schoolwork," rather than admit, "I'm frankly too lazy to mow your lawn." There may be times when we want our children to take an honest look at themselves, but there are other times when it's reasonable to put a good face on things.

Doing Chores

There are two kinds of chores: project chores, which I've already discussed, and what I call citizenship chores. These include all the ways in which kids join into the work of the family or another group because that's what members of a community do.

The most important thing about citizenship chores (setting and clearing the kitchen table, feeding the pet, taking out the trash, making one's bed, watching younger siblings, assisting an elderly neighbor, helping cook for the homeless) is the attitude with which they are approached. I care very much that Miles and Evan willingly take on these chores; and ideally, I'd like them to join in these chores without waiting to be asked and without expecting to be thanked, just as I don't want to have to ask my husband to help unload the groceries or to thank him for doing so, as if it's a great personal favor. I want their participation to be routine, to be assumed. I don't care whether my kids do a superb job of bringing in the groceries, clearing their plates, or carrying packages for a neighbor, but I do care that they self-initiate these efforts. I want them to develop an awareness of the work others do to keep a household running smoothly and to see themselves as participating members of the community.

Because these citizenship chores are about joining into the work of a community, I try, whenever possible, to have them be communal. John and I feel very proud of ourselves if we organize a family chore like sweeping the garage, raking the leaves, or reorganizing the kitchen cupboards, that we can all join into together. And I am apt to nudge my boys to join me in folding the laundry while we watch a television show together.

When I was a child, growing up on a farm in western New York, Sunday afternoons were devoted to "projects." The nine of us, plus assorted neighborhood children, would pitch in to build a stone wall, seal the cracks in the driveway, rake the leaves, or plant dozens of tiny trees. We learned about the strength in numbers. The work would go quickly with so many of us pitching in; and there were always the small pleasures of hearing chestnuts pop in the bonfire, of making a towering pile of brush to be towed away, and of watching the antics of accompanying pets and toddlers. We'd sometimes break into song together, or divide into conversation partners.

Now my hope is that sometimes our family chores will feel like projects and that my boys will join readily and happily into these chores. Naturally, sometimes all of us find it difficult to be enthusiastic about doing the chores. But I am still quick to speak out against a bad attitude. If my sons grumble or moan when someone asks for their help, I'm apt to say, "We don't want your company if you're going to be grouchy," then suggest they sit out until they're ready to be good-natured about the chore.

I'm equally vigilant about their attitudes toward little jobs like emptying the trash. If I ask Evan to take out the trash and he whines as he begins to do the job, this isn't acceptable for me. I tell him to skip it, to leave the trash, and I'll do it myself. I don't want him to ever think that I appreciate a chore which is done with a begrudging attitude. On the other hand, when one of my boys does a chore with a cheerful attitude, I praise the spirit even more than the completion of the chore itself.

I also care that my sons do citizenship chores without step-by-step guidance. If Miles is helping to clean up after dinner and needs to stop every two minutes to ask, "What do I do with these leftover peas?" and "Where do I put this frying pan?" and "Should I wash this dish out?" I usually tell him, "The job includes figuring these things out. You decide. Use your head." I don't want to micro-manage chores such as these. Ultimately it doesn't matter to me if Miles throws the leftover peas away or if he stores them in the refrigerator; what does matter is that he shows initiative and responsibility for his work.

Of course, there are some chores about which I am particular. If I care that my sons load the dishwasher according to my precise specifications, then I tend to watch like a hawk when they even come close to the dishwasher. How much wiser I'd be to simply take a few opportunities to *teach* my boys what I have in mind instead of micro-monitoring each step of the chore. If loading the dishwasher really mattered in our home, then we'd have dishwasher clinics. I do not want my sons to do their chores in a dot-to-dot fashion, totally dependent on my executive role.

The truth is, teaching my boys to join willingly into the chores of our family is no easy feat. I have to remind them often about the importance of such community efforts. But because my goal is that they self-initiate, I try to remind them before the dinner, for example, that I hope they find ways to help throughout and after the meal, rather than reminding them every step of the way—telling them to clear the table, wash the dishes, and put the butter away. If I need to remind them to help, I do so not by saying, "Would you put away the mustard?" but rather "I don't want to have to remind you to join into the clean-up."

It remains to be seen whether my efforts will pay off. But meanwhile, I'll continue to help my children learn the values and habits of hard work, and to learn not only from the chores I list on job charts, but also from the work that grows out of their collections, hobbies, pets, and projects.

CHAPTER 7

Reading and the Middle Childhood Years

When I taught third graders, many of my students covered their books with homemade book jackets, wore mismatched socks, and used fountain pens. There is nothing developmental linking the middle childhood years with fountain pens and mismatched socks. My students did these things because they were emulating me . . . and the middle childhood years are a time when children are eager to emulate the adults they admire. Now, decades later, my third-grade son carries a water bottle to school and it's not coincidental that his teacher has a water bottle of her own.

These middle childhood years have been called "the golden age of instruction," and "the eager period." Children during these years are "superbly equipped to learn just about anything."[1] Why then, during the middle childhood years, do many parents become less involved in their children's education? By second grade, fewer parents come to open houses, attend author celebrations, volunteer in classrooms, drive on field trips, and read with their children. Recently, a third-grade teacher in an upper-middle-class town told me that only one child in his class had parents who read aloud to him. "I wasn't surprised. That's what I've come to expect," he said. Whereas parents sit side by side with their five- and six-year-olds, supporting their reading, they tend to tell older children, "Go to your room and do your homework."

The sad thing is that, during these golden years of instruction, when we could make such a difference, we tend to pull back from supporting our child's reading. One mother explained to me, "We figured once Sarah could read, she should read by herself." Another parent said, "If the teacher has assigned our son a book, I figure he should be able to read it on his own." Another said, "I want Jerod to have good study habits and so I try to be firm. I send him off to do his homework in a quiet place, at his desk."

These parents have the best of intentions. They are trying to enforce the school's expectations, and ensure that their children grow into conscientious, diligent students. But I am troubled by the sudden shift from parents sitting on big soft chairs cuddling their children during first grade to the children suddenly sitting alone at their desks in their rooms, associating reading always with home-work. As Susan Fox, a third-grade teacher from Oceanside, New York, recently stressed, "Second and third graders are still so young. If I can only remember that half my students still believe a tooth fairy exists, how much wiser my teaching will be!"

Seven- and eight-year-old children are still very young as readers. Some of them are able to call out what most of the words say, but usually the stamina of their attentiveness as readers is still very wobbly. During these golden years of instruction, parents can make a world of difference by staying engaged and supportive.

I'm particularly concerned because just when we parents often stop lavishing children with love, laughter, and closeness during reading time, school also changes in dramatic ways. Often it's as if someone blows a whistle between either first and second grade or second and third grade. "Shape up! Play time is over!" the school announces. Whereas a year earlier, children read lying on the classroom carpet or sitting arms linked with a friend, they now often read alone, silently, at their desks. Or they may be divided into ability-based reading groups, in which each child takes a turn reading aloud while peers and the teacher call out corrections. A new sense of "hurry up," "do as you're told," "stay in line," and "quiet!" pervades the entire curriculum in many of these rooms. All too often, every paper must have proper margins and headings, handwriting must stay within the lines, and spellings are expected to be correct. And children often have to write about every book they read.

If there is a new rigidity in our children's school curriculum, we need to be especially careful to not also have a new rigidity in the home curriculum. Sometimes I think we confuse rigidity with rigor. I am all for rigor, but rigor has nothing to do with sitting upright in a chair or with working in isolation. During second grade and third grade, we'll want to help our children read and write for longer stretches of time, yes, but they can still do this wrapped together in a blanket with a teddy bear and a snack.

If we say, "Go to your room and do your homework; you're supposed to read a chapter a night," we may think we're supporting our children's education, but we are inadvertently teaching that reading is something to do alone and because it's assigned. What a different message we convey if we say, "What's happening in your book? Have you had a chance to read on yet? I'm dying to know if . . ."

When parents talk to me about supporting their children's reading, these concerns are voiced most often:

- I wish my child would read more. I wish my child *liked* to read more.
- I don't keep a close eye on what my child reads. She does seem, however, to be reading quite a lot. I think she may be starting and abandoning books a lot. Is this to be expected?
- I wish my child would read different, better, more advanced books.
- Now that my child can read, how do I help him read better? He resists reading aloud . . . should I make him? When he does read aloud, he gets quite a few words wrong. What should I do? What are the reading skills I should be supporting?
- I think my child's teacher has put my child into a low achievers reading group. Should I be concerned?
- My child is expected to write book reports and keep a reading log. She hates doing this. Should I be concerned? Are there ways I can help?

Promoting a Love of Reading

The secret to being a good reader is to read a lot. Good readers bring flashlights to bed and read long past the final "lights out."

Good readers find intriguing texts everywhere in their lives; they read cereal boxes, their big cousin's magazine, the advertisements in the junk mail. Good readers develop rituals for reading; they read before they fall asleep, on lazy Saturday mornings, or riding the subways. Good readers like to read.

But let's face it. All children don't emerge from first grade loving to read. Even if parents regard reading as the primary educational priority for our children, it doesn't always follow that our children will be avid readers. We have to accept the fact that it's entirely possible for children to grow up not adoring books. As I've pointed out several times, our children live in a culture that honors athletes and movie stars far more than artists and teachers. Among our children's peers, the basketball star receives far more recognition than the bookworm. Many of our children's friends will have parents who take time to cheer at all their children's soccer games but not to read with them. Children often have televisions, but not bookcases in their bedrooms. In our children's peer group, it's baseball cards, stickers, pogs, and beanbag animals, not books and poems, which are collected and traded. When children get together, they watch television or play together. Reading is seen as a solitary activity. And the rare child who does read a lot is sometimes seen as a child who "tunes out" from life.

Even in their classrooms, children usually are not given significant time for reading real books. In *Becoming a Nation of Readers*, researchers report that the average elementary school child spends 70 percent of the school day doing "seat work" with 1,000 worksheets a year.[2] Other researchers estimate that in an average school, children spend 2 hours a day completing worksheets and exercises, and only 12 minutes reading books. And when children are given the chance to read in school, their reading is often followed by an examination. Finally, many of our children are divided and labeled according to their so-called reading levels. Even many six-year-olds already know that there is a reader pecking order in their classrooms.

When we take all this into consideration, it's no wonder that many of our sons and daughters don't love reading as much as we'd like. There is no sense blaming ourselves when we find that our children are among the many who'd choose to do almost anything rather than read. This is a common, almost predictable problem, which needs to be addressed.

To do so, parents should stop asking, "Do my children like to read?" Rather than waiting to see if our child independently initiates reading, we should do everything we can to scaffold and support the likelihood that our child will read. A good starting place is to reduce the competition, by which I mean create conditions whereby reading is the activity children choose. It's unrealistic to think that most of our children will choose to read rather than to watch TV, play video or computer games, visit with friends, or talk on the phone. Therefore, we need to set limits. I wouldn't advise limiting television, for example, for the stated purpose of supporting reading or reading becomes the culprit. Nor would I make playing video games the reward for having read. But by curtailing the time our children spend with Nintendo and television, we will be taking an important step toward making reading an activity of choice.

I also build ritualized times for reading into our lives. During summer vacation, I made early-morning reading into a family ritual. I always linger in bed with a book and the newspaper. "Don't you just love to read first thing?" I ask when Evan stumbles in, rubbing the sleep from his eyes. "Go get your book and join us." If Evan instead loiters, I eventually say "Let me know when you've had a chance to read for a nice long time, Ev', and then I'll start breakfast." Soon Evan will begin to emerge from his bedroom on summer mornings with his book in hand, heading directly for his reading nest or toward John and me, if he wants us to read aloud to get him started.

In Chapter 4, I mentioned that I put my sons to bed early enough so that they can stay up another 45 minutes to read in bed. They feel like they're getting away with something (and I know *I'm* getting away with something), so it works all around. We also converted naptime into reading time once the children were older. Whenever we're home together on weekends or in the summer, we set aside about 45 minutes every afternoon for quiet time, when everyone heads off to separate spots with a book. Because my sons have never known life to be different, I think they believe everyone in the world has an afternoon reading time.

I like to make the reading environment pleasurable, too. I sometimes put juice or a graham cracker next to Miles and Evan when they are reading. And as I've mentioned, they have little nests where they read.

Helping Children Manage Their Reading Lives

In kindergarten and early first grade, whenever children read, the reading episodes tend to be free-standing ones. That is, the books kindergarten children read can generally be read in a single sitting. Children choose a book, read it, return the book (if we're lucky!), and then they're done reading. One of the ways in which children's reading lives change as they mature is that children eventually learn to sustain interest in a book over time. This may sound like a small accomplishment, but it's not. And it's something which requires parental support.

We can begin to help even very young children sustain their interest in reading by encouraging them to settle down with *several* books rather than with just one. If it takes just a few minutes to read a book, having a pile of several books makes it more likely that children will spend continuous time reading. Then, too, we'll want to celebrate if our children choose, for example, *two* Babar books, *two* Titch books, two books about baseball, or two versions of Goldilocks. When books are linked to each other in these ways, readers are more apt to think between books, to think across longer chunks of text. Also, of course, children who read several Babar books are doing something very similar to children who read chapter books about Ramona. At some point, perhaps late in first or second grade, children begin to read books that last longer than a single sitting, which also prompts more far-reaching thought. The *Little Bear, Frog and Toad, Henry and Mudge, George and Martha,* and the *Fox* series books all serve this purpose.

Children need help if they are going to stay with a book over several reading episodes. It's important that they don't have a lot of other books competing for their attention. That is, the book they read during independent reading time at school will hopefully also be the book they read for homework at home. It may (or may not) also be the book we read to them before they go to bed, but it will certainly be the book they read to themselves just before lights out. We also need to help our children pack this same book for school, and somehow we need to help our children remember that the book is in the backpack once they get to school. Hopefully our children's teacher will help them pack that book for home.

I once actually phoned Miles's teacher to ask her to help me teach him to bring the book he's reading at school back home for the night. I also once wrote a note to Miles's teacher asking that we work together to help Miles move along with some momentum in whatever book he was reading. I didn't care whether the book was started at school or at home . . . I just wanted to be sure the same book traveled between places. When he was learning to sustain his involvement in a book, I felt it was not helpful for Miles to try to juggle too many books at a time. Now, Miles's engagement in a book isn't at risk, and he can keep several books going at a time. I still try to ensure that in general he makes it through a book within a week or ten days. I think that children who spend a month reading a single book would be well off to read shorter books for now. It seems unreasonable for a child to try to keep the world of a book, the drama of a book, vital and alive when the child's engagement with a book stretches over such a very long period of time.

Another way to make reading pleasurable is to work hard to find books that your children will love to read. I often look at my sons' books before they do, steering them away from those that I think will prove to be uninteresting or too difficult for them. The right book can make all the difference in whether a child wants to continue to read.

For this reason, when Miles and Evan find a book they really love, I go out of my way to help them find another similar book. If they love one book by Beverly Cleary, I look for another by her. If they love a *Choose Your Own Adventure* book, I get them another like it.

We especially help our children love reading by assuming that they love it, even in the face of evidence to the contrary. When we pause in the midst of packing for a vacation to give our child an extra suitcase, saying, "You'll probably want this for all your books," we are helping our child grow into a person who loves reading. When we put a higher wattage light bulb in the bathroom fixture, saying, "It has been too dark to read in here, hasn't it? This should help!" we're being powerful mentors. When we see our children snuggled with a good book and say, "I'm jealous. I'm dying to get a chance to settle down and read like you," we're teaching our children to love reading.

Then, too, we support reading by attaching books to everything our children love. One of my nephews collects baseball cards, so for his birthday, I gave him a collection of Alfred Slote and Matt Christopher books. If my child loved horses, we'd subscribe to horse magazines and own all of those wonderful horse books from my childhood.

Of course, sometimes facing the problem head-on is necessary, and a long, intimate talk—or a series of them—is in order. During such talks, it's important that children be able to be honest about what reading is like in their lives. If the child says, for example, "I can't read; I make mistakes," our responses might include: "What's it like to feel that way?" or "Have you always felt so bad about your reading?" or "Has anything helped with your reading?" Questions such as these can set the stage for some open talk about this child's history as a reader.

The goal in such a talk is to let the child feel understood, and to help the child talk about the negative conditions that have caused such feelings. "It's not going to be like that anymore," we can promise. "As of today, we're going to take away that bad stuff that made reading hard for you, and we're going to give you what you need as a reader."

Finally, it never hurts to wear our own love of reading on our sleeve. Every summer of my life I've spent several weeks with my extended family at a lakeside cottage in Traverse City, Michigan. During one summer, I noticed that on the very first day, my father mysteriously disappeared for the morning, returning hours later with a stack of books. The books were all by Annie Dillard. I had given him one by her, *An American Childhood*, for Father's Day, and now he had a stack of her books! I asked, "Is there a library in this town? Is it nice? Can anyone use it or do you have a library card for it? Do you always read on one topic or by one author in the summer?"

I learned that for 52 years, my father has always gone to the Traverse City library on the first day of his vacation, and he has always had an author or a topic in his mind for his summer reading. "I couldn't imagine doing it any other way," Dad told me. For weeks before his summer vacation begins, my father considers the various possible directions for his summer reading. He always makes his final decision during a long morning in the Traverse City Public Library.

For me, the odd thing about this is that for every summer of my childhood, my father began his vacation with this pilgrimage to the library . . . and yet he never shared this with me or with my eight brothers and sisters! He has supported our education in countless other ways, but he never realized how powerful it would have been to share with us the quirks of his own reading life.

Steering Children to Read Better or More Difficult Books

Generally, two issues about our children's reading worry us the most: that our children won't love to read and that they will choose the wrong books. We see them reading a steady diet of *Goosebumps* books, for example, and despair. "How will they grow up with educated sensibilities if they read only light-hearted fiction?" And so we are tempted to steer them toward *Heidi* and *Hans Brinker and the Silver Skates*, or the children's versions of *Treasure Island* and *Julius Caesar*.

It is entirely reasonable for parents to wonder whether we should intercede in our children's book choices. We supervise our children's choice of television shows, so why not do the same for their reading? All stories are not created equal. Isn't it logical that we'd want our children to read books that will inspire and uplift them rather than reading only the violence-filled books that are popular with the peer group?

I am sympathetic to parents who want to be influential in their children's choice of books; I do, too. But I think most teachers would agree that uninformed parents severely handicap children's reading lives by pushing children away from the books that feel right to them.

The most common scenario is that parents see their child reading her way through a relatively easy series of chapter books and the parent calls the series junk. Soon the child comes to school carrying a child's version of *Romeo and Juliet* or some other adult classic. The plot, characters, setting, and language of the new book are all inappropriate for the child. The child is no longer reading the books that are popular with other children in the classroom community. She begins to live a charade, to pretend to read. She does everything she can to avoid reading, and even when she *is* reading, her mind is elsewhere. She grows restless and unengaged as a reader.

If parents are going to intervene in their children's choice of books, the parents need to be knowledgeable about what young readers read, about what creates difficulty in a book, and about children's literature. Too often, adults think that once children are reading chapter books, they can read any chapter book. This is far, far from true. There are chapter books that are relatively easy for many second or third graders, and chapter books that are enormously difficult.

In general, many of the books appropriate for second, third, and early fourth grade readers are part of a series. Parents who worry about their children reading *Goosebumps*, *The Babysitters Club*, or *The American Doll* books or a similar series need to understand that this is the age of the series book. When I was young, I devoured the *Nancy Drew* books. My children have progressed from the *Little Bear* books to the *Pee Wee Scouts*, then *Cam Jansen*, the Box Car books, the *Littles*, *Little House in the Big Woods*, and the *Superfudge* series. When children are new to chapter books, series books provide them with extra support. In a new book in a series, the plot will be new, but the characters, settings, and genre seem like old friends. When children read book after book from within a familiar series, this provides them with support that is not unlike the support children receive who reread a book or read a book that they have already seen on television or heard in a read-aloud. These are all ways in which children wisely give themselves the support they need as they move into longer texts.

And when children's reading lives are defined for a time by the series they're into, this makes it easier for us and for their teacher to help with book choice. If a child is reading her way through the *Anastasia* books, chances are that each new book in the series will be at a similar level to the one before it. She is, therefore, less likely to choose a book that stymies her. Furthermore, the gap between finishing one book and beginning the next can be more easily bridged when the next book is part of the same series. The next book is, essentially, the next chapter in the ongoing saga.

Series books also make having conversations about books more beneficial. For example, if Evan and I pause in the midst of reading the Box Car book *Surprise Island* to chat for awhile about Benjy, the youngest child in the series, comparing him to young Fudge in Judy Blume's *Fudge-a-mania* series, this supports Evan as he reads any future Box Car book.

Children can develop wonderful reading habits while they are making their way through a series. When children read *Goosebumps* or *The Babysitters Club* books, for example, they often gossip about these books with their friends, predicting how the books will go and empathizing with characters in the books. Readers of series books often collect books as eagerly as they collect baseball cards. They borrow, lend, and trade books; shelve and reshelve them; plead with parents to buy them the next volume; visit libraries to check out books; and ask for books as birthday gifts. They eye bookstore shelves to note when a new book is published; they compare books, and judge books; and they find that knowing books enables them to more easily join book conversations with kids they meet at camp and at Little League.

Naturally parents have series book biases. I, for instance, resist the *Goosebumps* series, but the truth is that what I dislike is not the *contents*, but the covers of these books. The fact is, I've never read a single *Goosebumps* book from cover to cover. I suspect if I did read one, I'd find them to be harmless.

There is no question that I steer my children toward the series books I prefer. I love the ingenuity and teamwork of the girl detectives in Elizabeth Levy's *Something Queer* series, in which the ratio of text to pictures makes these books easy for children to read. And so I did promotional work for these books. I read one of them aloud. Once Evan began reading them, we headed off to the library with him to check out half the series. Back at home, we cleared out a special shelf for *Something Queer* books in Evan's bookcase. This was a reasonable intervention. But wresting a book away from a child in favor of an adult classic would not have been the right thing for me to do.

In general, parents should avoid pushing adult books onto their children. There's time enough for these books once our children, themselves, are adults. Parents should also be wary of assuming that authors from long ago are somehow better than current authors. The field of children's literature has grown richer over the years. There are dazzling current authors. Parents who find themselves always pushing the classics from another era—books like *Misty of Chicoteague, Black Beauty,* and *Little Lord Fauntleroy*—would benefit their children by acquainting themselves with some of these new authors. The following lists include some of the great authors that many second, third, and fourth grade readers will adore:

Judy Blume	Ruth Stiles Garrett
Jeffrey Brown	James Howe
Clyde Bulla	Johanna Hurwitz
Ann Cameron	Robert Kimmel Smith
Matt Christopher	Dick King-Smith
(sports books)	Ursula Le Guin (*Catwings*
Beverly Cleary	series)
Pam Conrad	Beverly Naido
Roald Dahl	Barbara Robinson
Eleanor Estes	Robert Newton Peck
John Fitzgerald	Jerry Spinelli
John Gardiner	Gloria Whelan

Parents will also want to acquaint themselves with current authors whose books are especially appropriate for upper-elementary school readers. This list includes many of my favorites:

Avi	Patricia MacLachlan
Natalie Babbitt	Walter Dean Myers
Lynne Reid Banks	Scott O'Dell
James and Christopher Collier	Katherine Paterson
Paula Fox	Gary Paulsen
Jean Fritz	Cynthia Rylant
Jean Craighead George	Elizabeth Speare
Brian Jacques	Mildred Taylor
Madeleine L'Engle	Theodore Taylor
C. S. Lewis	Larry Yep
Lois Lowry	Jane Yolen

Sometimes when parents intervene to influence their children's book choices, the issue is not the quality but the difficulty of the literature.

Oftentimes, parents who are very involved in their children's reading life spend time urging their children to read longer and more difficult texts. This is an understandable thing to do . . . and can be a wise or foolish thing to do. After I suggested to my sister that she nudge her son Peter to advance from the *Henry and Mudge* chapter books to the more challenging *Cam Jansen* books, his reading took off. The books were rewarding to him in ways others hadn't been, and Peter's sense of himself as a reader was enhanced by the fact that others identified him as "the first grader who reads *Cam Jansen* books already!"

But urging our children to attempt more difficult books is often very problematic. I suspect that my son Evan has paid a price for the many times I've pushed him to read books that are on the edge of his comfort zone. As a result, he was, for a time, more dependent on me while reading than I would have liked. Whereas Miles always initiated reading periods, Evan would wait for me to say, "Can we read together?" And when Evan and I did read together, I was probably too active in helping him over the bumpy parts of the text he had difficulty reading. Evan needed my support in his reading, or believed he did, because his books were often a notch too hard for him. Looking back, I'm not sure why I didn't insist he read books that made him feel strong as a reader. Probably I wanted him to be a proficient reader so badly that I'd lead him toward books that were the books I wanted him to be able to read. This was my way of fooling myself, perhaps.

I certainly sympathize with people who nip at their children's heels, as I have done, urging them toward books which are a step up the ladder of difficulty. Evan never resisted my efforts, nor will many of our children. But this can still be a risky and even destructive thing to do.

The biggest problem one encounters among second, third, and fourth graders is that our children will read without thinking, that their eyes will travel across the print, but they won't be able to talk in any logical way at all about what they've read. This is a far more common problem than people would like to admit.

In general, my advice to parents is to let your children read and reread books at their own comfort level. Ideally, our children will also be working with wise teachers who will know when and if it's appropriate to nudge them toward longer, more difficult texts. But too often, classes are too big for us to feel confident that our children's teachers really know what's best for our children, in which case, we may be in a position of deciding whether or not it's appropriate to nudge our children ahead.

The crucial thing to remember is that *at no cost do we want our children to read without understanding a text.* The easiest way to detect this is for us to join children during their silent reading time, and for us to volunteer to read aloud *to* them. Ask, "Where'd you leave off in your reading?" then begin. Last night, for example, I read aloud this section of Rockwell's *How to Eat Fried Worms:*

> "Geez, you think it'll work?" said Alan to Joe. "Suppose it doesn't? He didn't seem to pay much attention today."

I didn't know the story, but Evan had been reading the book for awhile, so I asked, "What does Alan mean, 'will it work?' What are they trying to do? Who are Alan and Joe?" And referring to the title, I asked, "Are they really eating fried *worms?* Why?"

If Evan had been totally stumped by my questions, if he had acted as if he didn't have a clue why the book was called *How to Eat Fried*

Worms or what these boys were trying to pull off, then I'd have known he was reading a book that was beyond his grasp. My colleague, Randy Bomer, often asks young readers, "If I asked you to tell me all about this story, would you be worried?" If the reader nods, indicating that he'd have a hard time retelling the story, Randy tells that child, "Then put this book down and run away from it! Get as far away from it as you can because it's not good for you to be reading it." Children must learn that understanding what they read is the whole point.

Children need to know that something is drastically wrong when a book creates a meaningless jumble in their minds. This doesn't mean that it's necessary for children to understand all the details of a story. I don't think we need to go on a witch-hunt, asking particular little questions in order to detect whether youngsters have missed some element of the story. It's fine if children read a book and only come away with the main features of the plot (as long as they are encouraged to revisit books often, rereading favorites year after year). The concern is not whether children are missing some small element or other, but that texts yield meaning to young readers. I want to be sure that youngsters can make a movie in their minds as they read, that they catch hold to a story, that the book is interesting and sensible to them.

The rule of thumb is if a child can read 90 percent of the words so that they make sense (which doesn't mean accurately, but with logical errors that maintain the flow of the story), the child can figure out the 10 percent that is confusing. But if less than 90% of the text makes sense to the child, if the story ends up being like Swiss cheese with giant holes in the logic, then the text is too difficult. A child won't be able to maintain a hold on the story, and therefore won't be able to skip over or guess at difficult parts of the text. If our child is reading a text which is difficult, then it will be important for us to do everything possible to lessen the difficulty and increase the rewards of the child's reading.

How to Help Our Children Become Better Readers

Sometimes our children will read books which are a bit challenging for them. There are ways we can help with these books. Typically, parents sit and listen as children read aloud, and assist with difficult sections of the text. But when I have done this with Evan, he becomes very resistant, and I am not surprised. Once children have achieved a certain proficiency as a reader, they prefer to read silently. This enables them to slip over the difficult words or phrases, while following the central plot. And this is exactly what young readers *should* be doing.

The problem that arises when we ask children to read aloud is that they know we are checking on whether they are "really reading." Reading aloud becomes a test, not a way to share a great story. Children sense that we are testing them. Consequently, they grow tense, wondering "What if there are hard words ahead?" This happens often in some schools. Sometimes children sit in reading circles, with each child in turn reading a passage aloud while listeners sit in judgment (or at least this is what the child who reads aloud feels is happening).

My suggestion is that parents ask their children to read aloud only on occasion. And when children *do* read aloud, we will want to do everything possible to eliminate the test atmosphere. For example, it helps if we take turns reading aloud with our child. Or, in a book such as *Frog and Toad*, we can read Frog's lines, our child can read the part of Toad.

And when children get stuck on a word, we can make it clear that this is no big deal. All effective readers skip over or guess at some words, paraphrase sections of text, and resume reading. When a child encounters an unfamiliar word, there are several helpful ways to intervene. We can simply wait, letting the child attempt the word. We can whisper a prompt that might remind the child of what skilled readers do. "Give it a go," we might whisper, or "What would make sense?" If the child supplies a logical, but incorrect, word, it's reasonable to let this approximation stand. If the child supplies a word which in no way fits into the sentence, it helps for us to repeat the sentence with the new word sitting awkwardly in it, and voice our confusion. "That doesn't *sound* right, does it?" In this way, children will develop their own internal alarm systems which will, we hope, send them to take another running start at the confusing sentences.

It's also perfectly reasonable to simply read the problematic sections aloud, and in a straightforward manner give children the information they need. The most important thing we can do to help our children read is that we can do everything possible to be sure that they maintain a hold on the gist of what's going on in the story. The ideal way to support children's thoughtfulness and their hold on the sense of a story is to read sections of the story aloud. I may, for example, read aloud the first few pages of a picture book Evan is reading, or I read the first and fifth chapter of his chapter book. Evan recently brought me his new chapter book saying, "I want to get the tune of it. Can you just start me off?" This helped him not only with the sound of the text, but introduced the characters and setting for the story as well. I leave off only when Evan is hooked into the unfolding plot of the story. This helps young readers want to read; it helps them grow into the kind of readers who carry books everywhere.

I am also willing to read later chapters. I want Evan to stay connected to the drama of the story, and one of the best ways I can do this is to stay connected myself. Perhaps I'll read Chapter 6 to Evan and he will read Chapter 7 aloud to me; then Evan will read Chapter 8 silently to himself. (This is a good way also to support our children moving toward silent reading.) Before I read aloud my chapter, I might ask, "Will you catch me up on the story? What have I missed?" Or, sometimes I take a few moments to skim the sections I've missed, talking aloud as I construct for myself and reconstruct for Evan what's been going on. This helps both of us keep track of the unfolding meaning of the story.

I also keep Evan hooked into the unfolding meaning of the story by encouraging him to predict what will happen in a book, in a chapter, or on a page. Inviting readers to "talk back" to a story is another way to support the mind work of reading. As our children begin to look at the actual print on the page, to read the words and not just to approximate the story, they sometimes become *less* thoughtful than they were when they weren't yet decoding unfamiliar words in books. A child who mostly looks at the pictures of a *Little Red Riding Hood* book, for example, is more likely to notice that in one version, the wolf swallows the grandmother, and in another, the woodcutter arrives just in time, than the child who has just managed to work her way through the print of these books.

At first glance this will probably sound strange, yet there is a way in which it is also logical. When our children first begin to pay attention to print, it's as if they are wrestling with a new technology. Whenever any of us take on a new technology, for a while we seem to regress, because all our attention is diverted to the new technology. When we first write using a computer, we're too busy figuring out how to control the cursor to use insightful language. My colleagues and I say, half in jest, that when children are beginning to become independent readers, they can't read and think at the same time.

This is a predictable stage, then, but it's also a problematic one because in the end, reading is not about barking at the print. Reading is about creating worlds with words. The only way to read with fluency and expressiveness is to read closely hooked into the unfolding meaning of the text. It is very important, therefore, that we do everything possible to support the mind work of reading.

A simple and profound way to encourage our children to be thoughtful readers is to create structures that nudge them to talk back to texts. In Chapter 2, I suggested pausing often when we read aloud, asking children to "say something." Sometimes teachers I know draw little pencil lines here and there in the books. They ask children to read with a buddy, and when they reach the pencil marks which have been dispersed throughout the text, the partners pause and say something. Other teachers encourage children to pause after every page (or chapter) and to chat about whatever's going on in the story with their partner.

The way I support conversations about books varies considerably between Miles and Evan. Miles often reads books I've never read. Sometimes he tells me about a book, but I feel I'm just pretending to follow what he says. Without a knowledge of the book, it's hard for me to understand his summary.

To support Miles's conversations about books we have some conversations going that cross over books. Although the details of any one book might escape me, we can have ongoing conversations about such topics as:

- books that should have sequels
- a character who seems mean
- characters that are like characters from other books or like people we know
- books that are like other books or movies
- changes in Miles's reading life (how he can't put certain books down, how his teacher asks him to put Post-its in a book but he can't stop long enough to do so, how he's supposed to only read two chapters but finds it difficult to bite off such small pieces of a story . . .)
- how books suggest ways of living to Miles, as when a series of sailing adventure stories convinced him that he wanted to take sailing lessons; or when a book about boys in a cave made him dream of finding caverns in the hills near us

Assigning Children to Ability Groups

When parents pull me aside to say, "I think my child's teacher has assigned my child into a low/medium-level reading group. Should I be concerned?" my answer is "Yes." These labels can become self-fulfilling prophecies. And, sadly, children in the low-level reading groups tend to receive less attention and less positive reinforcement than children in the other groups; usually they are asked to do more low-interest drills and skills work; and they read many fewer real stories and engage in many fewer thoughtful conversations about books.[3]

I'd be concerned enough about this that if my child was a somewhat shaky reader, I'd watch like a hawk for indications that the classroom was divided into ongoing ability-based groups. This often happens without a teacher telling parents. When children work in a basal reader (or in any sort of a literature textbook), those children are probably divided into permanent ability-level groups. I'd ask the child, "Do you and a group of other kids meet often with your teacher to read and to do reading sheets?" In this way, I'd try to deduce whether ability-based groups exist in my child's school, and if they do exist, where my child fits into these groups.

There are children who enter school already having heard 5,000 books read aloud to them, while others enter school without having heard a single story. Some children enter school after having participated in thousands of conversations about how written language tends to go. Other children have never had their attention drawn to the black marks on a page. If one child reads before the other, this doesn't mean the second child is a slow learner. That second child may have spent her preschool years catching and studying dragonflies or building castles out of blocks. She may be poised and ready to become a remarkable reader, and simply needs the opportunity to reach her potential. Starting her off in a Buzzard's reading group and giving her "circle the 'sh' sound" dittos won't help.

So, yes, I'd be concerned if I saw an elementary-school teacher who didn't make an effort to muffle the divisions that *will* exist between more- and less-experienced readers, and I'd be concerned even if my child was in the high-level reading group.

What I'd probably do is to either try to move my child to a classroom with less rigid, pronounced divisions between ability groups, and different educational values; or else I'd ask for my child to be transferred to a higher-level reading group, or I'd ask for assurance that if my child showed growth in reading, that there could be a transfer at that point. Then I'd move mountains to provide that child with the support needed to become a stronger reader.

Some school systems offer a program called Reading Recovery, an early intervention remedial program that gives children intensive, daily one-to-one help for a limited length of time, often about 10 weeks. The goal is for children to outgrow the need for this intensive help. If such a program wasn't offered in my child's school, I'd probably try to visit schools where it was offered and read up on its methods (see Clay's book, *Becoming Literate*, Heinemann), so that I could give my child an approximated version of that program at home.

There are children who need extra help with components of reading. Some children probably need more direct and individual instruction in the printwork of reading than most children need. But all children need mentors who demonstrate a love of reading, who provide time to snuggle with books, opportunities to hear grand stories read aloud, and rituals for reading often in their lives. All children need people who believe in them as readers.

CHAPTER 8

Writing and the Middle Childhood Years

When our child is five and six years old, we, as parents, are enchanted by her lopsided letters, homemade spellings, and idiosyncratic ideas. Our child describes hiccups as jumping beans inside her stomach and we phone all the relatives to celebrate her poetic insight. Our child uses a colon at the end of each page and tells us it means "more-to-come," and we're breathless over her originality. We cover the refrigerator door with our child's stories and mail copies of her poems to the cousins.

Then our child enters second or third grade and so often it's as if our child has crossed a continental divide. Now suddenly we look at the lopsided letters, homemade spellings, and idiosyncratic ideas and see only what's not there and what's still wrong.

Our stomachs tighten when we look at our child's writing. "It's so brief," we think. "She can't spell 'said'," we notice. We begin compiling other errors, other worries. "The story jumps from one thing to the next," we think, dismayed at the illogical sequencing. We wonder what the other kids are doing in writing, and we are afraid our child doesn't measure up.

There is probably no curricular subject that creates as much anxiety for parents as writing, and this is no surprise. When a child writes, he puts his thoughts on the page. Writing reveals that child to the world, in black and white. Writing reveals his insights, his life experiences, his feelings. Writing reveals his spelling, his handwriting, his grammar. Writing reveals his intelligence, his soul. "Writing puts us on the line," Mina Shaughnessy has said, "And we don't want to be there."[1] It is also true that our child's writing puts us as parents on the line and we don't want to be there.

When our child does almost anything else in life, we are able to see and to celebrate the good part of what she's done. We admire the colors of her crooked tulips. We appreciate that she's tried to make her bed and overlook the wrinkles. When our child draws, sings, builds, learns history, sweeps the floor, paints, or buttons her shirt; we easily see through her errors to what she is trying to do, and we celebrate her efforts. But when our child writes, we lose perspective.

Our child's writing puts us on the line. We look at her sentences and we feel exposed and vulnerable. We hold our child's words and ideas in our hands and see only the errors. Last year, when Miles was in second grade, I was worried enough about his spelling that when Sandra Wilde, a nationally renowned spelling authority came to Teachers College to lead a conference for teachers, I asked her to come by Wooster Lower School, my children's school. Sitting in Miles's classroom, long after the students had gone home, I brought her Miles's teacher and his writing. Sandra looked at one page of his writing, then another while I waited for her prognosis. Watching her take in his mistakes, I thought, "What will she say? What's his problem?"

Finally, she looked up. "*You're* the problem, Lucy," she said. "His spelling is absolutely fine for a second grader."

"But look," I said, pointing to the spelling of 'because,' 'probably,' 'said,' 'when' . . ."

"Those are intelligent errors," Sandra responded. "And anyhow, his writing is 85 percent correct." She added, "Look on this page; there isn't a single error in the whole first section." Then she suggested, "Maybe because his handwriting slants backward you *think* he has more of a spelling problem than he has."

Later, the whole episode struck me as funny. Here I spend my entire life telling teachers and parents that they must learn to see through a child's errors to what the child has said. But when it came to *my* child, I read with a critic's eyes, searching for flaws.

Perhaps, unwittingly, we do unto our children as was done unto us. Experts say that dysfunctions in families recycle, generation after generation. Could this also be true of dysfunctions in our writing lives? When you and I were young, we put our thoughts onto the page and then teachers dissected our spellings and filled our margins with "awk!" and "run-on!" Most of us never had anyone who believed in us as writers . . . and so, without meaning to do so, when we read our child's writing, we reach for the red pen.

We are wise to care about our child's growth in writing and in spelling, but we are not wise if we let our care and our concern translate themselves automatically into corrections of our child's errors. Rather than reaching as if on autopilot for a red pen and rushing in to repair errors in our child's draft, we need to understand that when we hold a draft of our child's writing, we're holding not only a draft, but also a child in our hands.

A teacher recently asked the author Avi, "What do you do if a child has writing problems?" He answered, "First you have to love the child. If you can convince a child you love him, you can teach him anything."[2]

Avi was speaking to teachers who work with a new batch of 28 kids each year. How much more true for parents. Our children will encounter people everywhere who look at their pages of print and see only the spelling errors, who see only the missing "u" in because, who think only, "It's so brief."

We, as parents, need to be the readers who can see through the errors to what our child is trying to do. We need to see and to celebrate the new risks our child has taken as a writer, the new challenges she's reaching toward, the new punctuation she's tried to use (even if she's using it incorrectly), the new details she's added.

We need to remember that emotionally, children are not all that different from adults. If we were asked to write, and then to pass our writing over to someone more important, more powerful than us, most of us would feel afraid and anxious. We'd think, "Are my words, my ideas, okay?" and underneath that, we'd be thinking, "Am I okay?"

No one is more important or more powerful in a child's life than that child's parents. If we are not careful, we can be powerfully destructive of our child's confidence as a writer. We can be powerfully destructive of our child's voice as a poet, a storyteller, and of our child's ability to build worlds with words. If we're not care-full we can be powerfully destructive of our child's willingness to put himself on the line.

As parents, we are wise to care about our child's writing, but we need to remember that caring and correcting are two different things. We care for a child's writing by understanding that working with a child's writing requires extra restraint, extra sensitivity, extra thoughtfulness, and extra wisdom. When children bring us their captions, poems, letters, and essays, they are putting their lives—their fantasies, their thoughts, and their language—into our hands. What a responsibility it is to be an adult mentor in a child's writing life.

Finding Opportunities to Support Our Children's Writing: Mobilizing a Child to Write

This chapter represents my area of greatest expertise, and yet it has caused me more difficulty than any other chapter. Although I know ways in which teachers can support children's growth in writing, it is puzzling to determine what parents can do if their children are not having wonderful writing experiences in school. It's easy to imagine that children can have a reading life, separate and independent from school. And it's easy to imagine that children can weave mathematics and science and social studies into the everydayness of a home life. But it is less easy to imagine children having a writing life, separate and independent from the school's curriculum. Parents can't help children write with more skill and confidence unless those children write in the first place. If the school is not mobilizing children to write joyfully and often, how can parents do this? The first answer is that we need to support whatever our children *are* doing.

Recently I was working in a class of sixth graders who were writing memoirs. They had all written pages and pages of vignettes about their lives. All except Kenny. His memoir went like this:

My Life Story
I saw my father. We had Coke, and then we had a hot dog.
by Kenny.

It would have been easy to take one quick glance at Kenny's meager draft and then to exclaim, "Kenny, this is so short! You have to tell more. What else did you do in your life?" But what I've learned from working with hundreds and thousands of young writers is that the best way to help a child say more is to attend fully and deeply to what *he has already said*, and to let a child's words affect you.

And indeed, just as we could easily read Kenny's story with a scowl, we can also read it with a wide-open heart and be moved by it. For me, Kenny's story was touching, poignant. "My Life Story," I read. "I *saw* my father. We had Coke, and then we had a hot dog."

"Kenny," I said. "This is so huge. Geez, what happened?" He looked at me soberly, with his big brown eyes.

"Tell me *all* about it," I prompted gently, meeting his eyes. He repeated: "I saw my father. We had coke. After that, know what we did? We had a hot dog." "Oh, Kenny, I can picture it," I said, although of course this was only partly true. "You and your Dad . . ." "Yeah," he said. "I still have the can."

Bit by bit, Kenny began to talk to me, and I listened. When he paused, I touched his arm. "Kenny, do you have any idea how big this is, what you are saying? You have to put it down." That day marked a turning point in Kenny's life as a writer. A vast majority of children graduate from high school without anyone talking with them about their writing in process.

In Chapter 3, I described ways of encouraging four-, five- and six-year-olds to write. I talked about young children captioning their drawings, adding items to the grocery list, and posting signs on their bedroom doors. This is easier to do with younger children, who want to put their signature on the world; they construct stories and poems out of a handful of consonants as fearlessly as they construct castles and forts out of a handful of blocks. But for many older children, writing becomes a stressful endeavor. "How should I start it?" they ask. "I'm not a good speller," they say. "I make a lot of mistakes," they tell us.

My advice to parents is: begin early. If we support our children's writing when they are very young, by the time they reach the age of self-consciousness, they may have strong enough skills to overcome their misgivings and forge ahead. Howard Gardner summarizes the middle childhood years in this way: "Now for the first time, a child in the midst of singing or drawing will nervously ask, 'Is this right?' "[2] If we shore up our children's writing efforts early, they are more likely to cope better with the audience awareness and self-consciousness of the middle childhood years.

Parents who care about their children's writing will want to do everything possible to make it likely that their children receive good instruction in writing. It's fairly rare to find teachers who have an expertise in teaching writing. Years ago, a friend of mine, Don Graves, surveyed 36 teacher-training colleges and found they offered a total of 169 courses on teaching reading, but *no* courses on teaching writing. This has changed somewhat since but it is still true that many teachers haven't been given a lot of guidance in the teaching of writing. Consequently, teachers usually assign and correct writing, but spend very little time coaching children on the strategies writers use in order to write well. If we are lucky and our child has a teacher who encourages rough drafts and revisions, a teacher who confers with our child about work in progress, then we'll want to mobilize ourselves to support that teacher's influence in our child's writing life. If we back up that teacher, building her up in our child's eyes and doing everything possible to ensure our child rises to the challenge of her teaching, our child's writing can be totally transformed in a single year. This is most likely to happen if the teacher values the importance of creating a safe, supportive community in the classroom, and encourages children to tell the truth and put the details of their lives on the page. We need to support teachers in their efforts to steer our children in this direction.

We also need to be supportive of *any* writing that our children initiate. This isn't always easy. For example, Miles collects tiny Star Wars spacecrafts, and periodically he makes charts or lists in a small spiral notebook of what he has acquired, as shown in Figure 8.1. Sometimes he will even write soliloquies to accompany his dramatic play, as shown in Figure 8.2.

Miles wasn't writing these for my approval; he didn't show them to me. This was his "underground writing." He chose to do this writing, and he did it during his playtime, surrounded by his toys and his secret fantasies. Miles is a conservative, law-abiding, rule-

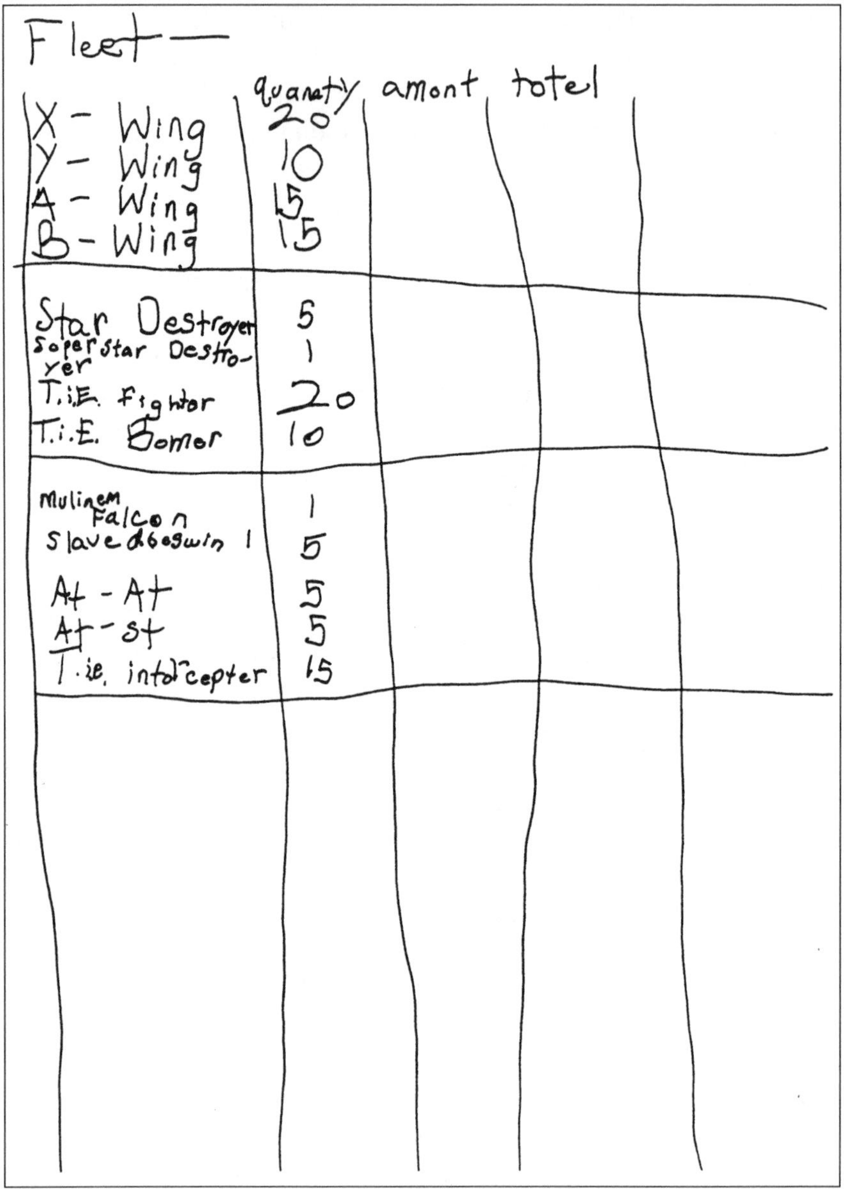

Fleet —

	quanaty	amont	totel			
X - Wing	20					
Y - Wing	10					
A - Wing	5					
B - Wing	15					
Star Destroyer	5					
soperstar Destroyer	1					
T.iE. Fighter	20					
T.i.E. Bomer	10					
Mulinem Falcon	1					
Slave d6o9win 1	5					
At - At	5					
At - St	5					
T.ie. intercepter	15					

Figure 8.1

conscious child who doesn't like to go upstairs when it's dark or to walk up to the counter at a restaurant to ask the waitress for a second soda. Yet he dreams of being king and solemnly publishes his inten-

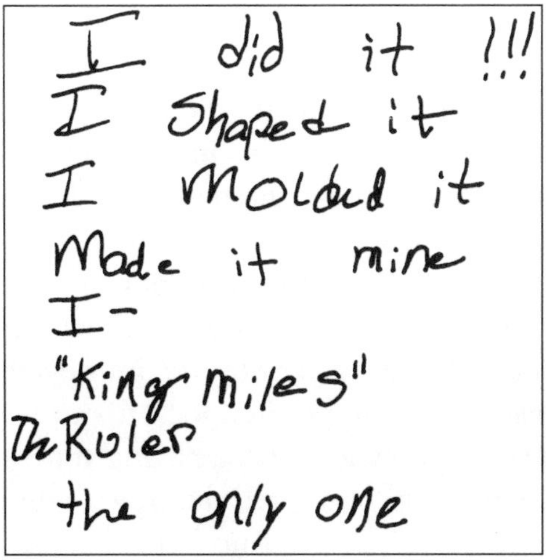

Figure 8.2

tions to regain power and rebuild an empire. I never got involved in this writing or in other pieces like it. I don't want such efforts to become adult-sanctioned writing. I want it to continue as Miles' private play. But I did buy Miles a new notebook and helped him make an audiotape of a Star Wars play he had written.

Evan, meanwhile, will periodically fix dinner for all of us and write out elaborate nametags and menus from which we can order the meal. The actual writing Evan did for his meals was limited. He wrote nametags and menus. But looking back now, I realize it's no small accomplishment for a seven-year-old to use writing to orchestrate an elaborately designed event.

All of our children will have their own reasons and occasions to write. We need to watch for these. If they want to make nameplates for their stuffed animals, we can find them wooden plaques. If they invent little songs, we can give them blank cassettes and show them how to use the tape recorder. If they write captions under photographs in their picture albums, we can offer to type them. If they author letters from Barbie to Ken, we can supply them with fancy stationery.

We make it more likely that children will have their own reasons to write when we help them to pursue their own projects. When a musician friend came to visit, I encouraged the boys to put on a concert for her. They lined up chairs facing a make-believe organ, and played for us with great aplomb. When children produce concerts, plays, and pet shows, it's easier for them to find reasons to write.

We need not sit around waiting for the day when our children initiate writing on their own; we can also nudge them towards writing. I encouraged a little boy to write the makers of his favorite mustard, telling them about his delight in their product. The child received a package of coupons for free mustard. I know of other children who have written to their senators and state representatives or to editors of local newspapers. Still others petition for improved playgrounds in their town and extended hours at their local library. One child I know learned that a beloved cat who had been living at the local library was about to be banished, so she organized children throughout the town to speak and write on the cat's behalf. Another child discovered that a pet store was giving out incorrect information on the care of geckos and protested by writing his own *Guide to Geckos*, which he asked the pet shop to distribute. Yet another child initiated a campaign to save a giant tree from being cut down. Children who engage in this sort of writing are often rewarded by responses from adults other than their teachers and parents, and this goes a long way toward promoting writing.

A Ritual of Writing

For children to write better, they have to write often. To ensure that this happens, I try to make writing an everyday activity. Miles and Evan know that just as we read and practice piano every day, we write every day. My sons each have a notebook, and they are expected to write at least a page a day in their notebooks or elsewhere.

My sister thinks it's unrealistic to believe most families will be willing to institute such a ritual, but my theory is that if parents expect their children to practice their musical instruments every day or go to baseball practice according to schedule, why not expect them to write every day.

Parents initially may want to consider instituting a daily writing ritual, for, say, the duration of a summer vacation or a family trip, or on Sunday nights. If parents want to support a ritual of writing, my first suggestion is to buy your children a special notebook for the occasion, and to buy yourself one as well.

I look hard for the right notebook. Thin notebooks that can be filled quite easily are less likely to overwhelm a child than fatter notebooks. I like notebooks which are lined and it is important to me that the bindings are constructed so that the notebooks lie flat when they are open.

Buying a notebook is much easier, of course, than sticking to a writing ritual. My advice is this: make this writing nonnegotiable; that is, *never miss a day*. In our summer notebooks, we tend to write Day 9, Day 10, Day 11 on the tops of the pages; and after a while, the progression of days provides its own compulsion to write. If you allow kids to get off the writing hook once, they'll try to get off it all the time. Even when the family is busy from morning until night, usually there are a few minutes for putting thoughts to paper.

Helping Children Develop Strategies for Writing

Once my sons knew they were expected to write each day, my energy could be directed toward coaching them to write better. If Miles says, "I don't have a topic to write about," sometimes I make a suggestion, such as, "Why not write about staying overnight at Peter's," remembering his animated stories about the visit. "Nothing much happened. There's nothing to say," Miles counters. "You could tell about how there was so much snow that we traveled by train . . ." I say, hoping this will get the creative juices flowing. Miles picks up the pen, robot-style, and wearily says, "So how do I start it? What do I say first?"

These scenes probably happen in all our homes. When I'm at my best, I don't let children lean too much on me for their topics, for I do not want to foster a dependency. Instead, I try to give children strategies for generating their own topics.

For example, I've told my students and my sons that sometimes I take my notebook with me and go sit somewhere, then write about what I see. Author May Sarton has told writers, "Remember to write about what you are seeing every day. If you are going to hold people's interest, you need to write very well. What is writing very well? It is seeing very well, seeing in a totally original way."

It is crucial to teach youngsters the technique of slowing down, paying attention, speaking in detail. My sons and I, then, sometimes take our writing and sit before a bit of our lives: a square of sidewalk, an old sneaker, an overgrown garden. We set up writing easels alongside Lego castles, a rabbit's cage, even messy bedrooms. It doesn't matter that the first sentence of these entries often begins with the refrain, "I see . . ." Figure 8.3 shows the entry Miles wrote about his garden.

Often writers move from observation to reflection, from writing the specifics of what they see to writing about what interests or

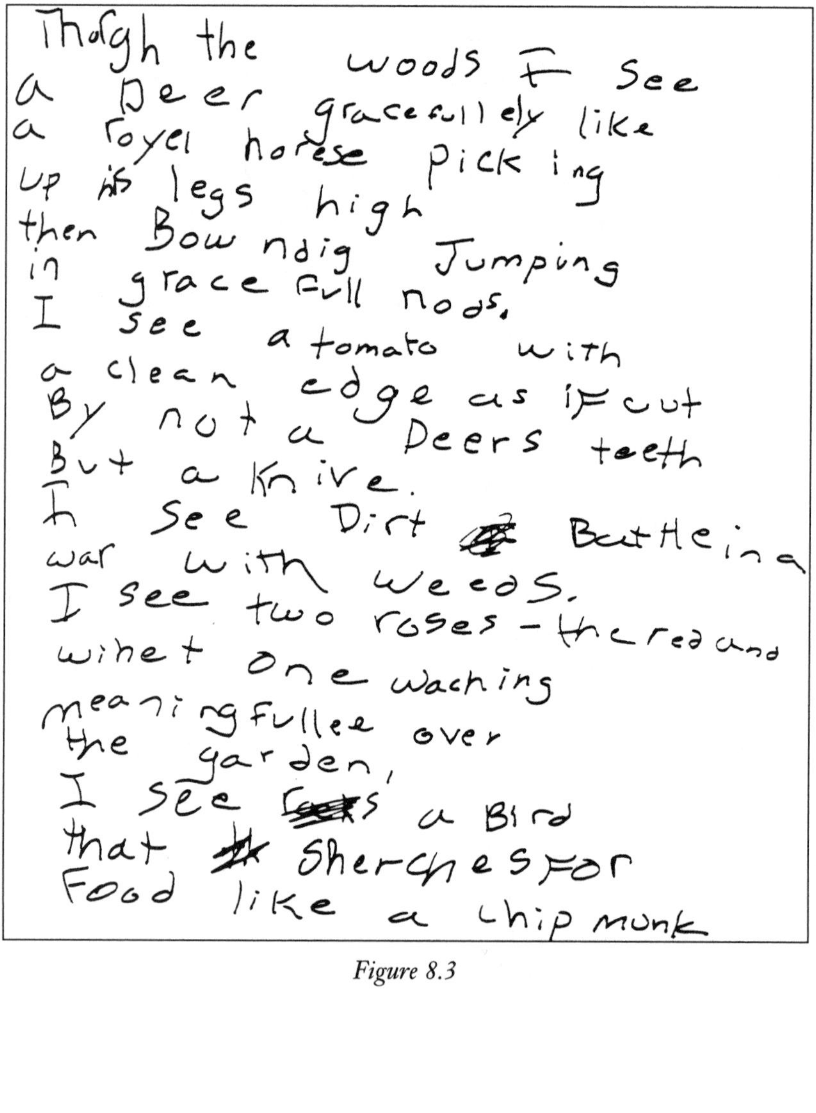
Thogh the woods I see
a Deer gracefullely like
a royel horse picking
up its legs high
then Bowndig Jumping
in grace full nods.
I see a tomato with
a clean edge as if cut
By not a Deers teeth
But a Knive.
I see Dirt But Hein a
war with weeds.
I see two roses - the red and
wihet one waching
meaningfullee over
the garden,
I see a Bird
that sherches for
Food like a chipmunk

Figure 8.3

disturbs them or makes them wonder. To help children do this, it sometimes helps to divide a page into two columns. In one column, they note the facts, the details of a moment; in the second column, they write what the facts make them think and feel and yearn for.

Another strategy my children use is to keep their notebooks open to a blank page while reading one of their books. When Evan read about the Box Car children excavating a bit of Navajo pottery, it reminded him of when he and Miles had found a sunken ship, half-buried in the sand on the floor of the lake. Soon Evan had filled his notebook page with memories of diving under the water to get a closer look at the boat. His entry didn't mention the Box Car book at all. This strategy is called "writing off from literature."

Sometimes children will reread and "write off" of previous entries. Brooke, a second grader, reread an entry she'd written in her notebook where she had catalogued things she cared about. With encouragement from her teacher, Brooke asked herself, "What's the big thing here that I want to stay with?" and she selected her mother as her subject. Again, Brooke's teacher asked her to focus, "Can you think of one moment, one image, that captures how you feel about your mother?" What Brooke wrote is shown in Figures 8.4 and 8.5.

In other cases, new writing "bumps off" from previous efforts, as

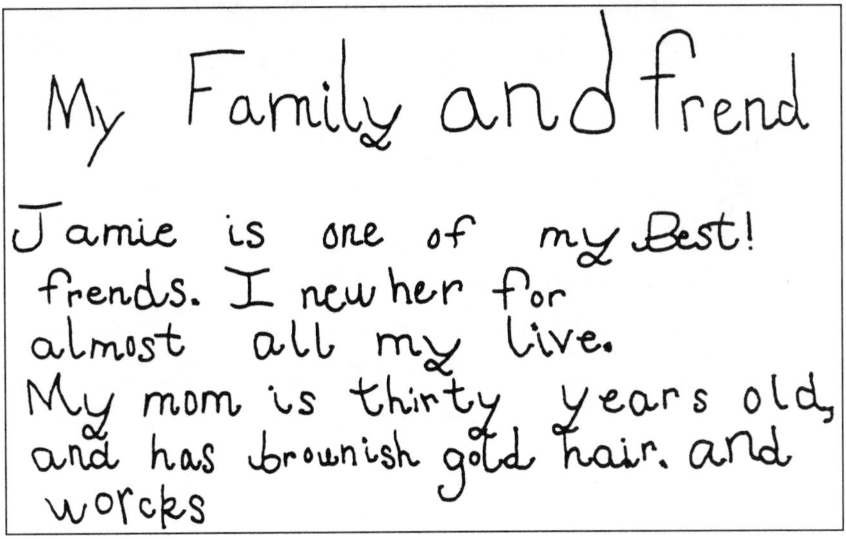
My Family and frend

Jamie is one of my Best! frends. I new her for almost all my live.
My mom is thirty years old, and has brownish gold hair. and worcks

Figure 8.4

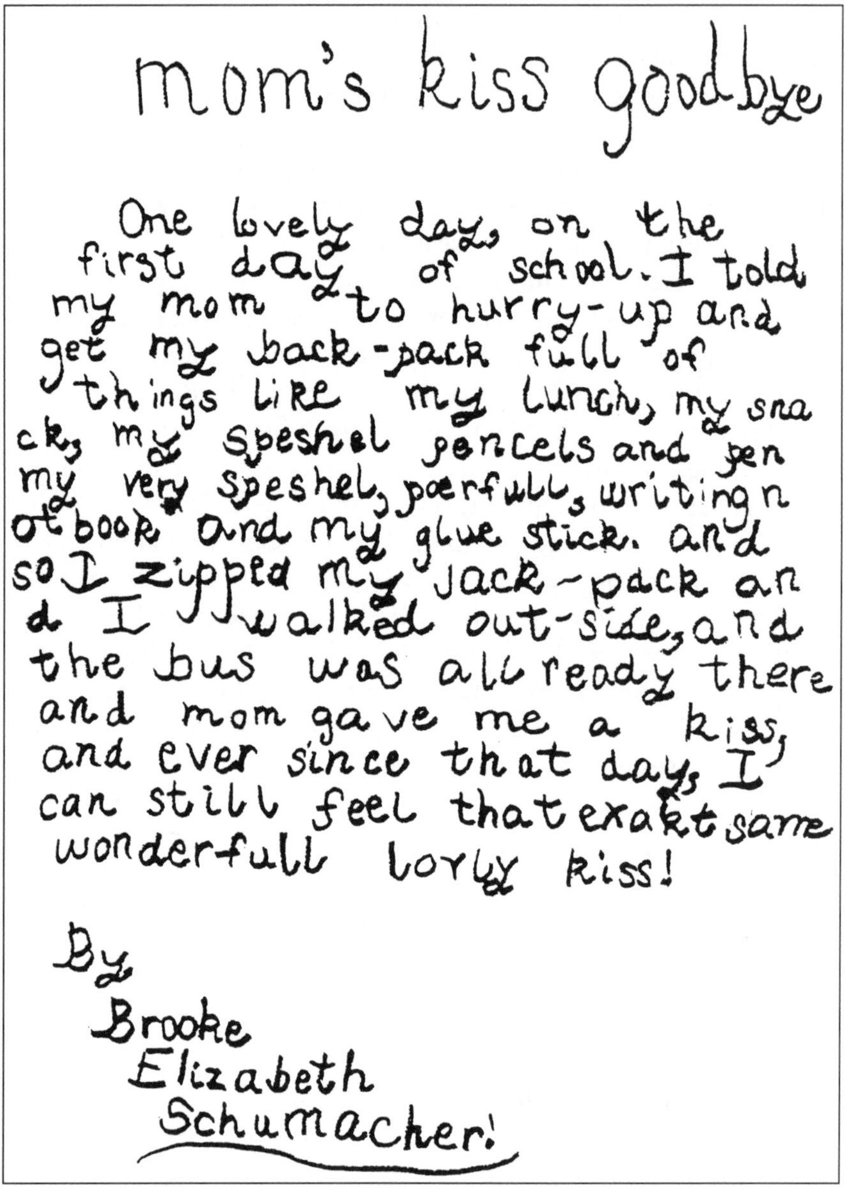

mom's kiss goodbye

One lovely day, on the first day of school. I told my mom to hurry-up and get my back-pack full of things like my lunch, my snack, my speshel pencels and pen my very speshel, poerfull, writing notebook and my glue stick. and so I zipped my jack-pack and I walked out-side, and the bus was allready there and mom gave me a kiss, and ever since that day, I can still feel that exakt same wonderfull lorly kiss!

By
Brooke
Elizabeth
Schumacher!

Figure 8.5

when Miles reread a few of his "computer city" entries and wrote a parallel entry about the forts and towns he has built all his life, in the woods, in the block corner, in his Lego worlds. In a similar vein, I have encouraged Miles and Evan to look over old family photographs, finding one to prop up beside them as they write. They don't describe the photos; they look *through* the photographs to the moments and write about those moments, as shown in Figure 8.6.

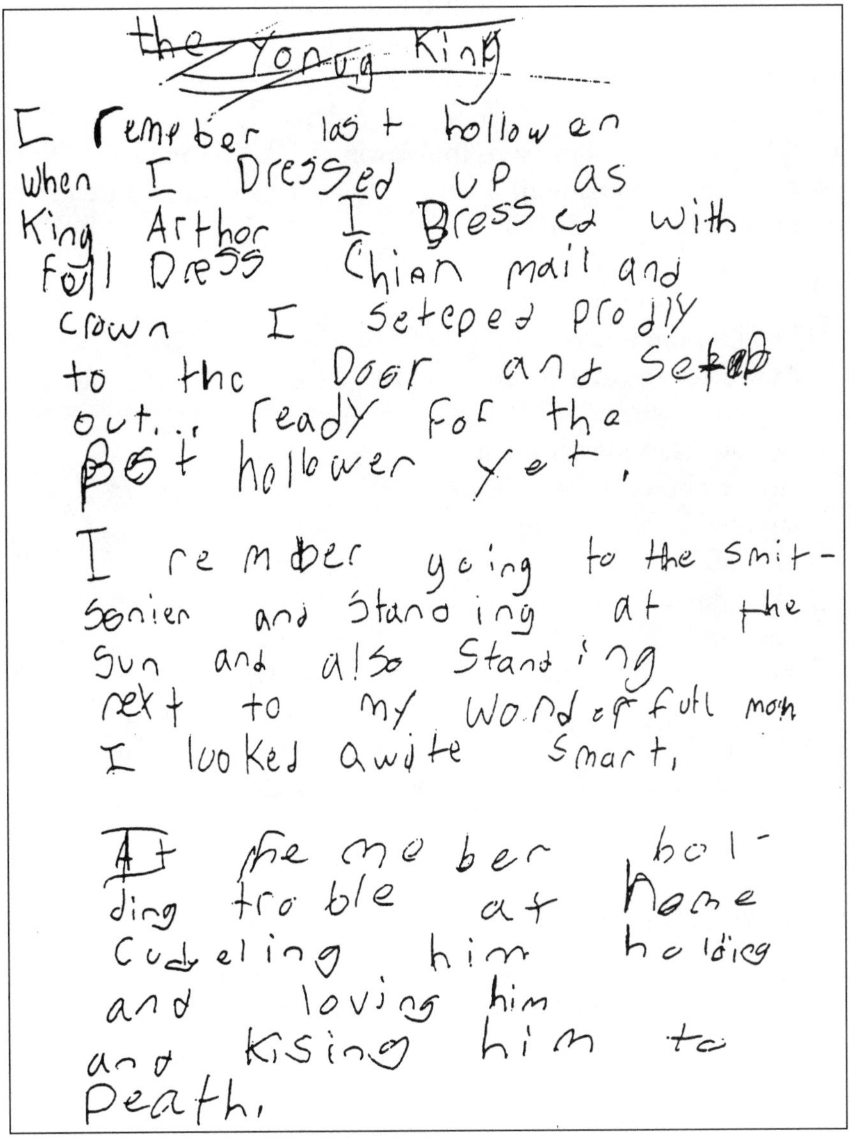
~~the Yong King~~

I remeber last hollowen
when I Dressed up as
King Arthor I Bressed with
full Dress Chian mail and
crown I seteped prodly
to the Door and Setep
out... ready for the
Best hollower yet.

I remeber going to the Smit-
sonier and standing at the
Sun and also Standing
next to my wonderfull mom
I looked awite Smart.

I remeber hol-
ding troble at home
Cudeling him holding
and loving him
and kising him to
Death.

Figure 8.6

Even a line from a book will act as "starter dough" for writing. One of our picture books contains the line: "The bad thing about being an only child is . . . ," and Miles has altered that to generate a page or two of vignettes, each one beginning, "The bad thing about having a little brother is . . ." Other moments evoke writing, too. If your daughter is ending a vacation, finishing a course of study, or saying goodbye to someone, her piece might revolve around the refrain of "I will remember . . ."

Another strategy is to make timelines detailing the chronology of a single event. When my sons took a winter hike, during which they used ice chunks to dam up the water flow in a stream, for example, they made this quick timeline:

Got in our snow clothes.
Hiked on the trail.
Drew faces and arrows in the snow.
Got to the stream.
Used sticks to loosen the ice.
Sent ice chunks to the big rock.
Dammed up the stream.
Got wet.
Hiked home.

Then, instead of writing a summary of the day's events, they each chose a single point on the timeline and wrote about it with as much detail as possible. This, of course, can turn any one adventure into an endless supply of writing topics, and dramatically improve the eventual writing.

Improving the Quality of Our Children's Writing

Every summer, several thousand teachers travel to Teachers College, Columbia University, to learn ways to improve the quality of their students' writing. The most important thing they learn is that it helps immeasurably when students focus their writing. "Pretend, when you are writing, that you are a photographer," I often say to children. "Instead of swinging about, taking a photo of an entire scene, a photographer focuses carefully on a single bird, for instance, sitting on the bough of a tree." Writers are the same. Instead of writing about "My summer vacation," a writer focuses on one aspect of the holiday, writing perhaps about finding a salamander under a stone. Byrd Baylor, the children's author, says it well: "Don't write about the whole ocean, write about one seed pod, one dried weed, one grain of sand."³

What a difference it makes when a child narrows his writing about his parrot in general to writing about taking a bath with his parrot! Or from writing about a weekend on his grandparents' farm to writing about tending the chickens.

Once a child has narrowed a topic down, I try to help the child write with tiny particulars. If Evan wanted to write about feeding the chickens, I might ask, "Can you picture what it was like?" If he answered with a quick summary such as "I opened the door and went in and got five eggs," I might say, "No, wait, slow down." I might repeat his words, leaving space for more details. "You opened the door and . . ." I'd pause to give him time to jump in with more details. If he didn't add details, I might prompt him further with, "What'd you see?" This is how I led Evan to saying and then writing this: "I was standing in a sea of clucking feathers."

We can help our child bring out the details in a piece of writing if our focus and our child's focus is on trying to experience the subject. If Evan and I sit side by side trying to picture that henhouse, trying to see it and hear it and feel it, then it's almost inevitable that Evan will find words to re-create the moment.

Recently, I worked with Lila, a fifth grader who was writing about moving from one house to another. She wrote:

> I recently moved to a new house. It's nicer than the old one, but I miss our old house. When I come into the new house and take off my shoes, I remember how I took my shoes off in the old house. *I miss coming home from school and leaning against the white walls of the old house.*

Lila's detail works for me because it's specific and concrete, yes, but it also works for me as a reader because it works for her as a writer. I know that it's true, that when she takes off her shoes in the new house, she remembers taking them off in the old house . . . leaning against those white walls.

Lila was able to write with this power because she was full of her experience as she wrote. Similarly, if we want to write about anger, the best way to fill our sentences with the short biting phrases that reflect anger is to experience that anger as we write. This is one of the secrets of writing well. Author of *Writing with Power*, Peter Elbow, says: "See the tree!" or "Experience the tree!" is better advice than "Give more specific details about the tree!"[4]

Admonitions such as "Can you be more descriptive?" make the youngster focus on the words, rather than on the tree or the chicken house.

We can bring out the descriptive details in our child's writing, then, by saying:

- "Can you close your eyes and picture it? What exactly do you see?" We might later add, "I can't quite see it. You say it's a blue ocean? Tell me more . . ."
- "Can you think of one particular moment? One time? Can you remember it? Do you have a movie of it in your head right now? How does it start?" Then if the child speaks in generalizations, we might add, "You say you got home and went upstairs? I can't picture it. *Exactly* what did you do?"
- "I'm dying to picture it. So there you were," . . . we almost reenact the moment . . . "What was it like? What'd you see?"

It also helps to bring new life to a piece by having the characters talk. If Evan says, "I told the chickens to get out of the way," I might ask, "What *exactly* did you say?" and encourage him to make it up if he doesn't recall. He then writes: "Scoot, chickens! I need to get through!"

Another important point to remember when helping children write with detail, and particularly with descriptive detail, is that adjectives and adverbs often weaken writing. This comes as a surprise to many of us. Instead of writing, "The cute, funny little dog," it's better to write, "The cocker spaniel puppy stopped abruptly, then eyed the spinning leaf overhead. Springing into the air, the puppy grabbed the leaf in his mouth." In general, writing is strengthened not by adjectives such as "cute" and "funny," but by specific nouns and verbs.

It's also important to guide children to write not only the external but also the internal story. For example, Evan wrote, "I stood on top of the giant sand dune, and looked down to Lake Michigan. Then I started to run." I encouraged him to take the time to write not only what he did, but also what he thought. Eventually, Evan added an asterisk after the sentence, "I stood on top of the giant sand dune and looked down," and at the bottom of his page, wrote an insert in which he told about what he noticed, wondered, pretended, felt, and imagined. After reading his expanded piece, I told him about the poet, Maxine Kumin, who reread her notebook and said, "I am too busy leading the life of a wife and mother now to unfold. It's all in the pleats."

When I work with children to bring out the internal as well the external story, I'm careful not to tell them, "Add your feelings." Generalizations of feelings such as, "I felt scared," or "I felt proud," often weaken pieces of writing. The trick is to expand such phrases and to include specifics such as Jerome did when he wrote:

> Yesterday Donny and I walked home together, eating ice cream. Soon our hands were sticky. Donny wiped his hands on the bushes and wished they held more raindrops. An instant later, it rained. It was a miracle.

The important thing to realize is that our children write well when they take what's there in their lives and let it affect them. The challenge is not only to *tell* the internal story, the challenge is also to *have* an internal story. So often we hurry here and there only half conscious of the life we live. Eve Merriam has written a poem that matters a lot to me:

> Hurry, scurry
> Worry, flurry
> There go the grown-ups
> To the office, to the store
> Subway crush, traffic rush

No wonder
Grown-ups
Don't grow up anymore
It takes
a lot
of slow
to grow.[6]

These days, it's not only grown-ups, but also children who hurry from one thing to another. Our children rush between Little League and computer class, birthday parties and piano lessons. For our children, as well as for us, there isn't always time to see, to wonder, to pretend, and to dream. How important it is for young writers to give themselves the slow to grow!

CHAPTER 9

Finding Our Way Through Today's Math

I remember as a child sitting at my desk in the bedroom under the eaves, plowing through page after page of little math problems. I remember working with a multiplication grid. And I remember the tools of math: the protractor, the plastic ruler, the compass, and the little see-through case in which I kept these tools. But mostly I don't have childhood math memories.

Math was never my thing. I rather liked being very good at English and very bad at math; they balanced each other, I figured. It was, however, a shock to find out that, as a teacher, I was responsible for teaching mathematics. How could I support 30 youngsters' education in math when math and I were officially enemies?

But that was 20 years ago, and since then, teaching math has become a special love, a thrill for me. How extraordinary it has been to face the math dragons, to work past my fears and resistance, and to relearn math first alongside my students and, more recently, alongside my sons.

Like thousands of teachers and parents across the country, I've had a lot of "unlearning" to do. The field of math has changed in dramatic hold-your-hat ways. Paper-and-pencil computation drills represent a much smaller part of what youngsters do today than when I was young. Traditional notions of mathematics have been replaced by higher expectations. We live in a world of calculators and computers, and children need more than ever to be analytical, creative, and flexible in their math knowledge. I have learned that the habits of mind that matter to mathematicians are also those that matter in writing, dance, music, science, and reading.

Changes in the Field of Math

The National Council of Teachers of Mathematics recently released a set of new standards for the field of mathematics. This isn't noteworthy; similar standards have been written for every field. What *is* noteworthy is that these standards have been almost universally embraced by leaders in math education across the United States. The new standards are part of a revolution in the teaching of mathematics that parallels the revolution in the teaching of writing. The long-standing debate about "new math" versus "old math" is a thing of the past. Among knowledgeable teachers of mathematics, there is widespread consensus that the time has come to adhere to a new concept of what it means to teach and learn mathematics.

In some school districts, of course, traditional curriculum in math endures; curriculum reform isn't easy in the best of conditions and this is probably particularly true for elementary-school teachers who tend to not be especially knowledgeable about the teaching of math. As a result, many children today do the same drill-and-skill exercises as did children 20 or 30 years ago. Remarkably, this reassures parents; they are comfortable with their children working through rows of problems in math textbooks that remind them of their own. Perhaps they feel more at ease helping their children with their homework. Parents will say, "Thank goodness my kid doesn't have that new-fangled math. I can understand what my kid is doing."

This attitude is understandable, but in the end, not in the best interests of the children. It is misguided to want yesterday's math curriculum for today. Students who've been educated through a traditional curriculum may perform adequately on standardized tests, for these tests tend to evaluate only low-level computational skills; but as the National Assessment of Educational Progress reports, these students will be sorely lacking in those areas of mathematics that require higher-level cognitive skills and understanding. Children who will come of age in the twenty-first century need a math education that enables them to understand math principles well enough to combine, adapt, and use these principles in ways we can hardly imagine. The new standards document finds our old, traditional math curriculum woefully lacking:

The present K-4 curriculum is narrow in scope; fails to foster mathematical insight, reasoning, and problem solving, and emphasizes rote activities. Even more significant is that children begin to lose their belief that learning mathematics is a sense-making experience; they become passive receivers of rules and procedures rather than active participants in creating knowledge.[1]

In schools that have adopted the new math standards, children can create their own ways of proceeding. When Evan's teacher asked her students to find a way to add 5 + 7, she did so anticipating they would come up with a whole host of strategies for tackling the problem. Lisa, for example, put her hand in front of her and counted her fingers. "One, two, three . . ." Then, in order to add seven onto her five fingers, she put seven buttons in front of her. Looking over the cumulative collection, she sighed and began to count up the total. She began counting the first finger: "One, two, three . . ." Then touching the buttons, she continued counting, "six, seven, eight . . ." In this way, Lisa reached 12 and then recorded her solution. Erik worked in a similar way, except he began by just glancing at his hand and saying, "Five." Then he laid out seven additional objects. That is, Erik's counting took off from the *assumption* of five. He began counting by touching the first of seven cubes. "Six, seven, eight . . ." Kerry worked like Erik, but she did her work mentally, with only small twitches of her fingers to accompany her. Andrew began by thinking of 7 as 5 plus 2, and then efficiently added the two fives together to make 10 and arrived at the solution of 12.

In Evan's class, the students use (or create) not only a host of different strategies for solving simple math problems, they also spend time as a class and in small groups talking about and demonstrating how they went about solving the 5 + 7 question. The emphasis is less on getting the correct answer and more on being resourceful in finding ways of solving problems. How different this is from the math of most parents' experience.

The pages of math problems which I worked on alone under the eaves of my bedroom were part of a traditional approach that emphasized arithmetic computation skills. The entire math curriculum focused on teaching students to add, subtract, multiply, and divide whole numbers, and eventually, fractions and decimals. Even today, children spend 90 percent of their math time on these computations.

The important thing wasn't whether I could apply or critique or analyze or think about or build upon or combine or use what I'd learned. It was enough that I could follow the math recipes and could use the rules. We were to add the ones column first, then the tens. I never asked why. I simply thought this was an inviolate, eternal truth. Only now do I realize that there is no other nation of the world in which people begin with the ones column. Only now do I realize that this rule of my childhood isn't particularly rational, that many would argue that it's the millions which matter, not the ones.

Children today who "invent" ways to solve math problems work first with more concrete, spelled-out, pictorial methods. Later they learn the symbolic shortcuts of my childhood. And so when Lisa added 5 + 7 first by counting out five on her fingers, she was solving the problem in a manner that was developmentally appropriate for her. And because she is surrounded by classmates who have devised shortcuts from her very concrete method, she has the opportunity to learn more expeditious ways of adding 5 + 7. But she can also do the work she needs in order to eventually comprehend what this math equation truly means.

Not long ago, I watched a class of first graders tackle a slightly more complicated problem. "How many numbers are there between 17 and 53?" the teacher asked. The children in this class know they can use or make charts, number lines, pictures, notes, and so forth, so it didn't surprise the teacher that a few kids immediately turned to their laminated "number squares," which are inside their math folders. These squares are laid out like this:

1	2	3	4	5	6	7	8	9	10
11	12	13	14	15	16	17	18	19	20
21	22	23	24	25	26	27	28	29	30

and so on . . . to 100.

One child put her finger on 17. Then, moving her finger down a line to 27, she counted "10"; moving her finger to 37, she counted "20."

This continued until she touched the number 47. Then she moved her finger along the number line, counting by ones. In this way, she arrived at her solution. Another child rounded 17 off to 20, and counted by tens to 50, added 6, and arrived at his solution. None of these first graders set up an equation in the following way (as I would have done in school):

$$53$$
$$-17$$

And significantly, when the teacher gathered the children to talk about the strategies used to solve this problem, it wasn't important to her that some children's answers were wrong by a number or two. She was more interested in having them describe and demonstrate *how* they went about solving the question at hand. It was also interesting to note that she never told the children that most grown-ups would have solved the problem by turning it into a subtraction equation, $53 - 17$, and proceeding from there.

"I don't think there is any one best way to go at a problem like this one," she explained to me. "We adults do most of our math mentally, and counting by tens is a way many of us would proceed," she added. "But also, I don't want to rush kids to the pen-and-pencil shortcuts. I'd just as soon they do things the long way first. This way the image of what they're really doing is there for them, underneath the shortcuts." She summed up her intentions by saying, "I want to teach them ways to think about and estimate with numbers."

When children are expected to explain (and later to write out) how they proceeded to solve a problem, this has important benefits. It helps kids to focus less on whether they are exactly right and more on thinking like a mathematician. The emphasis, the focus, is on being resourceful strategically. Therefore, when these first graders were asked, "How many numbers are there between 53 and 17?" it was not clear how they should proceed to tackle the problem. Part of their challenge was to decide which operation to use and to set themselves up to use it. One of the reasons I learned rules, like "inverse fractions to divide them," without having a clue what the rules meant was that no one ever asked me to talk about the logic of what I was doing. It didn't really matter to me if there *was* any sense behind what I was doing. What mattered was that I got the right answer. Because I never tried different ways to arrive at my answers, because I never saw different people proceeding differently to solve the same problem, there was something mystical about those formulas I learned. They didn't feel manmade. They'd come from some place on high, and my attitude toward them matched the old saying, "Mine not to question why, Mine just to do or die."

One big difference, then, between the traditional way of teaching math and the methods supported by the new math standards document is that more children today know there are many logical ways to go about solving any math problem; and they are encouraged to use any method or combination of methods that work for them.

More and more children today tend to work concretely and manipulatively first. For a five- or six-year-old, adding will usually involve piling up beans, buttons, or nuts. Then, after a child has been using concrete objects to add for a while, he will probably begin to just draw pictures of beans or nuts. Similarly, for a five- or six-year-old, subtracting will usually involve making a pile of things, then taking some away and counting the remainder. Very young children tend to multiply by using images such as eggs in birds' nests. For example, they will put three eggs in each of five little birds' nests; then they will count to find the total number of eggs. Geometry, too, is done concretely. Five- and six-year-old children list square things and not-square things in their kitchen, and use rubber bands stretched onto nails of geoboards to make squares. Even in the third, fourth, and fifth grades, when children encounter new concepts, they work first with concrete, hands-on materials. Miles has been making designs out of straws in order to understand three-dimensional shapes and angles.

All of this work has combined to put a new emphasis on problem-solving into today's math curriculum. The 1996 standards document states:

> We strongly endorse the first recommendation of An Agenda for Action (National Council of Teachers of Mathematics 1980): Problem-solving must be the focus of school mathematics."[2] To de-

velop such abilities, students need to work on problems that may take hours, days, and even weeks to solve. Although some may be relatively simple exercises to be accomplished independently, others should involve small groups or an entire class working cooperatively. Some problems also should be open-ended with no right answer . . ."[3]

A group of second graders worked for a week on this problem:

We've collected a lot of money toward our new class pet. Jane's family gave us $10.00. Katie's family has given $14.00. Evan's mother left a $12.00 gift certificate for us at the pet store.

Now it's time to shop for our pet! These are the prices at the pet store:

hamster	$6.00
gerbil	$8.00
wheel	$6.00
food (1 bag)	$3.00
treats (1 box)	$2.50
shavings (1 bag)	$2.00
nest	$10.00
toys	$3.00 each
water bottle	$2.00
food dish	$1.00
cage	$10.00

What should we plan to buy with our money? Get your friend's opinions and see if you can agree. What will we want to buy another time, after we have more money?

If we all bring in cans for redemption, about how much money do you think we can earn in a week? Are there other ways we could earn money for our new pet?

(Show your methods of exploring these issues.)

In order to work on this problem, the children needed to decide whether to buy one or several packages of food. "How much food was in each package?" they wondered. For this, they phoned the pet store for more information. Next they weighed each new shopping plan against their total sum of money. They also needed to estimate how many cans they might each collect, and determine how much money each can would yield. The work they were asked to do is very much like what the real world asks of us, as mathematicians, all the time. In real life, we rarely have all the information delivered to us on a platter. Often, we have to research to secure some of the data we need in order to solve a problem. And in real life, the biggest challenge often is to figure out which operation to use and how to proceed. Rarely is there one right way to go. They could have begun with a chart on which each child rated the priority of each possible purchase:

	FOOD	TREATS	CAGE	WHEEL	TOY(1)	WATER BOTTLE	TOY(2)	HAMSTER
Summer	3		2	5		4		1
Christian	2	6	3	4	5			1
Ariana	2	5	4	5		3		
Kate	2		3	6	4	5		
Briana	3		2		5	4	6	

Alternatively, they could have established a consensus about which items were requirements and which were options, and then asked people to vote yes or no for each of the optional items.

In real life, too, a lot of math is done through estimation and mental calculations. These second graders were often adding the approximate cost of selected items just as I do when I go to the grocery store with only $50.00 in hand. I keep a mental record of the approximate costs of items as I add them to my cart, just as these children did when they anticipated adding particular items to their shopping list.

Although the class pet problem is an unusually complex and multifaceted example, schoolchildren throughout the country work on open-ended problems that might take several days to explore. In Evan's class recently, children worked together to find as many different possible combinations of coins they could use to pay for an 80-cent ice cream cone. Then they had to figure out if they paid with a $5 bill and the ice cream man gave them all their change in coins, what would the coins be. Then, what *else* might the coins be?

Another problem the children in Evan's class had to solve was how much cloth they would need to make a tent big enough to cover all of them. And if they could only buy full yards of the cloth, how many yards would they need?

Evan was also asked to use cubes to make square shapes. He found that while one cube made a square, two or three cubes didn't; four cubes made a square, as did nine (3 × 3). He was asked to figure out how many cubes in all he would need to make a series of 10 ever-larger cubes. To solve the problems, he made himself a chart, which began like this:

CUBES THAT DON'T MAKE A SQUARE	CUBES THAT DO MAKE A SQUARE
	1
2	
3	
	4
5	
6	
7	
8	
	9
10	
11	
12	
13	
14	
15	
	16

Halfway through the work, the teacher asked Evan to see if he could estimate what the next number might be on his chart. Could he see a pattern in the number of cubes that *did* make squares?

In a fourth-grade math class, children might estimate and research and graph the average summer temperatures of various countries. Or perhaps they might study how each nation's latitude (and distance from the equator) affects its average summer temperature.

These examples illustrate that today when teachers talk about learning math within the context of problems, they mean something very different from what the teachers of most parents meant when they talked about "word problems." When I was young, my teachers gave us "word problems" that were really disguised computations. A typical word problem might have been:

> If Billy contributes $8.00 toward the new class pet, Jane contributes $12.00, and Evan contributes $12.00, how much will we have in all?

Teachers would have expected students to all proceed in the same way, that is, to turn the sentence into an equation and then follow the rules (adding the ones first, carrying, and so forth) to produce the correct answer. And teachers would all have used the same phrases that essentially revealed which operation to use. For instance, when my teacher wrote "When 12 cakes are shared between 3 children," we knew the numbers should be written as a division problem. If she wrote "You have 10 apples and you take away 6," that signified subtraction. The phrase "how many do you have in all" usually meant addition, although sometimes it meant multiplication.

Today children in math classes generally work collaboratively, and they do a great deal of their math mentally (as adults do) and are often working with approximations. Then, too, the talk in a math classroom is no longer the "How do I do this?" and "Am I supposed to add or multiply?" talk of my childhood. Instead, children say, "I have an idea!" and "Wait, wait, I got a different plan," and "Let's try your way, then my way" and "But would that make sense?" Children learn to work in collaboration on a problem, and they use fingers, charts, drawings, counting aloud, and every other resource imaginable to improvise their solutions.

Developing a Mathematician's Habits of Mind

Early in this book I told the story of the preschool director who believed that strong fingers were the most crucial prerequisite for learning to write. "It's all in the fingers," she said. There are parallel stories in math. Parents, in an effort to be sure their children do well in math, assign their four- and five-year-olds to a regimen of flash cards and workbooks. Preschoolers are asked to sit at the kitchen table practicing "their numbers" to ensure that they can draw the figures correctly. I've even seen parents turn meals into math drills. A mother puts crackers on a plate in front of her son and says, "How many crackers do you have?" The child eats two crackers, and the parent is there, waiting to turn the snack into a subtraction problem. "You had 5 crackers and you ate 2. Now how many do you have?" I saw a mother and child climbing steps together, counting as they mounted each new step. Noticing that I was watching, the mother proudly announced, "My older son counts stairs by 3s!"

I watch these interpretations of what it means to help our children be competent mathematically in dismay. I want to say to these parents, "Stop." I want to tell these parents that just as writing is not a little thing we do with our fingers but a big thing we do with our whole lives, the same is true for math. Just as we want to immerse children in the multilayered use of story rather than simply drilling them in alphabet letters, so too should we want to help children explore the full dimensions of real math in the world rather than narrowing in on the technicalities of whether their numbers are exactly right. Just as literacy involves so much more than the alphabet, mathematics involves so much more than the numbers one through ten. Just as our children will, for the most part, all grow up knowing their alphabet letters, so, too, they'll all end up knowing their numbers. But will they be curious, inventive, thoughtful mathematicians? Will they initiate math calculations in their own lives? Will they have an astute sense of time, space, design, proportion, ratio, and the like?

We prepare our children for the world of math by encouraging them to build with blocks, Legos, models. As a child balances his blocks, he develops a sense for equivalence. These two triangular blocks balance with that one square; this thick pile of blocks balances on that tall, thin pile of blocks. And as children work to make their structures stand firm, they work with angles; they learn that the best way to make a tower strong is to abut square blocks rather than triangular ones against it. When children follow directions to make a model, they learn to proceed logically, in a step-by-step fashion. They learn to let words create a mental picture and to then make a replica of their vision. This underlies most complex geometry. Children also learn how to handle setbacks, to examine with care what went wrong and to try what they've learned on another sequence of operations. All of this is far more essential to learning math than most parents realize.

Parents may believe that it is most important that children "know their numbers," when, in fact, being able to write the number "7" is no major accomplishment. Kids will learn to do this soon enough. When my sons were in first grade, both of them still wrote "9" and "7" backward much of the time. This made their math work *look* immature. I'd try to remind them of how the numbers went. But the fact that a child reverses his numbers says *nothing* about whether that child will be proficient in mathematics.

It is far more important that children have a felt sense of balance, equivalence, design, and patterns. The true foundations in math are best learned when children design jewelry and pretty margins, when they draw and execute plans, when they follow cooking and building directions, and make replicas and models.

In order for children to see math as part of everyday life, not a numbers drill, we, as parents, will want to let our children in on the possibilities in something as simple as a trip to the grocery store. We look at the clock to see what time it is, and estimate whether we can get to the market and back before the company arrives. We note the time, say 11:10, and estimate that shopping will take 50 minutes. After some quick, mental addition, we conclude that we can pull it off. In the car, we notice the gas gauge is on empty. We consider the distance between our home and the store, and compare it to the distance we were not able to make the last time, when we actually ran out of gas. Deciding we can make it to the grocery store easily, we head off. We arrive at the store and check the time, calculating whether our estimation was a reasonable one. We're still on track. In the store, we compare the cost of coffee in the smaller and larger cans. Intrigued to find the larger can isn't the savings we anticipated, we put two small cans into the shopping cart. We continue through the aisles, keeping mental tabs on the approximate total. Glancing again at our watch, we decide we have time enough to make a *quick* sweep down one last aisle.

Our entire trip was saturated in mathematics. Interestingly, much of the math we did was not in precise numbers, but estimates. And none of the math involved paper-and-pencil computations. It was all done mentally. For adults, the math we do is intuitive, but we can become conscious of this aspect of our lives and let kids share it. The result can have enormous educational benefits for our children.

Whenever my sons, John, and I eat out together, Miles and Evan always figure out the bill. At first this just meant getting the $20.00 out to pay for the $16.00 dinner, handing it to the cashier, and noticing the change they received. Now Miles calculates the tip for us and adds this to the cost of the meal.

We also gave the boys watches, and now I see them estimating time, checking time, and planning with time. We often begin our Saturdays with a family discussion about how the day will go. "Why don't you play until 9:00 and then you can practice the piano. We'll leave for Evan's soccer game at 9:30," I'll say. When it's approaching time for piano, instead of saying "Practice your piano," I simply say "Keep an eye on the time, guys."

When my sons join me in cooking there are myriad opportunities for them to use math. They know how to follow recipes, double recipes, and halve recipes. Our family calendar has also become a forum for math talks. We consider, "How many days (weeks, months) until . . ." The calendar also helps us to budget our time. If we see that a school project is due on Wednesday, we're reminded to start it early because with soccer and piano on Tuesdays, there's never time for much else.

My sister-in-law handles the allowance issue in such a way that her kids have learned to budget money. She gives each child the number of dollars that matches his or her grade in school. Virginia, in third grade, gets $3.00 a week for allowance. Joan has also established policies for buying birthday gifts and so forth. She pays for the gifts unless they are over a set limit, in which case the child pays the added cost. The details of the plan don't really matter, but I'm full of admiration for the fact that she has a clear, predictable system in which the expectations are spelled out clearly enough that her kids know what it is to have limited funds. As a result of such attentiveness, her kids are learning what it is to work with money—numbers. All of this and so much more is math.

Helping Children with Their Math Homework

Whereas I used to do my math homework alone at my desk in my bedroom, my boys do their math homework with me, each other, John, or their baby-sitter. They work in the midst of everything, at the kitchen table. One night the assignment will be to estimate and then weigh family members, first in pounds and then in another measure. What fun Miles and Evan have figuring out how to weigh us in jars of Ragu spaghetti sauce! They have great plans to hang me from the balcony, with as many jars of spaghetti sauce as necessary piled upstairs on the end of the rope, but they end up weighing the sauce and then converting my weight into the equivalent Ragu weight.

Even when the math is straightforward, I encourage the boys to do something extra with it. When Evan was asked to measure the length of each family member's arms, he included our cats, dog, bird, and rabbit. When Miles was asked to write five story problems, I suggested that he link them all together into one big problem.

Of course, there are many times when Miles's and Evan's one goal seems to be to complete their math in record time. Often I've found that when their teacher sends home an open-ended question like "What numbers combine to make 10?" they'll answer with just a slap-dash note: 5 and 5.

I know, of course, that they're being quite normal to do the fastest job they possibly can, but I always act dumbfounded at what I see before me. "I can't believe my eyes!" I say. "*You, YOU* of all people, with your interest in math, your talent for math . . . you do *this* and call it done? I *can't imagine* what your teacher will think!"

I try, meanwhile, to let my sons' teachers know that I hope they feel free to come down hard on my boys when they do shoddy work. Neither of my sons is neat by nature, but I try to weigh in as a person who cares at least a bit about the neatness of math. If Evan scrawls an answer with a crayon onto a page that's torn and smudged, it's hard for me to think he's taking his math work seriously. And so we've been known to get out the ironing board and iron to restore a page of math homework to a more respectable shape.

These, then, are the ways I help Miles and Evan with their homework. I encourage them to make more of their homework, to do it with a flourish and with spirit. I enjoy the idea of weighing each other with jars of spaghetti sauce, or of measuring each other not with inches, but with Tuckers (Tucker is our dog!).

When Miles or Evan make errors in their calculations, I sometimes intervene to say "Check number two"; but I also believe it's okay for them to make errors and to learn from them. In the end, I care more that they are tenacious, enterprising, creative, and spunky mathematicians than that they are always correct.

Furthermore, I am reluctant to teach Miles and Evan the tricks and rules I know. I learned this the hard way. When Miles was asked to multiply 36×23, I showed him how to line up the numbers as I'd been taught and to begin by multiplying the ones. Only much later did I learn that his teacher was hoping he would multiply 36 by 2 tens to get 72 tens, or 720; then to multiply 36 by 3 to get 108; and add the two together to get the final answer.

Nevertheless, I do try to keep my eye on the topics my sons are learning in school so that I can provide enrichment on those topics at home. This has included buying both a computer program and flash cards that drill them on math facts. The time comes when it's important that they have these facts at their fingertips. They are a minor but necessary part of my sons' math education. I also am not surprised that Miles and Evan have to relearn their math facts, because they often forget them after awhile. I expect to recycle our work on the times tables. I know children the world over need this.

Evaluating a Math Curriculum

Generally, elementary schools purchase and follow a single published math curriculum, a practice which has disadvantages. When educators teach "by the book" this asks less of them. As a result, teachers spend less of their energy and time learning to teach math than they do other subjects in which they have more ownership and more responsibility.

But there are also advantages to a school district following a standard math curriculum. One is that we, as parents, can quickly acquaint ourselves with the values and methods that will be part of our children's math program each year.

When parents look over a math curriculum, it is worth noticing whether it is organized in such a way that topics (fractions, measurement, multiplication, graphing, probability, decimals, and so on) are covered and then abandoned, or whether these topics continually cycle through the curriculum. In Evan's first-grade math curriculum, for instance, he spent a few weeks learning time. At the end of that period, however, he still couldn't tell time, so I set out to remediate matters at home. Only later did I learn that the curriculum for first graders in Evan's school only touches on the hour hand of clocks. Now I know that because his math curriculum is organized like a spiral, Evan will return to study time again in second grade, learning about the 15-minute, half-hour, and 45-minute intervals. I also now know that a great many of his classmates won't truly be able to tell time until third grade. It is, of course, crucial that I understand that the topics Evan explores will be revisited in even more complex ways.

The concept that children should learn aspects of math partially at first, then cycle back to these topics over and over doesn't always match a parent's idea of rigorous education. But this design for math curriculum is widely supported by research, which suggests that education is more successful when students come to understand a topic in increasingly sophisticated, complex ways. When a curriculum spirals in this way, even very young children explore what were once regarded as "fifth-grade" math topics. Probability, statistics, and fractions all have a place in the six-year-old's math education, even though none of these topics is expected to be mastered by these youngsters.

Parents also should pay attention to the role of manipulatives (concrete objects and physical actions) in their child's math curriculum. Most math experts today suggest that children learn a concept first by working in very concrete, physical ways, then by working with drawings that represent the physical objects. For example, as I explained earlier, instead of literally putting eggs into birds' nests, the children rely on drawings of this. Finally, they work with mental and jotted computations.

Various children will need more or less hands-on, concrete work. For children who are ready to work abstractly, it will be tedious to have to draw nests and eggs; therefore, parents may want to inquire whether their children can work with problems in their own ways.

In an ideal math curriculum, even when teachers must follow a published program, they will branch out from this, in order to provide enrichment for children who either need more support or greater challenges. Any topic can be explored with more or less sophistication and so children needn't be divided up by abilities, although working with heterogenous groupings of math students requires thoughtful management.

Parents who want to understand their school's math curriculum will also want to research the tone and relationships in math classrooms. Are children encouraged to collaborate, or do teachers separate children for fear they'll "cheat?" Do teachers encourage children to work together on their homework with parents and siblings, or do they prefer children to sit alone working through rows of problems as I once did?

A quick look at the homework will also reveal whether our children's math curriculum focuses on problem solving, as the new math standards recommend. Ideally, our children will not often be asked to complete 40 equations or work through rows of problems on pages 52 and 53 of a math book.

As I remarked at the beginning of the chapter, despite the new standards for math, the math curriculum in many schools remains much like the math curriculum of my childhood. The sad thing is that parents rarely complain when this is the case. On the other hand, parents frequently complain when school districts are more progressive and sophisticated in their treatment of math. One reason that schools get away with a narrow focus on out-of-context, low-level computation is that this is also the focus of most standardized tests of a child's math ability. Therefore it is entirely possible that schools that teach in antiquated ways could even have higher scores on standardized math tests than do the more-informed schools. Children who score well on the tests may have very little understanding of what they are doing, very little ability to apply math to real-world situations, and very little ability to reason in complex ways about math, but none of these deficits show up on most standardized math tests.

When children are comfortable with concepts such as probability, fractions, division, and time, this however does show up in real life. Children who think mathematically design boats and plan holidays differently, they shop for birthday presents and cook cakes differently. Most of all, children who are comfortable with math can combine and revise and invent their own ways of solving the complex problems of their lives.

CHAPTER 10

Helping Children Develop the Wide-Awake Curiosity of Scientists

Several years ago, Anna Quindlen wrote in her *New York Times* column:

> The lightning bugs are back. They are small right now, babies really, flying low to the ground as the lawn dissolves from green to black in the dusk. There are constellations of them outside the window: on, off, on, off. At first the little boy cannot see them; then suddenly, he does. "Mommy, it's magic," he says.
>
> This is why I had children: because of the lightning bugs. Several years ago I was reading a survey in a women's magazine and I tried to answer the questions: Did you decide to have children: a) because of family pressure; b) because it just seemed like the thing to do; c) because of a general liking for children; d) because of religious mandate; e) none of the above.
>
> I looked for the lightning bugs, for the answer that said, because sometimes in my life I wanted to stand at a window with a child and show him the lightning bugs and have him say, "Mommy, it's magic."[1]

To me, this excerpt says everything about the relationship between science and childhood.

Recently I asked my secretary, "Whenever you make a plane reservation for me, would you try to get me a window seat?" Her eyes met mine, and she nodded with an air of significance, as if to say,

"That's sweet; yes, of course, I'll help you get a good view." I didn't want to disillusion her, so I didn't mention that I like the window seats because I can sleep better there, leaning my head against the window. How I wish I was the person she imagines me to be! How I wish I did peer out at the cloudscapes and vapor trails. Instead, it is as if I'm always too busy or too tired to notice the miracles around me.

But when I travel with my sons, it's a different experience altogether. We press our noses against the windowpanes, peering out at the wisps and scoops of clouds, and at the patchwork world below. We notice and study and theorize over the airplane's wings; and we marvel at the miracle of us, a flying bus, suspended in air. We wonder over the clouds and mountains, research the weather below and above us, and imagine the difference we make in it all.

Even a walk from the house to the car is different when my sons are along. When I'm on my own, I tend to travel on autopilot, not seeing to my right or left. With my sons, we question the tiny balls of water, like beads on the hood of the car; and we notice the loud call of a bird, marveling how such a clear strong song can come from such a tiny bird, perched on the bough above us.

Robert Francis wrote a poem, "Summons," which was, I think, addressed to a lover, but I think of it as my poem to my sons.

Summons

Keep me from going to sleep too soon.
Come wake me up. Come any hour
of night. Come whistling up the road.
Stomp on the porch. Bang on the door.
Make me get out of bed and come
and let you in and light a light.
Tell me the northern lights are on
and make me look. Or tell me the clouds are doing
something to the moon
they never did before.
See that I see. Talk to me and show me till
I'm half as wide awake as you are.[2]

"Miles and Evan," I say, "Keep me from going to sleep too soon. See that I see . . ."

Miles and Evan are so wide awake, it is exhausting. In the car recently, Evan picked up a cassette tape and started to finger it. "Evan, Sweetie," I said, "Don't touch the black part of the tape." "Why not?" he asked, moving his hand to it. For an instant, I couldn't think what to reply. "You'll rub the music off," I said, aware as I spoke of the inadequacy of my answer.

Evan peered at the tape more closely, turning it this way and that. "How did the music get *on?*" he asked. I wondered the same thing. "How *does* music get onto an audiotape?"

Like Anna Quindlen, it's only when I have a child with me that I slow down enough to think about the world around me; that I sit at the window watching as the lawn dissolves from green to black in the dusk, waiting for those little flares in the dark. The children's author Jane Yolen wrote a beautiful book called *Owl Moon*, which I've mentioned several times. In it, a father takes his youngster out on a cold winter night to hoot at the edge of a forest clearing, hoping to see an owl, waiting for that familiar echo to wend its way through the woods. Although Jane Yolen writes the book as if it is the child's father who takes his youngster into the woods, we who have children of our own know that it is the child who lured that father to crunch across the winter snow, to stand under the full moon, in search of owls. Science education begins when a child says, "Look, look what I found," or, "Wait, I hear something." It begins with the child teaching *us* to see more, wonder more, notice more.

The Limitations of Following the Recipe

When our children crouch down to peer at a worm, it is not always easy for us to regard this attentiveness as a part of science. Instead of trusting that science lives in our front lawns or in our kitchen cabinets, we look for prepackaged science. At stores, there are science kits for sale. In one there may be some plaster of Paris, a rubber cap, and the directions for casting a footprint; or a coil of wire, a battery, and a lightbulb. Classrooms sometimes have similar kits. One in a fourth-grade class contained a little cardboard bureau with drawers labeled "20 Wheat Seeds," "10 Radish Seeds," "12 3-oz cups," and "6 water sprinklers." It was part of a program called Science-in-a-Box. Directions included detailed instructions of how children were to plant their garden experiments. The children were supposed to follow the script, planting five mustard seeds two inches down in the soil, and five seeds one inch down.

None of this fits with my image of what matters in science education. My goal isn't "Science-in-a-Box," but instead, science-out-of-a-box. I want children to get their hands in the soil and leaves, or root among wires and batteries, funnels and tubes, and say, "I wonder . . ." or "I have an idea!"

In our home, we support science education by letting our kids "have a go" at the world. For a few years, when Miles and Evan were four, five, and six, whenever one of our machines broke, the boys would carry it to their workbench and set to work, using their electric screwdriver (a must!) or their hammer to wedge or smash open the case of the tape recorder, the telephone, the waffle iron . . . and soon they'd uncover coils, wires, control panels, and other marvels.

I'd like to say they then carefully examined these, drawing the inner workings of the machines, comparing these to nonfiction books I supplied at just the right moment so they could study how the machines worked. But in truth, they just destroyed the machine and then combined its parts with other parts, creating their own versions of computers, spacecrafts, or watchamacallits. But listening to them, their talk was not the talk of someone following another person's recipe ("Okay, I planted those five seeds, now what am I supposed to do?"), but rather, it was the talk of an explorer. "I can't believe it! Look at this! It's stuck. I don't know how to get it out. Maybe I'll try a bigger screwdriver . . . There's more stuff underneath!"

Miles and Evan messed around in similar ways in the kitchen, making what they called "potions." Once, they poured together corn syrup, molasses, orange juice, and salad dressing, then added one egg, still in its shell, and put it outside on a winter evening. "Don't touch our experiment," they cautioned me. When I asked what the experiment was about, they said, simply, "We want to see what happens."

If I were a better parent, no doubt I would have pursued that conversation more. "What happens with what?" I could have asked, and coached them until they had a hypothesis ("The stuff will eat away the eggshell."). Then I could have helped them set up a control (perhaps another egg out on the back porch in just a container of water) and we could have recorded and charted the temperatures and all the rest. But I don't usually do a lot of this. John and I simply looked at each other, and smiled, sharing the pleasure of their early efforts at being scientists. The next morning, we reminded them of their experiment, and asked with interest, "So what happened?"

In retrospect, I wonder, should we have done more? Was it a good idea to launch our kids' lives as scientists simply by letting them mess around? So I asked my sons what I should tell parents to help them help their kids in science. Evan replied, "You said it, Mom. Grown-ups have got to *help*, not be the boss. It's the kids' science, not the parents'. The parents shouldn't say, 'Why don't you do it this way?' " Miles added, "And they should never say, 'It won't work,' or the kid will learn not to try, not to keep trying."

Eleanor Duckworth, a science educator from Harvard University and author of *The Having of Wonderful Ideas*, would probably agree with Miles and Evan. In her book, she reveals that, as a post-graduate student, she was hired to work on an elementary science study despite the fact that at the time she had no background in science. Reflecting on this, she says her naïveté about science was a great boon for she became a "sample child" for her colleagues on the team. "I spent a lot of time exploring the materials and issues that they came up with. . . . Three seemingly unrelated items came to-gether in a way . . . I got hooked and have been ever since."[3] Then Duckworth wrote something that I regard as crucial: "It was the first time that I got excited about my own ideas. My struggle had always been to get in on what I thought somebody else knew, and knew to be important. This was the first time that I had a sense of what it was like to pay attention to my own ideas."[4]

Of course, when children deconstruct and reconstruct machines or combine kitchen liquids into nauseous potions, it's unclear whether they really are paying attention to their own ideas or simply making a mess. But for Duckworth, an engagement with ideas came from the stuff, the materials. She said, "I spent a lot of time exploring the materials and the issues they came up with."[5] This is true for children, too. An egg, still in its shell, set outside on a winter night raised issues. Raisins, added to a liquid concoction, raised issues. Miles and Evan didn't begin by formulating questions about freezing or dehydration; they began with childlike pleasure over pretend-play, but this time, they were pretending to be scientists. As Joseph Elstgeest says,

> It may be the clouds in the sky, or the birds in the undergrowth; it may be a bumblebee on the clover or a spider in a web, the pollen of a flower, or the ripples in a pond. It may be the softness of a fleece, the "bang" in a drum, or the rainbow in a soap film. From all around comes the invitation; from all around sounds the challenge. The question is there, the answer lies hidden, and the child has the key.[6]

To encourage our children to do the messing around that is such a part of childhood, we must give them access to the stuff of science.

Once I saw a toddler sitting on the ground at our local playground using his hands to bulldoze piles of sand. The child's mother hurried to her son's side, frantically brushed his hands off and said, "Don't touch that sand! Who knows what dog might have peed in it!" A week or two later, I saw a three-year-old peering through the iron mesh fence at the ballpark to watch his sister's softball game. His mother loosened his fingers from the fence and scooped the child into her arms, saying, "Stay away from that fence. That ball may come right over here and crush your little fingers." At the time, watching the Little Leaguers swinging hopelessly away at their batter's T, I couldn't resist chuckling at the notion that one of those little six-year-olds might ever, in a million years, send a ball soaring across the field, Babe Ruth style, to hit bull's-eye onto the child's waiting fingers. Later, thinking about the episode, I stopped chuckling. How common it is for us to think only about the possibility of crushing a child's fingers, and not to consider the possibility of crushing a child's spirit! What a message we send when we pull our child back from the fence at the ballpark! Do we really want our child to sit on the sidelines, worrying whether balls will zoom through the air onto his waiting fingers? Do we really want a child to look at the sand and the earth and think, "Is this safe to touch? Might a dog have peed here?"

When I say that science education begins with giving our children the stuff of science, perhaps I really mean it begins with giving our children access to the stuff that is already there and encouraging them to do what they will with it. We needn't buy plastic octopuses and sharks that adhere to the bathtub walls; all we need is to bring little tubs, plastic sprayers, sponges, and straws into the bathtub . . . and more importantly we need to stop worrying over whether our child will drink the soapy water or get suds in her eyes. How different our bathroom looks from the clean, simple bathrooms I see in magazines, where there is just a single yellow rubber duck sitting on the edge of the tub as the child's only signature! We often have a fleet of boats beside our bathtub, testimony to my boys' lively obsession with making boats that float without tipping over, and more recently, with making submarines that sink *and* float. Miles and Evan use orange juice containers and plastic bottles as the hulls of their submarines, and insert Lego people in them. When these are full of air, it's a challenge for them to devise a system for submerging the boat. Miles and Evan will work hard and long trying to figure out principles of sinking and floating, and as they do, they are doing the work of a scientist.

This doesn't mean that they keep lab reports on their bathtub play, or that they record their hypotheses and their procedures. Science is far more organic than this. Duckworth, in describing her goals for a school science program, writes:

> The materials should allow opportunities for a variety of different ways to find out—some patient-watching, some resourceful tool-making, some clever experimental design, some sudden insight, some constant repetition, some imaginative guessing, some tight logical thinking, some trying out a tentative idea, some frustration. . . .[7]

The outdoors, the kitchen, and the bathtub, all are central to our children's growth as scientists. I'll never forget a walk I took with friends when Miles was still in the baby carriage. My friends had a four-year-old, and early during the walk, the little boy Taylor gave his dad a rock to hold, then another, another, and another. Later, Taylor added sticks to the collection. Skipping off, Taylor lost interest in the rocks and sticks, and we proceeded to walk. Arriving home, Taylor's father asked him, "Where should I put those rocks and sticks?" "You still have them?" I asked, astonished. "Of course I still have them," he said. "Taylor asked me to hold them."

Later, when Miles and Evan were old enough to ply me with sticks and stones, I tried to live up to Taylor's father's example, and I often felt grateful for the lesson he had taught me. I even bought a little display case for my sons' treasures. I also use pottery bowls, set in the center of the coffee table as containers for their stones, remembering that the focus of many elementary science programs is to give children opportunities to sort and categorize their collections.

Deepening the Engagement with the Stuff of Science

I admit I found it hard to encourage my kids to save and categorize stuff without wanting them to progress to the next step of labeling things. When Miles and Evan began spending hours in the "mining center" they created on a little rock outcrop in our woods, chipping away at the cliff to loosen bits of quartz and mica, I bought them a guidebook to rocks and minerals, anticipating that they would take great pleasure in identifying their jagged, glittery stones. But they glanced at the book for no more than two seconds, then headed back into the woods with their red wagon, loaded with chisels, hammers, and jars, bumping along behind them. I started after them, book in hand, then stopped midway and retraced my steps. Perhaps someday they would care about the Latin names of their rocks, but for now, it was something else altogether that motivated their excavations.

Once our children start school, there is less time and support for messing about with rocks, sand, water, raisins, and the rest. Once school starts, we, as parents, tend to focus on helping our children read and write, add and subtract, and know facts and labels. The sad thing about this is that just as our children get old enough to pursue their own wonderful ideas, to become deliberate problem solvers, we tell them to clear off the kitchen table and get out their papers and their books. If we pay attention to science at all, it is usually to teach facts and definitions, the names of planets and insects, the meanings of words like orbit and evaporate. What a mistake! Our children are natural scientists; they become spellbound by ant hills and pulleys, vapor trails and animal tracks; and so science gives us an extraordinary forum for teaching them to be inventive, inquisitive, analytic, persevering explorers. What habits of thought could matter more?

When possible, then, I try to be as supportive of my children's investigations and explorations now as I was when they were preschool age. My hunch is that we can help our children grow in big and important ways if we continue to honor their collections and their magic potions.

To that end, I try to give my sons mentors, and these come from unlikely places. Last summer, my husband hired a mason to install a patio in our backyard. With great pleasure, John reported that he had managed to schedule the work during a week when the boys and I would be away from home. "You can avoid the mess totally," he said. "You'll come home to a finished patio!" John expected me to be pleased, but I wasn't. "Reschedule it, pleeease," I pleaded. "The boys will want to watch."

The patio project proved to be more than mere fun. For 10 days, Miles and Evan watched the show, enthralled from their chairs lined up at the worksite. After a few days, I found the boys making secret plans behind a bush. They were surreptitiously making their own "rabbit patio" on a corner of our lawn. Each day they'd watch Angelo's progress, then follow the example he had set, using his leftover sand and stones. "We tried to keep it extra secret so Angelo wouldn't see," the boys confided.

Angelo didn't leave behind any bricks, so Miles laid a wooden ladder in the middle of our lawn, filling its quadrants with a thick mortarlike mixture of sand and water. When I found this on the lawn and protested, Miles told me, "We had to do it in the sun. We saw it on television; people bake bricks in the hottest, sunniest place." When Miles and Evan lifted up their ladder mold carefully and their huge squares of sand collapsed all over our grass, I regretted that this one time, at least, I hadn't told them beforehand, "It won't work!"

But for the most part, I find that my sons need the same things now as they needed when they were younger: access to stuff, opportunities to experiment with no particular purpose in mind; time to raise questions and ideas; encouragement to dream and to explore their own wild schemes; and chances to experiment without adults saying, "It won't work."

I think Miles and Evan especially need John and me to pay attention to their ideas so *they* pay attention to their ideas. And so when I see them messing about, I often ask, "What are you planning?" even when I suspect they don't have any plans or intentions at all yet, just as I ask the child who's piling blocks on top of each other, "What are you making?"

At first when I asked, "What are you planning?" or "What are you trying to find out?" Miles and Evan concocted answers on the spot. "We're testing to see what happens," they said, partly evading my question and partly pretending to be people with plans and intentions. And my role was to go along with the drama. "What have you noticed so far? Does any of that help you predict what'll happen next? What's your hunch?" I asked as if certain that they've taken the time to develop a hypothesis. This is how I helped Miles and Evan role-play their way into being the kind of researchers I want them to become.

Over time, I have found that Miles and Evan have become more intentional and purposeful in their experiments. Last summer they made another potion; it looked as gloppy and smelled as awful as their earlier potions. I noticed it only because part of the mixture involved a large quantity of my expensive beauty salon shampoo. When I asked about it, I was surprised to learn that there was a deliberateness and thoughtfulness behind the potion that had not been there in their earlier potions.

"We wanted to kill the red ants that bit Evan's foot," Miles explained, "so we decided to make a bug-killing potion." Nodding in agreement, Evan explained further: "We started with some things the ants would like. So we could attract them. We put in Cheese Whiz and sugar and our toothpaste, because it's sweet. Then we wanted something to drown them in that smelled like it might be poisonous, so we got your shampoo." Miles added, "A lot of it, and some salad dressing. And then we wanted it to have sticky parts in case the drowning didn't work. We wanted something to act like the sticky paper Virginia uses in her barn to trap flies, so we put lip-vaseline and some of that red lip stuff, which was hard to put into the jar." Pausing, they remembered one more ingredient. "We added a little rock so you could shake it up because things kept getting stuck to the walls."

Apparently after all this, when Miles and Evan went outside to try their bug-killing potion, they opened up an ant hill with their shovel and found hundreds of ants carrying white eggs "to save their children." Seeing this, Miles and Evan revised their plans. Instead of killing these families, they decided to construct an ant farm for them. Although this didn't work, how much closer this was to the real work of science than any of the Science-in-a-Box kits that line the shelves in stores and make up the curriculum in schools!

Promoting Thoughtful and Sustained Research

How does one promote thoughtfulness in children's early work with science? In part, the answer is through conversation. We and our children need to have the kinds of conversations out loud that we hope eventually will happen in our children's minds.

We need to have conversations with children about what they see in the world around them: the raindrops and puddles, the little animals and the insects, the soil and the logs, the batteries and machines. It is not important that our children know the names of things; it's important that they know what to expect of things. What are the habits of mosquitoes; what are the properties of clay?

Eleanor Duckworth suggests that it's also important for children to be able to think of things to do that can tell them more than they could learn by just observing the clay or the mosquitoes. What will happen if they put the clay, the toys, or the batteries into water? If they put them in the dark? She writes that it is helpful if children know that "they sometimes must repeat what they do over and over again, before they can believe the results, and that they know when to count and measure, and how to think of factors that might explain what happened. . . ."8

To help our children to think like scientists, then, we can ask such questions as:

What have you seen so far?
So what's your hunch?
How could you find out?
What could account for that?
How could you see if that's a reasonable expectation?

For such conversations to happen and to subsequently become internalized—that is, part of our children's thinking—science projects should last for more than one sitting. One of the problems with all the Science-in-a-Box projects and other follow-the-recipe experiments is that, often, they are one-time projects.

It's a different experience altogether when, for example, a child and a parent return often to walk a favorite path. "I think the repetitiveness of our walks helped to enrich them," Shirley McPhillips says of a walk she frequently took with her son Shawn. "We'd notice how everything along the trail had changed; and each day's walk was connected to earlier walks, and to earlier conversations. One day I might notice a patch of wildflowers, picking one to press inside our guide on the page where it belonged. The next day, my son would notice a patch of the same flower, and we'd wonder if one patch was there first, if one patch was the parent flower patch."

One day, Shawn turned over a stone, and oh the excitement of discovering a new world! That day, he sat on his haunches for a long time watching ants carrying little white things (which he later learned were egg cases) this way and that. Soon he wanted to turn over every stone and log in the forest. Eventually, Shawn no longer followed the trail; he went into the woods, to the right or the left, and his attention was no longer undirected. Now he had one thing on his mind. The McPhillips' home was filled with jars and jars of sand, leaves, and ant colonies. Shawn learned from his dad that he could contain his small creatures in their jars if he smeared a vaseline ring around the tops of the jars. He researched what his ants needed to survive, to thrive. And he waited for the ant cases to hatch.

Presently, he made himself an ant notebook, and filled it with tiny careful drawings of his ant villages. He read books and critiqued them, writing such comments as: "That's not how it is for my ants." "These two books each say something different." Thus, Shawn's research became deeper and more directed as he focused on a single interest. Like many other children, Shawn was, for a time, obsessed with one topic.

In her book, *The Making of a Scientist*, Anne Roe reports that when she studied 64 individuals who grew up to become scientists, she found that all of them had "a singular purposefulness" in their adult days as well as in what is known of their youth.[9] For every person Roe studied, the individual's connection to science came especially from the opportunity to research an inquiry, to pursue an obsession over time.

Biologist Sir Julian Huxley's obsession was with birds, and it began one day when he was eight:

> We had a bird table and there I learned to differentiate the tits . . . and one day down Charter House Hill, I saw a queer little bird, blue-grey above and russet below; it was just a common nuthatch, but to me it was a revelation.[10]

Huxley's interest in birds continued throughout his school years. "I kept an elaborate bird diary, noting which species of birds I saw each day, their approximate number, whether they were singing, the nests I found (with the number of eggs or young) and notes on peculiar behaviors."[11]

If your child becomes interested in insects, encourage her to focus on a particular insect. Shawn will develop an expertise more easily if he is interested in red ants than if his interest is in all creatures that live under logs. A Julian Huxley will become an expert more easily if his focus is on woodpeckers rather than on all birds. Whether it's ant eggs or birds or ways to submerge a submarine, we need to support our child's single-minded and tenacious interest for as long as we can, even if it seems that she is developing a "one-track" mind.

Of course, it's important that the object of study be present in the child's life; that the child can watch, record, draw, chart, question, theorize, and investigate, rather than just read up on a topic. A few years ago when I learned that a colleague was taking a course with the science educator Eleanor Duckworth, I phoned my colleague to ask, "What are you reading?" "The moon," she answered. "*The Moon*," I repeated, adding the title to my list of recommended books. "By whom?" "The *moon*," she said again with emphasis. "By God."

In her graduate course in science education at Harvard, my colleague was asked to observe the moon every night for half an hour. I couldn't imagine this. "What happens up there?" I wondered. I later learned that Duckworth had been watching the moon for 16 years and meeting for week-long retreats with other moon watchers, who then collaborated to make sense of what they had seen. Duckworth says, "We're surprised to find that everything that seems simple has depth unimagined for investigating and finding out more about . . . you just look at the phenomenon; and if you ask yourself what you can find out about it, you notice all kinds of things which keep leading to deeper understandings."[12]

When teachers in Duckworth's courses first begin to record what they see, they tend to believe they already know all about the moon. "Very soon," Duckworth says, "they find out things that surprise them. Like sometimes on bright, starry nights, there's no moon to be seen. How come? And sometimes, you see it tonight, and you go out a couple hours later and it's not there anymore."[13]

How important it is for children to realize they can make their own wonderings and ideas. How important it is for them to build theories out of what they see and think. What better readers they will be if they have first spent a few nights (or a few years), observing and thinking about the moon.

But observations alone are insignificant. The scientist, young or old, needs to make something—an idea, a theory, a hunch—out of this fact, this observation. The scientist needs to ask, "What do I make of all this?"

A quote from John Bronowski, a scientist, reads, "There is nothing on the face of a fact that tells you what it means." Recording a pattern is not research, cutting an article out of the newspaper is not research: These are invitations to do research.

We can guide our children to develop hunches, theories, and ideas if we direct them to slow down and pay attention to all that is around them. One group of fifth graders studied five ecosystems (terrariums) for six weeks. Every day, they observed their terrariums for 45 minutes, writing and talking about whatever they saw. Most of us would, at most, give these terrariums a passing glance. But research *is* paying attention, looking longer.

I asked these fifth graders to explain to me why these little worlds were so endlessly interesting to them. One student answered, "Say you see a spore in the moss; every day it could be different if you look closely. Different things happen around it and to it. You ask questions, you get clues." Another noted: "You can wonder, 'When did it start growing?' and you can look at how fast it grows now, every day, and then count back. There might be spores forming on other plants, too."

This conversation continued, with the students interrupting one another in their enthusiasm to tell me all they could study if they found a single spore growing in the moss. Listening to this, I felt humbled, for I know that I tend to rush my sons from one fascinating science subject to another.

Miles and Evan often beg us to take them to a place called the Discovery Zone, a building in town filled with a giant metal obstacle course made from red bars and yellow rope netting. At the Discovery Zone, they race frenetically through the apparatus, somehow accumulating credits, which they then trade in for prizes. Watching them, I always wonder, "Where's the discovery in the Discovery Zone?" Likewise, children often race frenetically through a too-full curriculum. In one semester, they cover weather, the human body, Kenya, and machines, all while moving from one list of vocabulary words to another, from one chapter, worksheet, or experiment to another.

When I was young, we spent hours in the swamp behind our house. It wasn't much of a swamp, really; it was more a seasonal muck-hole at the base of our toboggan hill. But to us, the swamp was a place of endless mystery and magic. Clumps of trees grew out of the water. I regarded these as islands, and named each one; and often, I'd pole my homemade raft to them. I collected strings of frog eggs, too, and incubated them in a glass bowl at the center of our kitchen table. Thinking back to that swamp, it seems to me I launched more investigations, developed more theories, imagined more possibilities, and researched more hunches during my hours in the swamp than I ever did in my science classroom. Growing ideas takes time.

CHAPTER 11

Social Studies: People, Places, Dates, and a Habit of Mind and Heart

Last week, parents gathered at my sons' school for a "Morning Coffee" to discuss the topic of social studies education. One of the mothers opened with: "We need to be sure the basic facts are being taught. There are children who couldn't list the continents if they tried!" Other parents nodded their assent, while I gave myself a quick quiz. On my fingers, I silently counted, "Europe, Asia, Africa, North and South America, Antarctica . . . and . . . um . . . yes, Australia." With a glad sigh of relief, I joined the chorus of nods. Of course, definitely, we need to be certain our children can list the seven continents.

At home that evening, I was comforted when Miles was able to deal with the continent question far more decisively than I. But then he added: "It's on the placemats at the pizza shop."

What if the list of continents hadn't been on those placemats? Like most parents, I want my sons to know the continents, to know Thomas Jefferson, Paul Revere, Franklin Delano Roosevelt, and to know that California is on the western coast of the United States and Massachusetts, the eastern coast. But I try to remind myself that the goal of social studies education is not for our children to do well in a Jeopardy quiz show or a Trivial Pursuit game.

It's pleasant that Miles hit the jackpot with his answer to the continents question, but not essential. What does matter is that our children are fascinated by stories of long ago and far away. What

215

does matter is that our children know what it is to be "on about" an inquiry (finding resources in people, places, pamphlets, maps, and libraries; cumulating information from all kinds of sources and seeing parallels, contradictions, and surprises among the different sources). What does matter is that our children understand that people everywhere build worlds for themselves, including systems of government and religion; and that our children appreciate that their own world is just one of many.

Now, thinking back on that Morning Coffee, I wish I'd said that as important as it is that our children know there are seven continents, it's even more important that they have ways of using that information.

Inviting Children to Explore Social Studies

When Miles was in nursery school, he surprised his teachers by building the Berlin Wall in the block area. I confess, it surprised me too. I wasn't prepared for his fascination with history, geography, and science. He'd pore over books or listen to the news, asking a million questions. I'd answer those questions—badly I admit—and Miles would be off and running, carrying with him his own idiosyncratic and incomplete notions about countless subjects.

Perhaps because I'm a teacher and perfectionist, I found it frustrating that he rarely mastered any subject. His own improvised study of social studies was nothing like a school curriculum in which topics are introduced and covered with some degree of completeness. Instead, it was as if Miles built little outposts of knowledge on countless different frontiers. He'd pick up bits of knowledge about Fort Ticonderoga, Thomas Jefferson's Monticello, and Martin Luther King, Jr., but not understand the eras surrounding the episodes. He never quite got anything straight or complete in his mind. And he'd latch onto the oddest, tiniest facts; reading about birds, he learned that ornithologists don't wear nylon "because it's made with oil."

Thinking back now, it seems to me I needn't have worried that Miles had lots of half-developed, not quite-right, unintegrated ideas about geography, government, and history. How could it have been otherwise? It's not possible, of course, for a child to simply put on the garment of an educated adult's understanding of history or geography. Instead a child has to construct that understanding, and an understanding of any one historical era relies on an understanding of so much else. To envision Colonial America, a child needs to piece together some notion of England, France, Africa, America, and the Atlantic Ocean, and an understanding of time, government, religion, agriculture, commerce, and of how history is made.

This is as it must be. Adults cannot give children a fully developed, packaged, complete understanding of all this; children have to build this understanding over time. And so we need to invite children to try on ideas, to imagine possibilities, to make their own— sometimes wrong—connections and theories.

"Paul Someone rode his horse to tell people that the British were coming," a little boy said to his teacher. She nodded, "That's right. Paul Revere did ride out to Lexington and Concord saying, "The British are coming!" Then she paused for an instant, as if she was turning the story over in her head, pondering it. "What do you think about that story?" Soon the teacher and the first grader were deeply engaged in a talk about how people get to be famous. "Why?" they wondered, "is Paul Revere one of America's most famous people if all he did was ride on his horse, warning people?"

When that little boy said, "Paul *Someone* rode his horse . . ." I wonder if I would have seen what the child *almost* knew and responded, "That's right!" I hope so. I wonder if I would have accepted the child's approximation of the story as this wise teacher did, and invited him to think more about the story as she did. I hope so. But perhaps, instead, I would have worried whether the child had his facts straight. Perhaps I would have focused only on the missing surname—Revere—spelling it out to be sure my student mastered it this time.

As I said in the previous chapter, in science, children need to be given free access to the "stuff" of science. "I spent a lot of time exploring the materials," science educator Eleanor Duckworth explained, "and the issues that they came up with." In Chapter 10, I told about how, for Miles and Evan, an egg, still in its shell, outside on a winter's night, raised *issues*. Raisins, added to a liquid concoction, raise *issues*.

The challenge of social studies education comes in part because there are no raisins, no eggs on a winter night, for children to hold onto and weigh and measure and question and investigate. The "stuff" of social studies, the facts, theories, and stories from long ago or far away, is more abstract, more negotiable, and more difficult to hold onto. Yet it is still important for young learners to mess about, to see that events, that snippets of information they have about history, can raise issues. "Paul *Someone* rode his horse," the child says. As adults we tend to be so afraid that the facts and stories might not be exactly straight in our children's minds, that we don't help children think freely about whatever they sort of, halfway, know.

If we want our children to be powerful learners of history and geography, it's important to help them feel at home with half-straight facts, vaguely remembered stories, and approximated maps. I'm reminded of the first grader who wrote a beautiful picture book about dinosaurs. The book opened with the question, "Where are the dinosaurs?" On each of the following pages, the child wrote, "Are they in the library, hiding behind books?" "Are they invisible so we can't see them?" The book ended with this summation:

> No, they died a long time ago and this is the story. A long time ago, about a hundred years ago, the dinosaurs were all around. Soon a volcano exploded and the smoke didn't let dinosaurs breathe so they all died and that's the story.

We can look at that child's book in dismay, seeing it as all wrong ... or we can look at it in admiration, amazed that this youngster used what she knew to construct an explanation for one of the world's mysteries. We can certainly mention that dinosaurs died long before 1897, but meanwhile we'll understand that for this child, a hundred years ago may represent the far horizon of her imagination.

In a similar way, it's constructive to encourage kids to draw maps even if those maps will never make it into any atlas. Miles has always enjoyed making maps, all of which have been seriously flawed; his drawing of the United States at one stage contained just California,

Texas, Florida, and a *very* large New England. One of Miles's early world maps is shown in Figure 11.1.

Over time Miles's maps have become more accurate, in part because of his earlier efforts. These early drafts are instructive to him. Perhaps he dismisses the entire continent of Australia on one map, but as his world knowledge widens, eventually he will take careful note of Australia's size and shape. Once Miles has drawn a map with a huge New England, thereby articulating his theory of New England's size, that theory stands ready to be revised. He is all the more ready to take note of New England's actual size on a map, revising his earlier notion.

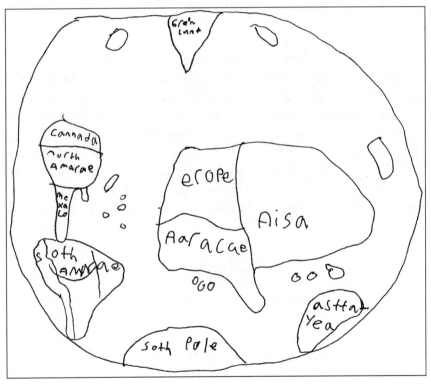

Figure 11.1

My hope, then, as a parent, is that I'll invite my sons to have theories about geography, history, and government, even if these theories aren't exactly correct or complete. If we can appreciate children's approximate timelines and welcome their peculiar maps of the world, if we can invite children to start building on their snatches of historic and geographic knowledge, they ultimately will become more powerful learners.

Teaching the Facts

But what does all this mean for the traditional ways of learning social studies? Is there still good reason for children to assemble wooden puzzles of the 50 states? Is it helpful to quiz them on the state capitals? How important are social studies terms: longitude and latitude, piedmonts, steppes, and mesas? And what about teaching kids to use encyclopedias in order to write research reports with footnotes and subheadings?

These are important questions, and well worth our attention. To begin to answer them, consider this: If we ask our child, "What is the capital of New York State?" it's far more important that the child understand what a capital is, how and why cities become capitals, and which buildings, positions, and functions exist in a capital, than it is to be able to answer "Albany." But is it also important that a child knows to answer "Albany?" I don't have simple answers to these questions. When my nephew Peter was six, he could fill in every state on a blank map of the United States, and he was well on his way to knowing every state capital as well. I wished Miles and Evan could do as well. I wished *I* could do as well. For Peter, puzzles are great fun; he likes to learn such details as state capitals and the times tables. But kids are different. And what's important to parents differs as well.

If it's essential to parents that their children know the state capitals, for instance, then it becomes important that the children know these facts. If we want our children to know the major rivers of the world, we should teach this to them. If we want them to know Asian history, we should teach it to them. When I said this to an audience of parents, a few became angry: "*We* should teach it?" they stormed. "What about the teachers? Where's our tax money going?"

"My son has such gaps [in knowledge]!" one said. "He doesn't know the name of the Atlantic Ocean!" I sympathized. I was recently stunned when I discovered that Miles, at the age of nine, didn't know the months of the year. "How could this be?" I ranted. None of us likes to face the inadequacies in our children, the gaps in their knowledge. But Miles isn't stupid. The fact that he doesn't know the months of the year doesn't—shouldn't—shake my confidence in him. And surely I can't hold his teachers responsible. I know that at my son's school, as at every school across the country, teachers begin most days with work on the calendar. But the fact that they teach the calendar in no way guarantees that my son or any other child will learn it. Yes, he has gaps. So do we all.

It's probably unrealistic to believe a school system should cover any particular social studies curriculum. As Lydia discusses in the appendices, social studies is a broad topic, including economics, government, anthropology, art history, geography, world history, American history, and more.

Traditionally, a certain group of topics has been covered in schools. We expect kids to know the names of the early explorers of America. After all, *we* learned about Columbus, Magellan, Lewis and Clark, and de la Salle. But the truth is, Magellan isn't necessarily more crucial than Humboldt or Cook, who we probably don't know much about. It's just that somewhere along the line Magellan got into the canon, into the body of "accepted school knowledge."

That canon is being questioned today. Many are suggesting—demanding—we fix the oversights, indeed slights, to people of color and women in history texts. Others suggest we think again about whether American history should be taught in such ethnocentric fashion, that there should be more world studies and less American studies. As the debate rages over these issues, perhaps each of us will need to find our own answers to these questions. If we want our children to know certain information, perhaps we should take it upon ourselves to teach them. Meanwhile, I recommend that all of us focus less on ensuring that our children have control over certain facts and focus more on teaching them to develop the skills and attitudes to be lifelong learners.

Reading Nonfiction Texts

When I was in fourth grade, I remember reading nonfiction books and encyclopedias for my Switzerland report. I conducted my research in the town library. I can still recall how scholarly I felt, turning the tissue-thin pages of the *Encyclopaedia Britannica*, copying down the facts onto my index cards. And oh, those index cards; how I loved the mounting weight of those cards, the physical evidence of my hard work. I wrote subject notes in red and author notes in green; and I recall how I loved to unzip my pencil case to choose one pen or the other. Always, I was scrupulously careful to change the big words into small words, because over and over, I had been told, "Copying is against the law." I imagined police officers coming to handcuff and carry off anyone who forgot to use their own words.

For me, nonfiction reading evoked an atmosphere of pencil cases, tracing paper, index cards, and the hush of a library. Nonfiction reading is very different for many children today. I heard two first-grade girls, huddled over a book about whales, read, "When baby whales are born, they are two feet long. Within two years, they are as big as their mothers." "Imagine that," one girl said to the other, "being as big as your mother when you are only two years old! What do they eat to get so big?"

The girls read on and eventually came to a page that said that whales eat tiny microscopic plankton. "Huh?" said the girls, totally baffled. Rereading the line, they said, "This makes no sense!" Rather than "turning big words into small ones," they were turning small facts into theories, hunches, and inquiries.

Similarly, I remember watching Miles, when he was six, pore over a junior atlas, his eyes darting all over the page. "It can't be," he muttered. "What?" I asked. "There's a chart here that shows half the world's people live in Asia! Could it be true?" A little later, Miles was again surprised. "Mum!" he called. "Canada is bigger than the United States of America! Can you believe it?"

Children who read research materials in this way fit new information in with what they already know; they change their minds as a result. They use books to launch conversations, to move from one section of a text to another, and from one text to another. They question what they read, all the while making and negotiating meaning.

Even before children can read, they can be minds-on readers. I witnessed three kindergartners who were participating in a week-long "reading center" during which they pored over books about turtles. The five-year-olds gleefully noticed that two of the books had pictures of turtles' butts. In both, a female turtle was laying eggs in a hole in the sand. "How come this turtle has 3 big eggs and that one has 10 little ones?" they asked. Turning to their other turtle books, they fanned through the pages looking for another picture of "a turtle's butt." Although they were only five, these children were already integrating information from a variety of sources, noticing discrepancies, and clarifying information.

How do we help our children to become active, thoughtful readers of nonfiction? What happens, for example, when a fourth grader in a social studies class is asked to read a selection such as this from a social studies textbook?

> In this chapter and the next, we shall see what the civilized culture of Sumer was like. We shall see why people liked civilized society and why other peoples copied Sumer. Once humans had invented civilization, they never lost it. However, no civilized society so far has lasted for more than about 2,500 years. Most have lasted for a shorter time.

Probably this text on the ancient civilization of Sumer would not be a good place to begin. Generally, it's easier for children to be assertive, critical, constructive students when they already know something about a topic firsthand. For this reason, during the early grades, children usually study topics they are familiar with. They may study families, neighborhoods, or their town, for example. In my sons' school, however, second graders study the Inuits and ancient Egypt, and I am skeptical over the rationale for focusing on topics so utterly remote from my sons' experiences.

The sample text on ancient Sumer poses other problems. For one, the text isn't logical; the third sentence, for example, seems to contradict the sentences that follow it.

Once humans had invented civilization, they never lost it. However, no civilized society so far has lasted for more than 2,500 years. Most have lasted a shorter time.

The focus of the article then jumps to a definition of an archeologist. The focus jumps again; and once more, the text seems to be contradictory:

Many scholars believe that Sumer was the earliest civilization. No one knows for sure who the Sumerians were or where they came from.

The article continues to discuss the ancient civilization of Sumer, with no further mention for more than a page of the archeologists introduced in the chapter's opening.

Children don't tend to read such writing comprehensibly, because they don't have a lot of images, experience, stories, and theories to bring to bear on such topics. Another problem is that this text is poorly written, which is unfortunately true of many textbooks and a fair number of nonfiction books as well.

All of this brings me back to the point that we, as parents, are wise to encourage our children to read nonfiction texts about topics that have meaning in their lives. Because my parents live on a farm, when my sons read the computer *Sim Farm* manual about the "animal containment policies" that govern some farms, they have their own images to draw on as they read. Crowding chickens so that they can't turn around means something to my sons because they've opened the door to my mother's chicken house, and stood amidst the sea of clucking birds.

As a matter of practice, I pass along to my sons the newsletters I get from their school about upcoming celebrations and new policies. And when I came upon an article in our local newspaper about the controversy over whether to sell the town's last farm, I showed that to Miles and Evan, too. When John and I are sorting through brochures while planning a vacation, we assume the boys will want to read these as well, so they can cast their votes for favorite places. Obviously, none of this is part of an official study program, but reading such materials in the normal course of their lives leads my sons to be more expectant, active readers when they do encounter texts on ancient civilizations or baby whales.

It is, of course, tremendously helpful to embellish school courses by providing related experiences at home. When Miles was reading about the Revolutionary War in school, we watched the video *Johnny Tremain* at home. How many more images he then had to bring to the texts he was reading! Of course, a visit to the Old North Church in Boston or to Fort Ticonderoga would have helped my son's study of the Revolutionary War even more. Even discussions about current wars around the globe would have helped.

But just the simple act of leafing through and talking about a book can help. When our children read about a subject such as the Revolutionary War, we can skim through the text, pointing out important subheadings, mulling over the drawings, and reading the captions, before they settle into reading the text.

We can also help our children read nonfiction well by suggesting they pause often, to "talk back to" the text. I often read aloud to my sons the nonfiction books that support their school studies. This helps them really think about the text. Often I tell my boys ahead of time that I'll pause every few paragraphs and that in those pauses, we'll each need to say something. Sometimes I go so far as to suggest that we each say something that begins, "The thing that surprises me here is . . ." This may seem gimmicky, but it's effective. When we read or listen with this attitude, we are more open to what someone else has to say. Alternately, I invite my kids to say something that begins, "The big idea I'm getting here is . . ." or "What I really wonder is . . ."

Getting only the facts isn't, or shouldn't be, the goal of nonfiction reading. As my colleague Randy Bomer often says, "A good nonfiction reader isn't just a Xerox machine." The effective nonfiction reader is always cumulating and synthesizing information learned from various sources. The good nonfiction reader relates what's on the page to what he has observed, assumed, or believed.

Recently I asked a group of teachers to read a *US News and World Report* article about teachers' unions and to notice what they did as readers. One said, "I read two or three sentences, and then thought,

'Who wrote this?' and checked the author's name and bio. I didn't know the author, but as I kept reading, I was thinking, 'Where does this guy stand on these issues? What camp is he from?' " Another teacher agreed. "I kept weighing whether or not I agreed with his arguments."

In a similar fashion, young children too can learn to read with a critical eye, asking, "Who is this author? Do I agree?" Children will develop this sort of authority most easily if they bring their own knowledge to their reading. When my sons read about caring for cats, because we have three cats, Miles and Evan immediately assimilate new information with their preexisting mental files. They assume they have a more or less equal relationship with the author. The author knows about cats, but so do Miles and Evan. When a book admonished: "Be sure to brush your cat's teeth every day," Evan laughed aloud, instantly critiquing the author's information.

One class of first graders were full of questions when two of them discovered, in the midst of a study on the Olympic Games, that they could only find articles about gold medalists from the United States. "Why do you have to be from the United States to have a story written about you?" they wanted to know. They were beginning to understand what it means when an article has a "slant," an "angle." This is what inquiry is all about.

There is another way to read nonfiction. It is possible to become totally caught up in the drama of real life, just as it is with fiction. As we read about other places, other times, we vicariously live those other lives. As Samuel Eliot Morison once said, "History is one-tenth fact and nine-tenths imagination."

One of the greatest historians for children is the author Jean Fritz who has written historical novels and picture books. She describes her love of history this way: "I like to step back to the time of Columbus and try to experience a world in which the known geography was perched on the edge of vast regions marked on maps, 'Here Be Dragons.' What would it be like to believe there were dragons thrashing about on your horizons?"

And so we will want to encourage our children to read history as a story, to weep and cheer for other people in other times and places.

We'll want them not only to read but to play, dream, and think history, and to do so with empathy, imagination, and zest.

Helping Children to Care about Social Studies

We can also help our children to care about social studies by demonstrating how their interests connect with geography and history. For example, my nephew Peter loves sports; he collects baseball cards, and creates imaginary teams in his mind. He also follows the Olympics avidly. Because teams are based in cities across the United States and the world, it's not difficult to nudge Peter to locate his favorite teams on U.S. and world maps. From that can flow conversations about why Scandinavia has so many cross-country ski champions, why Nigeria has so many world-class runners, or why Russia is the home to so many champion figure skaters.

My niece Brady has an American Girl doll, and this has led her to read all of the American Girl doll books. What a natural extension it would be to take Brady to visit historical sites related to those dolls and their historical eras! Or to read historical fiction from those same eras!

For other children, an interest in social studies can grow out of a passion for horses, skiing, goldfish, or music. Each can be the thread that connects children to an engagement with geography, history, and the like.

Children's play, too, can be an avenue to social studies. At the famous Bank Street College of Education, blocks are central to a great deal of the social studies work in primary classrooms. A child may begin by building a block boat and constructing the story behind that boat. The child will soon have named the river along which the boat travels; created and named the harbor and the pier; considered how goods and people are transferred to the boat; imagined the trip the boat will take; and chronicled the sights it will pass by.

Computers, too, can give children access to social studies. I'm not an authority on computers, but I know enough to be dazzled by what my sons learn when working with programs that simulate farms, communities, and towers. Because of the time they've spent creating and managing their virtual environments, my boys think about such things as the relationship between taxes and an operating budget. They are aware that towns sell bonds to finance new projects. They think about the merits of different locations for airports, rivers, schools, and industry. They are aware of trade-offs between civilization and ecology.

When I read parts of the newspaper to Miles and Evan, they listen differently because of their work with the computer; they converse differently with adults and other children because of the computer. And this education happens in 20 minutes a night (in lieu of television) and is regarded by them as play!

Of course, we can give our children a computer program about Ancient Rome and find that they either avoid the program altogether or use it as yet another "I-shot-you!" game. We can take our children to museums and find that the display they like best involves the wild pigeons *outside* the museum.

John and I recently took our sons on what we hoped would be an educational field trip to Washington, D.C. While Miles gloried in the chance to imagine himself as a senator, making laws that would rule the land, Evan, on the other hand, was most interested in the hot tub at the hotel and the guards and pigeons outside the important buildings.

What are we to do when our child does not show an interest in history, government, and the like? The truth is, Evan's response to the trip to Washington, D.C., was entirely in character. Whereas Miles hit the jackpot with the continent question, Evan wasn't clear whether Connecticut qualified as a continent! It's convenient to chalk this difference up to their different ages, but I know that Evan probably never made Berlin Walls when he was in nursery school, nor does he often imagine himself as a friend of Thomas Jefferson. Last weekend, during a long family trip, we paused the car at a bridge's tollbooth to pay a toll. "Why'd we do that?" Evan asked, as if he'd just seen his first tollbooth ever. "Why'd we give him money?"

John and I looked at each other, intrigued. Evan is seven, and only just now taking in the fact that we pay road tolls! John answered Evan's questions, explaining a little about the way roads and bridges are financed. Then I said, "Evan, I really love the way you noticed about those tolls and asked about them! It's great the way you pay attention to things in the world."

As we drove on, John and I talked quietly, wondering if we'd unwittingly created the differences in our sons. How often have we read snippets of the newspaper aloud *to Miles*, implicitly buying into the notion that our eldest is the one who is interested in government and current affairs? Do we tend to give exotic coins only to Miles? Do we tend to direct only Miles's attention to the line of flags outside the concert hall? What powerful messages we are no doubt sending to both our children! Is it any wonder that Evan creates his identity in opposition to his brother's?

John and I are now rallying ourselves to the idea of nurturing Evan's interest in history, government, and the like. My first step in this new regime was my response to Evan's tollbooth observation. "I love the way you notice ... and pay attention to things in the world," I said, speaking on faith that these qualities will emerge more in Evan if I support even just the most sputtering sparks of interest.

Now, in retrospect, I know that it wasn't enough to take Miles and Evan to Washington, D.C., and to just sit back and wait for them to take an interest in what I considered important. If I wanted Evan to be intrigued by the Capitol buildings and monuments, I should have helped this to happen.

In contrast, my friend Randy Bomer is planning to take his children to Washington, D.C., later this summer. Far in advance, Randy began to think, "What should we read together; what should we do or talk about together today to make it more likely that the trip is more meaningful to my children?"

Randy wants to ensure that not only his eldest child Jake, but also his five-year-old daughter Samantha, finds the trip interesting. On other trips, of course, it's Jake whose interests need to be stimulated. Randy found he had to work hard, for example, to lure his nine-year-old son to spend a recent Sunday afternoon at the Metropolitan Museum of Art in New York. His daughter was all for the idea, but Jake was adamantly opposed. "All they got is pictures of God," Jake complained. And so Randy told Jake about the rooms full of armor;

and when they set off to spend an afternoon at the Met, they started with the knights.

What caught Jake and Samantha's eyes first were the jewels in the hilts of swords. Randy said, "I know beforehand that this is how these trips will go. We'll survey the rooms of the museum until something draws us in." As Randy's family toured the armor room, they recalled other gems and precious stones they had seen at the National Museum of History. They compared jewels from the various swords and wondered why some knights had better jewels than others.

Later, while visiting a room full of paintings, they paused in front of a Rembrandt painting in which the man had a chain across his chest, studded with precious stones. From a distance, the stones seemed to gleam. Jake and Samantha found, however, that by standing very close to the painting, the effect of the gleaming jewels was actually created by a cluster of single white dots of paint.

Later, in the gift shop, Randy and his wife Katherine announced to the children that they each could buy one postcard, but it had to be a postcard of something they'd seen together. Later at home, Samantha noticed that her dad's postcard was of the Rembrandt that had occupied so much of their attention that afternoon. "You got that one," she noted, and they talked for awhile about the artist, his craft, and especially his jewels.

As parents, many of us have taken a child to a museum or a city, and heard ourselves complain afterward that our child wasn't interested. How often have I complained, "They just raced through the museum, giving a quick scan over things!" How often have I bemoaned the fact that my children don't linger over each (or any!) item in a museum, studying it with care. I've even complained in front of my kids about their lack of interest in museums and monuments. Now I kick myself for this. The irony is that I take my kids to these places to strengthen their connection to other times and other cultures. Yet instead, I end up letting these trips become proof that at least my youngest *isn't* a member of the club of historians! If I convince Evan that the trip to the monuments and museums is social studies, and if I convince him that his experience of that trip proves he's not "good at social studies" my elaborately planned trip does a lot more harm than good.

What I am learning is that I shouldn't wait for my sons to become interested in history, or government, or geography. I can actively cultivate an attitude of engagement. Evan will be more interested if he knows more. By reading and talking and storytelling with him, I can stimulate a readiness to be interested.

Social Awareness As Social Studies

How do we nurture an appreciation for other people, other worlds, other customs? How do we encourage our children to be advocates for justice? How do we mentor them to become responsible participants in the systems to which they belong, and responsible critics of these systems? By teaching respect for the differences in people.

Let's assume a child says, "Look at that guy. His skin is so dark." Parents might be tempted to respond by hushing the child: "Shhh, that's rude." But what is the message of such a warning? Surely we don't want children to think it's rude to notice that someone's skin is black. Instead we should support our child's awareness. "Yes," we can respond. "He's African American. His skin is beautiful, isn't it? And look at his hair; it's different too."

There was a time when I probably would have tried to educate my children to be "color-blind." I can hear myself say, "The color of a person's skin doesn't matter. It's what's inside that counts." But it's dishonest and disrespectful to say, "The color of someone's skin doesn't matter," because our racial identities do matter. Being African American or Latino or European or Korean matters; it is a huge part of who we are. Thus, I want my children not to be afraid to talk about or to notice or to wonder about other races. I want my children to notice differences in language, too. If we pass people who are speaking Spanish, and my child says, "They're talking funny. What are they saying?" I wouldn't want to hush my child but rather to say, "Yes, they are speaking Spanish, I think. People from different countries speak different languages."

Children are often experts on people. They know all about their classmates' lives; your son may know that a friend's father left Laos in the dead of night, and swam far into the ocean to a waiting boat. Your daughter may have a classmate who is Jewish, and knows he celebrates Passover, that he has different beliefs about Jesus. Evan loves his friend Summer's dark brown skin, and likes to line up everyone's arms in his class to admire the different shades of color. He thought Summer was very lucky when she was chosen to sing Martin Luther King, Jr.'s song to the whole school. He wonders if we, in our family, have songs that belong to us. In all these little interactions, we can teach our children ways of living in the world.

Miles has soccer practice Wednesday nights behind the local high school. I teach at the university that night, so John takes both boys. The next morning, I get a report. This morning Evan gave me his report. "I like it because I play with Jimmy; he's Teddy's four-year-old brother. We sort of have a play date every Wednesday. This time we went down below the school to a basketball court. We were playing (Evan reenacts the scenario, bouncing an imaginary ball) and I noticed a big kid playing beside us (he reenacts the backward and upward glance). So I thought, 'Why not?' (he reenacts how he stopped bouncing his own basketball and really looked at the 'big kid' playing beside him). So I scooted in, got away *his* ball, and threw it up for a basket. And he played with us. All night he did."

Evan then went on to tell me how he'd asked the "big kid" his age, which was twenty-four, and what he did for work. "We played chicken-in-the-middle," Evan told me, "and we made up teams but it was two on one and he had to play with one hand . . . we lost but he gave us some pointers. But we gave him one pointer, too. Know what it was?"

I couldn't imagine what pointers my seven-year-old non-basketball-playing son and his four-year-old compatriot had taught to this strapping young man. Evan explained. "He started smoking a cigar" (Evan sometimes uses slightly wrong words; I suspect he meant a cigarette), "and we told him he might die and he shouldn't smoke. He put it out. He stepped on it and crushed it."

Perhaps it seems strange that I include this scenario in a chapter on social studies. But I think that these fleeting vignettes are critical to social studies education. I'm pleased that Evan plays so willingly with a child who is several years younger than he is. He even regards their time together as a play date. This is, of course, an everyday thing for many of our young children. But as parents, we should smile to ourselves when children of different ages play together. There are forces in the world which divide us, as people. Especially as children get older, they often end up playing only with kids of their own age, or their own gender. We need to notice and support times when our children work and play with people who are different from themselves.

But I'm even more pleased that Evan had the chutzpah, the gumption, and the trust in other people necessary to playfully, with a twinkle in his eye, "steal" the big kid's basketball away from him. And to then go on to ask about his work . . . to play collaboratively . . . to suggest he stop smoking!

Evan may not know his state capitals, but he is very interested in issues of social justice and equity. He notices when fathers in books are drawn as gruff, cold people; and he will tell anyone who will listen why that's wrong. When a classmate was given five minutes of time-out during recess and he regarded this punishment as unfair, he spoke up in her defense. When that didn't work Evan decided he would take the punishment with her. "No teacher knew why," he told me, "but Summer said that if I got a wrong punishment some-day, she would do the same thing for me." This, too, is social studies.

If only we could all have this awareness, confidence, and interest in people who are different from us. If only we could all be as ready as our children are to work, play, and learn together. This social consciousness, this respect for and engagement with other people and other lives, coupled with a willingness to live according to one's principles are the true foundation of social studies education.

CHAPTER 12

A Lesson Without Words

It is time for my portion of this book to end. As I pass the baton on to Lydia Bellino, I feel some of the same bittersweet feelings I felt that September morning, years ago, when I stood at the end of the driveway with my firstborn son, waiting for the familiar glimpse of yellow through the trees as the school bus rounded the bend of our lane. I will always remember Miles, with his school bag as big as he was, climbing the tall stairs to that bus, then waving to me from the window. Sending our children to school is a giant thing.

I've worked to build a strong partnership with my children's school. There have been bumps along the way, and often to get over these bumps, I've turned to Lydia for counsel. Her inside perspective on schools, principals, teachers, boards of education, and state legislation, along with her forthright, sensible approach have given me a compass to steer by while trying to navigate my children's experience at school and my role in that experience. Because I want my readers to benefit from Lydia's perspective, too, I have asked her to write the appendices that comprise the remainder of this book.

As I look back over this book, fingering the pages, revisiting the anecdotes, rereading the chapters on talking, reading, writing, playing, and the rest, I realize there is one subject I haven't addressed, and it may be the most important subject of all. I learned about this subject, as I learned about so many things, from living side by side with my parents.

When I was twelve, my mother, who is a physician, took me on her rounds at Gowanda State Mental Hospital. We stood for a few minutes at the bedside of a young woman who had been in a coma

234

for a decade. Bending down to the woman, my mother asked, "Do you want some soda?"

The woman stared blankly at us.

"Orange or Coke, which?" my mother asked.

The woman stared blankly.

"Coke?" my mother said as if the woman had nodded. My mother responded, "Okay, Coke it is." Then turning to me, she said, "Would you get Denise a Coke?"

Two hours later, on the drive home, my mother asked me, "Did Denise drink her Coke?"

"Oh," I said, "the machine was empty."

There was a long pause. My mother looked at me sharply. "So what did you do?" she asked.

"What could I do?" I said. "The machine was all out."

"Lucy, she's still waiting for that Coke," my mother said.

In my mind, I protested silently. "She's *in a coma*," I wanted to say. "She doesn't know anything." But I knew enough to keep silent.

My mother pulled the car to the side of the road. She glanced behind her, then made a U-turn, and we began retracing the 45-minute drive to the hospital. We stopped halfway at a grocery store, and my mother emerged with a bottle of Coke. I don't recall that my mother made any long speeches that day or any day but I will never forget what she taught me.

INTRODUCTION TO APPENDICES

In the opening chapter of Beverly Cleary's well-loved book, *Ramona Quimby, Age 8*, Ramona sits at breakfast thinking about the first day of school. Cleary writes, "She did not want anything to spoil this exciting day. . . . Her stomach felt quivery with excitement at the day ahead, a day that would begin with a bus ride just the right length to make her feel a long way from home but not long enough—she hoped—to make her feel carsick."

Parents, too, have quivery stomachs on that first day of school, and this is true whether your child is just starting nursery school, heading off to fourth grade, or is driving away to college. Throughout my years of work as a teacher, a reading specialist, and school principal, parents have often told me that they wish someone would invent a magic cupboard in which they could shrink into toy-sized people so that they could sit on their child's shoulder throughout the school day, steering the course. We laugh at the image, but we don't laugh at the very real knowledge that we have to do everything possible to help our children once they've left the home and headed off into the world of school.

What parents do not realize is that they are a very real presence in any school. Their attitudes, values, habits of learning are ever-present in a school classroom. When parents have a home curriculum that supports tenacity, hard work, independence, initiative, enthusiastic learning, a love of reading and writing, and all the other things Lucy has described, this makes a significant difference in a classroom.

Nevertheless, it would be helpful if every parent could shrink into a two-inch version and ride along to school in their child's pocket.

Then, perhaps, parents would be able to discern what their child's teacher values. As it is, most parents take only brief peeks into classrooms and hear snatches of information about curriculum. It's hard for parents to know what to make of what they see and hear. Thus, many resort to simply counting computers in their child's classroom, as if somehow this one fact will reveal the nature of that classroom, that school. No parent truly believes that the number of available computers is so important, but a machine is visible, easy to count, and clearly a bonus.

In these appendices, I want to help parents to see the more subtle elements in their child's classroom. Journalists have a rule of thumb: the more a person knows, the more that person can learn. I want to help parents know more so they can be more discerning students of their child's school experience. I want to help parents understand why most classrooms do not look like the classrooms of their childhood; to understand what teachers have in mind when they arrange desks in clusters and provide large carpeted areas and classroom libraries. I want parents to understand what rigor can look like in classrooms, to see past the arrangement of the room and begin to understand the choices their child's teachers and school system have made, the course they are on. Some parents want phonics but don't understand the difference between phonics and phonemic awareness. Many parents want their children to have access to computers but don't understand that in some classrooms computers are used simply for games.

When we travel to foreign countries, we carry guidebooks to help us negotiate terrain that is strange but wonderful. I intend for these appendices to function in a similar way.

APPENDIX A

How to Pick a Preschool or Kindergarten

In the long history of decisions that parents make on behalf of their children's learning life, choosing a preschool or kindergarten is probably one of the first. More than half of today's young children attend some type of preschool. Alarmingly, the character and quality of these early childhood programs is very inconsistent. Early childhood experts are particularly concerned over programs that push very young children into academic, subject-specific instruction that relies on workbooks and worksheets, activities that take precious time away from the hands-on active learning through play so crucial for young children. When children feel unsuccessful at completing their workbook pages, they may regard themselves as failures even before they begin kindergarten. Another problem is that children who attend these academic nursery school programs sometimes lag behind in social development, compared to children who are more accustomed to having choices, working in groups, and engaging in many play situations. It's important for parents to know that kindergarten teachers consistently agree that the programs that best prepare children for kindergarten are those that support child-centered learning.

Preschools

Child-Centered Preschools

Classrooms that follow the child-centered approach are apt to be organized into what are often called centers, areas, and opportunities for active, involved learning. A center may be a table, a corner of floor space, or a cluster of easels. Centers may have building blocks, art supplies, plants, animals, musical instruments, or sand and water tables. Teachers set up these environments partially in response to what they notice their students working on. During the school day, teachers move among children, encouraging them to initiate and pursue their own ideas in these centers; that is, children will not merely follow the teacher's preplanned activities, nor will any one center always involve the same work.

While the children are in centers or small groups, the teacher listens to them interact, and talks with them in order to understand and extend their ideas. Ideally, teachers take notes as they observe, using these notes to plan the curriculum for the class and to evaluate individuals. In child-centered preschools, teachers do not create or direct lessons without the input from the children. This means, for example, that the curriculum will never be the same, year to year, nor will the morning group's schedules match those of the children in the afternoon session.

The children in child-centered nursery schools tend to play and work in small groups or in pairs. They are apt to talk a great deal with each other and to move freely and purposefully about the space. The rooms hum with energy.

Montessori schools fit broadly within child-centered school approaches, but they are unique because they place a particularly strong emphasis on children's development unfolding through play. Although Montessori schools originally had specially designed furniture and materials, many today vary in how closely they follow Maria Montessori's original educational ideas.

Cognitive Preschools

In other, more academic or cognitive programs, the values are very different. Conceivably, the same variety of materials may be available in nooks and corners of the classroom, and teachers may even refer to these areas as centers. But a discerning observer will quickly see that the roles played by the teacher and the children in these classrooms are different from the roles played in the child-centered classrooms. In nursery schools that I will call cognitive, the teacher is more likely to preplan all the activities. Consequently, the talk at the sand table or the block area is more apt to be teacher-directed. A closer look may also reveal that in these classrooms all the children often engage in the same activities at the same time. For example, all the children might work on an arts and craft project, starting it and finishing it at the same time. A classroom assistant might even prepare all the parts of the craft project without the children's participation. Each child, then, merely assembles his or her project with help from the teacher or the assistant. A greater emphasis is likely to be placed on the finished product. In these classrooms, it's not unusual for the bulletin boards to display 24 matching snowmen—and miracle of miracles, the snowmen all *look* like snowmen! This may make a lovely display, but as a parent, such a display makes me wonder whether my child had the chance to conceive of and carry out his or her own art project.

Likewise, in classrooms that follow a cognitive approach, children may be instructed to write on lined paper and to use fat pencils. They may also fill out preschool worksheets intended as preparation for kindergarten reading and math. Teachers in cognitive nursery schools are apt to talk a lot about helping children "become ready" for school.

Combination (or Middle-of-the-Road) Approach

Nursery schools that claim to integrate "the best of both approaches" do so in a variety of ways. Some may divide the day into periods of time for academic work and for "free play." Although teachers in these environments often claim they value both play and academic reading-readiness exercises, a discerning visitor can see that the teacher's role during playtime is merely that of a supervisor, watching to be sure no one gets hurt. If the teacher doesn't "dig in" or get involved with children's play, then it's a stretch to call such a classroom "child-centered."

The first question I'd want answered by such a school is whether teachers truly incorporate the best of the child-centered approach. Do they take their cues from children, letting even the academic work evolve out of children's interests? If children are writing, are they writing signs for their block area and labels beneath their drawings? This, in my eyes, would represent the best of both approaches. If, on the other hand, the school conducts letter-of-the-week drills, I'd have a hard time believing this incorporates the best of two approaches.

The best way to determine the philosophy of a nursery school is to visit that school. The school's philosophy may be full of words such as "child-centered," but a quick visit to the room might reveal that every initiative in the classroom is authored solely by the teacher.

Visits enable us to identify where a school stands in terms of its awareness of the importance of talk, play, exploration, active involvement, collaboration, and the like. More than this, during these visits, parents can try to see the school through the eyes of their children. When we actually witness the nitty-gritty details of a school day, we can anticipate the problems our child may have. Sometimes, parents are surprised simply by the length of the day, or by how often activities change during the day, or by how long children are expected to stay engaged in an activity. Parents of very quiet children might watch how a teacher encourages such individuals to become more involved in class. Watching a classroom function, we can imagine our own child within that room.

What to Expect in Kindergarten

Kindergarten is changing. Once regarded as an optional introduction to school, filled with playtime and chances to interact with other playmates, today kindergarten is more often regarded as the start of school. Many kindergartens even have eligibility requirements and "readiness programs" with academic demands. Some teachers expect incoming kindergarten children to be able to sit for long periods of time concentrating on workbooks or worksheets. Some children take tests prior to beginning the school year, which are designed to measure the children's abilities. Based on these tests, certain children are placed in specific kindergarten programs.

I do not agree with this frenetic trend to hurry children toward paper-and-pencil drills and skills. But I think teachers are wise to recognize that important learning about literacy and math can take place during kindergarten. There are myriad wonderful, child-centered ways to help our children grow as readers, writers, and mathematicians, even when they are just five years old.

In this appendix, I discuss several issues that concern many parents of children in kindergarten. These include age eligibility, the length and structure of the kindergarten day, testing, and the different philosophies of kindergarten programs.

Length of a Kindergarten Day

It's surprising to many parents that full-day kindergarten is still not the norm. With such a high percentage of children attending preschool and with so many families in which both parents work, many parents assume that most school districts have all-day kindergarten programs. In fact, only a little more than half of the kindergarten programs in the country are full day.

Half-Day Programs

The most common kindergarten program is half day, and these range from two to three hours, with one class coming in the morning and another in the afternoon. The morning kindergartners arrive at school with the rest of the older students and leave school by noon. The afternoon session begins around noon and lasts until the end of the school day, and these children are dismissed with the older students. Some school systems allow parents to choose which session they would like their child to attend, but most decide for the

244 RAISING LIFELONG LEARNERS

parents. In some schools, there is a "turnaround" policy, whereby, midyear, the morning children switch to the afternoon session, and vice versa.

Both the advantages and disadvantages of the half-day kindergarten seem to circle around the issues of time and expense. Supporters claim that the shorter day allows children to adjust more successfully to school life and to make the transition to the full-day schedule later. Furthermore, a shorter school day may make all the difference for a child who is experiencing anxiety over separating from his parents. A half-day kindergarten gives young children a chance to socialize with new friends and to have a few hours of instruction, while allowing time to participate in library programs, playdates, and unstructured play at home. In addition, those children who need special services from a speech and language teacher or a resource room teacher can sometimes have their time with the specialist scheduled before or after the half-day kindergarten program. This prevents the usual "pullout" necessary when there is a full day of school. The half-day program is also a lot less costly to a district than a full-day program. In half-day kindergarten programs, school districts need only half the number of kindergarten teachers and kindergarten classrooms.

On the other hand, the half-day kindergarten often presents a child-care problem to parents who work outside the home. And these kindergarten programs may seem like a regression from full-day preschool programs. Parents worry that the shorter day means the curriculum will be unambitious and that no rigorous instruction will occur. This may or may not be the case. Some three-hour kindergarten programs can offer a lot of rigorous teaching and learning. Kindergarten teachers may make the decision not to have show-and-tell, snacktime, outdoor play, and so on when they have only half a day with children. These teachers choose instead to spend most of their time reading to and with children, writing with children, exploring math, and delving into science and social studies.

A final concern that both parents and educators have about half-day programs is that each kindergarten teacher is required to work with two classes of children, allowing less time for a teacher to plan for individual children; in some cases, the morning and afternoon instruction may be exactly the same. Obviously, when this happens, it suggests that the teacher is not planning in response to the children's interests. Consequently, parents worry that there is a rushed quality to the program, and many kindergarten teachers bear this out, reporting that there is a lot more they would like to do if only they had more time with the children.

Full-Day Programs

As you might expect, supporters of the full-day kindergarten claim that the increased time with children gives teachers more time to assess the needs of the children; to individualize instruction; and to teach reading, writing, music, play, science, social studies, and math. Some say that the longer day actually reduces pressure on children because teachers do not need to rush through instruction as they do when the children are in school only for a few hours. Many parents are pleased because they feel their child is properly prepared for the full day of school, both academically and socially. Children in full-day kindergarten programs are likely to have the opportunity to receive instruction in special areas like music, art, physical education, and even computer classes on a more frequent basis than children in half-day programs.

But full-day kindergarten programs have their weaknesses, too. Many children have difficulty adjusting to a full day away from home. Some have long bus rides to and from school, and are exhausted by the end of the day. For others, issues of separation from parents make the longer day seem even more stressful.

Whether in a full- or half-day program, kindergartners often find the jump from nursery school to kindergarten to be a big one. Even a larger school building can be imposing for children, who find it frightening to move from their classroom to the lunchroom and to the special-area classes. Children manage these transitions with various degrees of capability. Sometimes schools will schedule all the special-area classes for kindergartners in the afternoon, freeing the morning of interruptions.

Extended-Day Programs

There are also two different versions of an extended-day schedule. When my daughter Marissa was approaching kindergarten age, I was asked to serve as a parent on a district committee appointed by the board of education to examine the different ways the schedule of the school day could be structured for kindergarten. Until then, I, like many parents, thought there were two choices: half day or full day. It was interesting to discover that there were also two versions of the "extended day."

In one extended-day model, the teacher has a kindergarten class that meets five mornings a week. Then, on Monday and Wednesday, one half of the class stays for the entire afternoon. On Tuesdays and Thursdays the other half stays. On the fifth day, either the whole class has a full day of kindergarten together or the entire class has a half day. In the latter situation, teachers use the afternoon to meet with each other or with specialists who work with the children in their classes. This extended-day model is clearly a more costly option in terms of cost and space than the model in which each teacher works with two half-day classes of children. A district must have many more teachers and classrooms available if this model of extended-day kindergarten is implemented.

The most important advantage of this extended-day structure is that the teacher has only one class of children, and the school isn't assuming that all kindergarten children are ready for a full week of 9:00 to 3:00 school days. Also, every child can go to school in the morning, which is generally regarded as the best time for teaching and learning. This schedule also allots time every afternoon for the teacher to work with children in small group settings. If a group has been identified as "at risk," these children can get extra help without being taken out of their regular kindergarten classes. These children, for example, might stay for a full day on all four days, spending two of them with a specialist such as speech-language teachers or early-intervention teachers. The small groups also allow teachers to partner children in ways that work best socially. Supporters say this type of extended day is the best of both worlds. The day is not as abbreviated as a half-day program, but it's also not as intense as the full-day program. Children spend some full days at school with lunch and special classes such as music or physical education, and other half days at school to allow children time with their families or daycare providers.

The second structure for extended day—the one used in my own school—is a more economical arrangement for a school system. This structure requires that each kindergarten teacher has two classes, a morning and an afternoon class. But the children stay for four hours. The morning and the afternoon classes overlap midday for about an hour and a half. During this time, both groups of children are in the school. Each day, during the overlap time, children have an extended period of instruction in a special-area class, either music, art, library, or physical education. The overlap also allows the children to eat lunch in school and play together. Most parents and educators who support this type of program like the idea that the day isn't quite as short, and are glad that children are not pressured to stay in school for full days until first grade.

The Age Debate

Each board of education establishes policies concerning the structure of the kindergarten day, and in almost every school district, the board also decides on a cutoff date to determine when children in the district are eligible to enter kindergarten.

In the United States, about 98 percent of children attend kindergarten prior to entering first grade, but the exact date by which a child must have turned five in order to be eligible for that year's enrollment varies from state to state. Recently, many states concerned about early failure or lack of readiness of children have tried to ensure greater success by directing that children must turn five by September of the school year, rather than by the usual December date.

Since a board of education usually doesn't make decisions without some community input, parents can assume that their school district's kindergarten cutoff date was determined with advice from a number of other groups. Districts may send out districtwide surveys to determine the preferences of the community on this subject.

Boards of education may hold a series of public meetings to encourage input; others may form advisory groups made up of parents, kindergarten teachers, administrators, and other interested community members.

The age debate tends to involve several issues: Some educators claim that when a school district requires children to turn five before they enter kindergarten, they simply create an older average group of children. They say that this does not necessarily mean the children will be any more capable; they will be older, but they won't have spent more time in school.

Other educators say that it's appropriate to set earlier cutoff dates to create older classes of kindergarten children, because kindergarten children pass readiness tests more frequently if they are chronologically more advanced. Of course, districts *could* deal with this problem by abandoning inappropriate readiness tests, but they probably would not do so because the problem is not the tests themselves but the curriculum. In the districts' efforts to be "rigorous," they may have created kindergarten curricula that aren't appropriate for all kindergarten children. If inappropriate whole-class instruction from commercial workbooks is a large part of a kindergarten curriculum, this will put some children at risk of "failing" kindergarten. The districts' solution, then, is to hold these children out an extra year, so they will be better prepared for worksheets when they arrive.

Allowing some children to enter school at a later date gives them more time to play. And when there is no room for play and exploration in a kindergarten, it makes sense for children to be older before they begin school. But there is another solution, one that involves making kindergartens more child centered. I'd prefer kindergartens to change to be ready for all children, rather than expect children to be mature enough for an inappropriate early childhood program.

Finally, there is also public concern that the decision to raise the starting age of kindergartners affects children who cannot afford private nursery schools more than those who can.

Each year, when I receive the new group of children in our kindergarten, I work with many members of the teaching staff and the parents to place each child in one of six kindergarten classes.

When this process is complete, many teachers will comment on the range of ages of the children in their classes. Parents are not alone in recognizing that some children are much younger and some are much older than others in the class. I think there is an overemphasis on age. Parents sometimes think that older children will have a greater chance to succeed in school, and certainly this is true if a child is more mature, independent, and eager to learn, but these qualities often are not associated with age.

As principal, each year a number of parents ask to meet with me to help them think through whether their child is ready to enter kindergarten earlier than scheduled. In some instances, the child has just missed the cutoff date by a few days. The parents may tell me that their child has been in preschool for several years and that she is more than ready to start kindergarten. The parents want to know if I can make an exception and allow their child to enter kindergarten.

I generally tell them no, and parents are often upset that I adhere to such a rigid policy; but the truth is, most school districts have an eligibility date because they do not want the decision to be left up to a parent. When a board of education sets an eligibility policy, it is trying to ensure that the age composition of the kindergarten classes is balanced. The school system knows that it is helpful to have some children who are older and more experienced in a class and some who are younger.

Parents who have the resources and are concerned because a child has missed the cutoff date in their district may opt to send their child to a private kindergarten accredited by the state. The following year, when the child has completed an accredited kindergarten program, he can be placed in first grade even though the child might be younger than all the other children in the grade.

When parents ask me whether their child will be challenged by our kindergarten curriculum, I find the question difficult to answer. Everyone has a different idea of what an academically challenging kindergarten program might be like. Parents sometimes assume that if a child knows the alphabet and numbers, she has mastered the kindergarten curriculum; further, they assume that a child who already knows the rudiments of reading and writing will be bored by spending a year in kindergarten. This is not necessarily the case. In many kindergarten classes, when children choose books to read, some can read books with long, complex sentences, while others "read" wordless books. Some children will pretend to read while others attend to the print. In writing, too, children work at a wide range of levels. Some use only initial consonants to write captions under their drawings while others write "books" filled with sentences, and spell with enough conventional phonics that their stories are readable.

The kindergarten curriculum will only be boring if it is set up around single-skill ditto sheets and regimented whole class instruction geared to one particular level of achievement. If, on the other hand, there is room for choice and for individuality, each child can work at his or her own level.

In any case, I am cautious about pushing a precocious child on to first grade. Even if the child knows a lot about written language, his life experiences aren't as broad as they will be a year later. And the child may not be emotionally or socially ready to be in first grade. Children who are pushed up a grade may feel pressured to excel and perform, and their eagerness to learn can be diminished in a few short years. Such a child may, despite all our efforts, become bored at school.

There are parents who deliberately hold their children out of school, even though they make the cutoff date, to purposely delay their entrance to kindergarten, choosing to have their children spend an additional year in a preschool program. Or they may send their children to a private kindergarten program and then a year later, enter them in kindergarten in the public school district.

Parents who make this decision do so based on their feelings and knowledge of their child's readiness or social and emotional maturity. They may have observed their child in preschool and determined that their child is less mature or less ready for kindergarten than the other children. The preschool teacher may have advised the parents on this decision, based on her observations of the child's interactions with the other children and how well the child has managed in the preschool program. Other parents choose to hold their child out a year simply because they believe that the additional year will give their child a jump-start on kindergarten.

Kindergarten Philosophies

The philosophy of any kindergarten program is reflected in the environment, the teaching, and the assessment beliefs and practices. Everything in the classroom reveals the teacher's approach: the charts and wall displays, for example, as well as the furniture and room arrangements. These elements are important to evaluate. Are the displays for the parents or are they truly for children? Does the teacher organize instruction around commercially packaged programs, or are there lots of books and "real-life" things like plants, fish, and building blocks in a classroom? Are the children assessed through standardized tests? Ask these questions and the answers will reveal the philosophy of a kindergarten. On the whole, the difference I described between child-centered and cognitive nursery schools also pertain to kindergartens.

Two philosophies are especially prevalent among kindergarten teachers. The first, the cognitive approach, looks at children in terms of what they don't know when they enter kindergarten and tries to fill the gaps. Screening and readiness tests are used to assess a child's deficiencies. Typically, remedial pullout programs might be used to fill in gaps in children's knowledge. This is sometimes called early intervention, a misnomer since children who have just arrived in kindergarten have not yet had a chance to learn with the rest of their peers. Thus, it is questionable whether it's wise for the school to pull certain children out of the classroom in order to remediate their skills. Some schools go so far as to divide kindergartners into different levels; the "highest" group of children receive different materials from the "lowest" group. In classrooms that follow this philosophy, all kindergartners may have workbooks, but children who demonstrate a knowledge of letters and sounds may be given simple books to read, while others are given worksheets focused on certain alphabet letters. Materials and teaching practices may consist of commercial letter-of-the-week programs, math worksheets with accompanying workbooks, and mastery assessments. These materials are used on a regularly scheduled basis. A full week might be spent playing games and working on craft projects and drills on a single alphabet letter. Proponents of this philosophy will often follow scripted lessons from a teacher's manual, and often separate playtime from learning; and learning is usually deskwork.

Another philosophical stance views children in terms of what they know—their strengths. These child-centered kindergartens emphasize collaboration. Children have choices in literary activities; they collaborate in pairs, in small groups, and with their teachers. They read their writing to one another, they share books of their own choosing, and their play is closely connected to all the literary classwork. Handwritten signs label the structures in buildings in the block area; housekeeping areas sport shopping lists and notes; and child-authored classroom rules are posted. The easels and bulletin boards around the room display the best of children's literature along with the writing efforts of the children in the class. Children have access to a range of reading materials including board books; concept books; label-list books with picture and word matches; rhyming and nonrhyming poems; stories with lots of repetition and familiar words; songs and chants; and plenty of nonfiction books representing the range of interests of children in the class. The teacher plans lessons based on observations and the notes he takes while observing the children, as well as on his knowledge of early literacy. Lessons are designed to extend what children already know about language and literacy. For example, when the children write, the teacher coaches them, while assessing each child's knowledge of letter-sound correspondence. Children often spend a great deal of time in centers filled with the same materials that one sees in nursery school classes, only these are more literacy and math related.

Kindergarten Tests

For decades, schools have tested or screened incoming kindergartners. This marks the beginning of the child's educational testing record, and it usually starts as soon as a child is officially registered to enter kindergarten. Parents have a legal right to know about these tests, and every parent should ask two questions when informed that the school will test a child: Why are you testing my child? What will the school do with the information and knowledge it gains from the test?

Kindergarten screening was never intended to reveal in-depth information about a child. Originally it was intended as a step in evaluating children for handicapping conditions. The goal was to ensure that a school would be ready to provide any special support or further evaluation a child might need. The point is, parents should be clear that the purpose of a kindergarten screening is not to determine "readiness" for kindergarten. Kindergarten screening should not be used as the indicator that a child should be held out for a year because she is not ready; nor should screening be used for grouping or labeling a child, or for placing her in a special program such as extra-year developmental kindergartens. The screenings are not comprehensive enough to be used in these ways.

Many kindergarten screening tests are published; and most cover the same general areas of development: cognitive, speech and language, and physiological. The cognitive part of a screening is designed to give teachers information about a child's ability to understand concepts and follow directions. It may also show how well the child pays attention or how comfortable a child is holding and using a pencil. Your child might be asked to point to pictures in response to questions like, "Can you point to the dog in the middle?" or "Show me the toy nearest the door." The purpose is to assess which concepts your child knows. Words like "nearest" or "middle" might be used in sentences or illustrated in a multiple-choice arrangement for a child to circle.

In the speech and language portions of these screening tests, a child might be asked to repeat particular sentences containing specific sounds. The articulation or misarticulation of words is noted; this initial screening may identify a child with special needs. It is important that parents realize many misarticulations are developmentally appropriate, and not all children are able to master certain sounds at the same time. Even missing teeth can prevent a child from articulating a certain sound.

Speech and language screenings might also assess your child's ability to listen, recall, and retell what he has heard. A child might be asked to listen to a story and answer questions that require an understanding of words such as "who?" or "where?"

The screening also includes an evaluation of a child's gross motor abilities and coordination. A teacher might ask a child to hop on one foot, to walk backward, or to jump for example.

In most school districts, once the screening is completed and the results are compiled, the kindergarten teachers and teaching specialists meet to review the results and discuss the children who seem to be at risk based on the screening information. All are aware that the screening is approximate and problematic; it's a one-time, out-of-context testing situation. Each child's performance is undoubtedly affected by the new and unfamiliar testing conditions. These factors are taken into account by supplementing the results with information provided by parents in questionnaires and interviews. We also listen closely to the observations of the teachers who conducted the screening. This subjective information is often more valuable than any of the test scores.

In my school, this meeting often prompts skepticism among the teachers about the screening process. We worry that we may be alarming parents, children, or ourselves when there may well be no good reason for concern. Still, we have no choice but to do this screening process. My public school is under state mandate to conduct a screening for new entrants, and kindergarten children fall into this category. In the end, the results of kindergarten screenings are not intended to measure everything a child knows or to predict future success in school. Educators know that kindergarten is a stage of rapid change and development. Kindergarten teachers in districts where the screenings are done in the spring or early summer say that the results are often irrelevant by the time a child arrives for the first day of kindergarten.

Each year, parents ask me if their children will be given any tests at the end of kindergarten. They are often relieved when I tell them that we do not assess young children with formal tests, that instead, their children's teacher ends the year with a narrative progress report. This report assesses children on important learning goals that directly reflect the tasks and skills they work on every day in kindergarten.

That said, parents should know that there are districts that do require children to take a standardized achievement test when they complete kindergarten. In New York, it is estimated that more than

84,000 standardized tests are administered to kindergarten children each year. If a child has not performed well enough on the end-of-the-year "readiness" test, that child may be labeled as not ready for first grade and be placed in an extra-year transitional class, separated from his peers, or retained. Retention can seem like the right thing for a child, but often it is not the solution people think it will be. In fact, research studies of children who were retained in early grades show that, on the whole, they made no significant gains, and tend to have low self-esteem and poor attitudes toward school. The decision to place a child in a transitional class or to retain a child for another year in kindergarten is something a parent must be involved in, and should never be made based only on a test score.

What You Should Know about Your School's Curriculum

When parents meet with me to talk about my school, they always ask "What is the school curriculum?" Parents ask this lightly as though it is simple to lay out our school's curriculum. But the truth is, for me and for any other administrator, it is not at all simple to describe the curriculum of a school.

Probably some parents might expect me to respond by giving them a stack of curriculum guides, books, vision statements, and the like. Every school principal has these documents on their shelves. When I do give these to parents, they leave my office seemingly satisfied. I think these parents are comforted with the thought that they're carrying our school's curriculum with them, that they are piling the school's curriculum onto the car seat beside them.

In fact, what they have gotten are papers that a team of teachers may have written five summers earlier, some of whom may not still be in the district at all, and certainly are *not* teaching their child. Consequently, that child may be studying with a teacher who has given only a cursory glance at these spiraled curriculum guides.

On the other hand, one of the curriculum guides may represent the ideas that are especially important to me. Because of my ongoing involvement, almost every teacher in the school may follow this one curriculum guide. If parents sit down with one of the curriculum guides hoping to understand our school's philosophy, they may find it's still hard to figure out where our school stands, because often the curriculum guides have been written by groups of teachers who believe different things about a subject. The language of these guides is often deliberately vague, to accommodate different approaches to a subject.

My point is not that parents shouldn't ask, "What's your school's curriculum?" but that they need to understand that the curriculum written in guidebooks and policy statements may not match the actual curriculum that lives in classrooms up and down the halls of a school. Parents need to understand that, although in some ways, schools do have a curriculum, often it's actually teachers who shape the curriculum an individual child will experience.

Nevertheless, in every district and every school, there are some underpinnings that unify curriculum. In my school, our relationship with the Teachers College Reading and Writing Project provides a very real, tangible support to our school's approach to teaching reading and writing. Many schools have such long-standing relationships to universities and staff development organizations. Parents who learn about these relationships can learn about the direction their school is moving by reading the books or by attending the courses that accompany this staff development.

Parents who want to learn about the curriculum which underpins a school should also want to determine whether the school purchases and follows any published programs. If a school uses a basal reader, for instance, this will be the program that has the most important effect on the school day, because instruction in reading occupies almost two and a half hours each day. (This is discussed in more detail in a separate appendix on the reading curriculum.) Many school districts subscribe to a published math program and to a published science curriculum. Parents need to read these published materials, acknowledging that some teachers will rely more or less on these.

Parents can also learn about a school's curriculum by investigating the expertise of people who live and work in a school. In one school, for example, the principal was once the science and technology staff developer for the district. That fact alone should have indicated something to parents about the curriculum in that school. In many schools full-time support people for language arts work alongside teachers. This makes a day-to-day difference in the curriculum throughout the school.

It's helpful, also, to find out about the learning culture that has developed among teachers in a school. If teachers meet over lunch to brainstorm about how to help struggling readers, or to teach poetry or hands-on science, this tells a parent something about the curricular energy in a school.

Furthermore, parents can inquire about the curriculum within particular disciplines. I'll highlight some of the major issues of each discipline next, and will devote an entire appendix to reading.

Writing

There are three approaches to writing often found in elementary schools. One has been described as "the particle approach," that is, dividing writing into parts and teaching children each part in a step-by-step fashion. With this approach, very young children do not write words, but are only drilled on alphabet letters and blends. Once they have shown some mastery in these areas, they progress to writing sentences; they may even learn the four kinds of sentences (declarative, interrogative, exclamatory, and imperative). They are taught to write and punctuate complete sentences. Only when children have mastered the sentence do they move on to the paragraph. Eventually, children are taught to write "kinds of paragraphs," which may include cause-and-effect, descriptive, narrative, and sequential paragraphs. By the time children are in upper elementary and junior high grades, teachers assign them to write five-paragraph essays, beginning with an introductory paragraph shaped around a thesis statement, followed by three supporting paragraphs and a conclusion. Obviously, this type of writing, also called expository writing, does not exist in the real world. This writing instruction, then, is geared toward teaching students to accomplish "school writing."

The particle approach to writing is based on a philosophy of teaching and learning that has been likened to an assembly line. If a tennis coach followed this philosophy, students would practice dropping the ball for a week. When they mastered that, they would swing their rackets for a week. Perhaps, years later, children would finally get the chance to engage in a tennis volley.

Obviously, the particle approach is in opposition to that described by Lucy earlier in this book, whereby children are invited to write and live like real writers from the start, and are coached to revise for clarity, grace, meaning, and structure. This is known by many as "the process approach to writing," or as "a workshop approach to writing." Most elementary school administrators across America today will at least *say* that they subscribe to a process approach to writing, but parents should monitor closely what's actually being taught in order to judge whether this is true. They should ask: "Are children writing on their own important topics most of the time? Are teachers moving among children during writing workshops, coaching them to revise for elements like meaning, focus, language, and detail, as well as helping them to spell and punctuate correctly?"

The third approach to teaching writing could be called a pattern or formula approach, in which youngsters study a genre of writing (haiku, tall tales, the friendly letter). The teacher explains the characteristics of a particular kind of writing, and students are then asked to write according to the prescribed form. Teachers who value this kind of writing do so because this approach allows them to connect reading and writing. Likewise, some students prefer this writing approach because they can lean on the form and structure of a particular genre. Rather than thinking first and foremost about content, these children often focus on following a technique. For example, if students are writing poetry they may be asked to work with a particular rhyme scheme, a a b b a, for example, and on being sure that the third and fourth lines are shorter than the rest of the lines. Sometimes teachers may even work with the whole class to generate a list of rhyming words that students can use during this kind of writing.

Teachers who use the pattern approach often teach writing through whole-class lessons rather than individual conferences. Usually, there is no emphasis on revision. Once students have written their pieces, teachers collect and correct them rather than conferring toward revision. Often these units result in the whole-class displays parents see in the hallways of a school.

Social Studies

When parents ask about curriculum, social studies is usually not high on their list of concerns; but if they *do* ask about social studies, they are likely to find that there are different approaches and philosophies in this area of the curriculum, too. In many school systems, the social studies curriculum is guided by a state syllabus or framework. In New York, the syllabus outlines the concepts, content objectives, and skills objectives for children at each grade level. The state education department also issues program guides with examples itemizing how teachers can develop each concept. Skills to be developed are outlined, and the state suggests activities and resources for developing these skills. When there is a state syllabus, districts can choose to purchase a textbook series that matches the framework, or they can write their own curriculum.

Whether or not districts operate within state guidelines, they have the option of purchasing textbooks for every child in every school throughout the district. When districts opt to do this, textbook companies provide the philosophy, core materials, manuals, and guides for teachers. The teachers at each grade level generally are assigned a particular period of history to cover. Usually, as a child progresses through school, each year builds on the previous year, although children cycle back to essential concepts and skills. If the school follows a published textbook approach, parents who want to understand the social studies curriculum should peruse the books students use and ask about supplementary materials, keeping in mind that when a district follows a particular textbook, usually creative, industrious teachers will design their own curricula to accompany the textbooks.

In some school systems, teams of teachers at a particular grade level might work for several weeks during the summer to write curriculum guides based either on the state social studies syllabus or on their own school's curricular outline. These curriculum guides will be valuable to these teachers, but they tend to be less valuable to other teachers who have had only a peripheral voice in their development.

In the end, many classroom teachers author their own plans for the day-to-day work within broad social studies topics. And whether the school system supports a textbook series or a teacher-authored curriculum guide, other issues arise around social studies and how it is taught in schools. Some teachers will approach social studies as a self-contained subject, separate from other subjects, while others will integrate it with language arts or science. Parents who hear that a particular teacher has integrated her social studies program with other disciplines may wonder why. The teachers I know best acknowledge that there are good reasons both for doing this and for not doing this. It's not always ideal that the language arts program exists in the service of social studies, just as it's not always ideal that every book a child reads needs to relate to a topic such as westward expansion.

Ultimately, the one factor that determines the quality of a social studies class is the teacher. A teacher's style very much affects how the instruction goes. Regardless of what they are teaching, or whether social studies is integrated with other curricular areas or not, some teachers will present social studies in a lecturelike fashion. In this type of class, children will listen, take notes, and answer their teacher's questions. There may be some whole-group discussion, and the homework will often include writing answers to questions posed by the teacher or the textbook. In another classroom, the teacher may teach the same material, but the tone and texture of classroom life will be altogether different. The room will hum with activity as children work in small groups to role-play, reenact, probe, and think about what they are learning. Children will initiate investigations, lead discussions, raise questions, and invent theories.

Parents should realize that a child's work in social studies is very connected to his work as a reader and writer, specifically because some students have difficulty reading nonfiction books, and especially textbooks. Teachers try to help by prefacing subject lessons with lists of words related to particular content, but often it's not just the unfamiliar words that makes reading social studies so difficult. The textbooks often are obtuse, ponderous, and dull. The best way for teachers and parents to help is to let children know that the subjects behind the curriculum are fascinating and rich. It can make all the difference if a parent shows their child that they too are interested in reading about the annexation of Alaska or the geographical features of our country.

Science

Parents rarely inquire about a school's approach to science, and when they do, it is usually in a perfunctory manner; that is, they check that science is covered, or ask which topics will be addressed over the course of a year. It's very rare indeed for parents to ask about a district's philosophy toward science education or about the methods used in the science curriculum.

Children think very differently from parents. They're often head-over-heels in love with science, and yearn for the chance to delve more rigorously into this area. Although they do not have the words or knowledge to ask about a school's philosophy or methodology, children quickly discern that there are major variations in the ways some teachers handle this discipline. Consequently, parents would be well advised to take a greater interest in their school's approach to science. A knowledge of science is fundamental to the human experience of this world, and especially to our children's ways of being in the world.

It is usually easy to answer parents' questions about the topics covered in a school's curriculum. Typically, schools try to maintain some balance between the earth sciences (geology and ecology), the physical sciences (mechanization, technology, electricity, sound, and light), and the natural and life sciences (plants, animals, migration, and evolution). Many elementary-school teachers would prefer to delve only into the natural and life sciences, and need to be nudged to cover topics such as energy and machines.

But the most important questions about a school's science curriculum do not revolve around the subjects that are covered. Rather, parents should ask about scheduling and methodology. Parents should try to understand how science fits into the schedule of their child's week, because, usually, teachers find they have more subjects to cover than they can possibly shoehorn into their days.

Naturally, teachers cannot possibly do all things equally well; every teacher must determine priorities. Many elementary-school teachers, especially in the primary grades, devote more time to reading, writing, and math than to social studies and science; the first three are often taught during the morning hours, "prime time." Subsequently, teachers must choose whether to teach a little science and social studies each day; focus on one; combine social studies and science into a single cross-disciplinary thematic topic; or alternate the pattern, so as to spend six weeks on science, then six weeks on social studies.

Elementary-school teachers tend not to have had a great number of education courses in science or in the teaching of science, so it's not unusual for them to opt for a solution that allows them to give more attention to social studies than to science. Teachers may, for example, immerse their students in a long-term study of Colonial America, and on the side, have children plant beans in milk cartons. Teachers sometimes circumvent the teaching of science by taking on topics such as space or inventions and treating these topics as social studies units. The process goes something like this: The subject of inventions begins as a physical science unit on machines; it becomes a unit on inventions, which then becomes a unit on famous inventors rather than the inventions. The result is that children spend their time in the library rather than the laboratory, and research with index cards, footnotes, and outlines, rather than with pulleys, stop watches, and weights. Thus, parents may want to peruse a list of science topics with an eye toward determining whether these topics are actually suited to the *process* of science. They should ask: "Is this a topic through which children can engage in primary research?" Dinosaurs and the planets, for example, are often presented more as social studies than science.

The most important question for parents to ask about the science curriculum is: "Are children given opportunities to inquire as scientists into their own hunches and theories?" If children have regular, consistent opportunities to roll up their sleeves and dig into the "stuff" of science the answer to this question is yes. The study of science should include sunshine, dirt, water, living things, bottles, tubes, magnets, and gears.

That said, sometimes even when classrooms are full of the "stuff" of science, they may not be places that support children pursuing their own theories, and this issue must be evaluated, too. Science class often resembles a cooking class, with children simply following someone else's recipes for experiments. These canned experiments *can* be launchpads for children conducting their own inquiries, but too often they are as far as children are allowed to go.

Math

Math is an area of the curriculum that many parents regard as important as reading, although one parent might bring his own insecurities about math to the inquiry while another parent wants to make sure that her child who loves math will be sufficiently challenged by the school. The bottom line: Both parents want to make sure that the school's curriculum will help their children become confident mathematicians and problem solvers; they want their children to value math and see it as a meaningful part of everyday life.

When parents ask about math curriculum, then, school administrators will tell parents about their philosophy of teaching math; and their teaching beliefs will often be reflected in the math series the district has chosen for the school. In some cases, this means a math textbook from the same series at every grade level. Or, rather than the district representatives selecting the math program, the teachers may have articulated a district philosophy and selected the math materials. For example, such a teacher committee may choose several math resources to use for instruction across the grades, which may include hands-on materials in addition to math texts.

As Lucy mentioned, parents should also be aware that, with the national emphasis on higher standards in all curriculum areas, the widely accepted standards from the National Council of Teachers of Mathematics (NCTM) are having a slow but detectable effect on how math is taught. The NCTM is encouraging school districts to reexamine curriculum guides and materials to be certain they reflect these higher standards. Therefore, in many schools, parents will find that teachers work with both the school math book and through their own teaching strategies, extending the ideas presented in the textbook. For example, teachers will encourage students to use mathematical language to explain their thinking or to justify their conclusions. And rather than teaching computation facts as ends in themselves, teachers will use problem-solving techniques as a starting point in lessons with students. When presented with a problem, students learn to think about which basic operation to use and to apply the facts in a meaningful context. Students are just as likely to gather data to construct their own graphs from their experiences as they are to analyze data from an existing graph in the math textbook.

Many school administrators will also tell parents that literature is often used in their math programs in the primary grades to help children realize that math is a part of everyday life. Books such as *How Many Ways to Get to Eleven* by Eve Merriam and *Who Sank the Boat?* by Pamela Allen encourage young children to think mathematically, and promote discussions that enable children to explain their thinking and understand that there is more than just one way to approach a problem. The use of computer technology has also affected math programs. In many schools, teachers are always researching quality software to support their math programs. Parents may want to ask if their school uses computers in this way.

Computers

Frequently, today, parents inquire about the use of computers in their children's programs. They want to know: "How many computers are in each classroom? Is there a computer lab in the school? How often do the children get to use the computer?" But parents should also ask: "How do you use computers to help students learn? What is your philosophy toward computers?"

Some schools do fairly well at helping children become more computer competent. Often a computer specialist works in the school or district with the teachers and students. Other schools offer minicourses or after-school clubs that teach keyboarding and computer games. Still other schools have the necessary software and hardware to enable students to create specific multimedia projects. Certain schools schedule weekly time in a computer lab; in other schools, labs are set up for classes to sign up on an open-scheduled basis. With all this program variation, what do parents need to notice? In classes with only one computer, they should determine whether the computer is used as a place to go when work is completed. Are computer programs another form of rote exercises that might just as well be from a workbook? Are the games mostly about choosing the right answers?

School districts like mine are hoping to expand the use of computers between home and school. They regard computers as tools for the study of subjects such as social studies, where students can learn how to access and gather information, critically read primary documents, and communicate with students from other locales.

School districts also have to decide among having a computer lab, placing a number of computers in each classroom, or a combination of the two. People who argue against the lab believe that having computer stations in the classrooms is the only way that computers can be truly integrated into the curriculum. But the availability of only one or two computers limits the options. Proponents of the lab believe that whole-class instruction in a place without distractions, and a computer for every child, is the most efficient way to provide instruction.

Libraries

More often today, libraries and librarians are not separate from the classroom and the ongoing curriculum, but extend and support the ongoing curriculum. And like everything else about public schools, school libraries are undergoing radical changes.

The most obvious change is that many of today's librarians are called "media specialists." This change is meant to represent a change in role as well. Many libraries today are on-line, books are bar coded, and libraries are equipped with computers. Children using these libraries are as apt to be traveling the Internet or poring over CD-ROMs as reading a novel.

Furthermore, not only have libraries changed, but the niches they fill in schools have altered, too. When I was a child, classrooms rarely had well-stocked libraries. Now children regularly check books out of their classroom libraries. These books are carried between home and school every night, and they are the books that have the most social support in the classroom.

For the librarian to support classroom teachers, he needs to open blocks of time for focused work with individuals and entire classes. For example, when a class of fifth graders in New Jersey became interested in their town's enforcement of pollution laws, they used the school library constantly as a place from which to contact the Chamber of Commerce, research local laws, role-play an interview with their mayor, and research school policies on recycling. This was possible only because their librarian was ready and willing to help teachers and children as they invented a curriculum together.

Of course, in some schools, the library is less involved with social studies and science and more involved with the literary curriculum. One school library, for example, supports a Parents as Reading Partners program, which lasts for many months, and brings parents and grandparents in to read to and with young children. Other libraries support schoolwide Author Studies, often culminating in visits by favorite authors.

But no matter how much school libraries have changed over recent years, books and reading are still at the core of what they do. As such, they offer crucial support to a school's reading curriculum, which is the topic of the next appendix.

Reading: An Essential Part of Your Child's School Day

When parents ask: "Are you a phonics or a whole-language school?" rather than about the general curriculum, I know they've been reading headlines such as, "Skirmishes on the Reading Front" or "Filling in the Holes in Whole-Language." Underneath this question are the unstated questions: "Can I trust you to teach my child to read really well?" and "Can I be absolutely sure my child will come out on top as a reader?"

No teacher or principal could or would ever promise that any particular child will become a strong reader. Success in reading, like success in any other subject, depends on a confluence of factors— including a child's home life. Of course, I sympathize with the parents' need to feel assured that the school district can guarantee that their children will flourish as readers, but no single one approach to teaching reading can make such a promise. No matter which approach a school uses, there will always be those children who progress in leaps and bounds as readers, while others advance more slowly.

When parents ask about our approach to reading, frequently they want to understand where the school stands in regard to the current national conversation about reading, because the media has portrayed an image of schools in a face-off. On one side of the line are the so-called whole-language schools, and on the other, the phonics schools. Given this portrayal, it's not surprising that parents are

concerned. The problem is that every parent has a different interpretation of what it means to be a whole-language school or phonics
school. For example, some parents who visit my school and see
groups of children sitting in a circle on the carpet conclude that the
teachers must be whole-language proponents. Other parents who
hear teachers explain how to spell the /ch/ sound while children are
writing stories assume a phonics approach. Although my school
teaches phonics rigorously, I would not regard it as pure phonics
based, because we teach phonics as a real tool for children to use when
they write and when they read. We do not isolate phonics and spend
hours each day practicing a particular letter sound. The teachers in
my school think instructing children to read and write well requires
more sense of story, more thoughtfulness, and a greater command of
language than a mere sequence of isolated worksheets.

Independent Reading

Experts in the instruction of reading may not agree about every
aspect of a reading curriculum, but they will agree that for children
to flourish as readers, they must spend time in school and at home
reading books of their own choosing. To that end, in almost every
elementary-school classroom, teachers set aside time for kids to
hunker down with books. This time is often referred to as "independent reading," "reading workshop," DEAR time (drop everything
and read), or SSR time (silent, sustained reading).

Although almost every teacher includes this time—we'll call it
independent reading—in her day, there are important differences in
the ways teachers approach this part of the reading curriculum. The
most significant differences revolve around the centrality of independent reading, the issue of choice and control, the teacher's role,
and the nature of home-school connections. Some teachers allot
only about 10 minutes a day to independent reading, often at the
beginning or end of the day, during snacktime, or just after recess.
Whenever, the message is the same: Independent reading is relatively inconsequential.

In such classrooms, it's interesting to note which aspect of reading
is given attention. There are teachers, for example, who think that

it's more important for children to be able to list the characteristics of a haiku or a tall tale than it is for them to be active, involved, planful readers. Others consider it more important that every child fill in sequences of a sound on worksheets or memorize the definitions of words rather than to read. I question these priorities.

In contrast, there are teachers who regard independent reading as the center of the reading curriculum, evident from the fact that even on busy days, when the firefighter comes to talk to the class and the children attend both music and art classes, time is still set aside for independent reading. These teachers will often invest half an hour a day in independent reading, not 10 minutes; and they will not use this time to catch up on their paperwork. Instead, these teachers will be vitally, actively involved in coaching their young readers.

Teachers also think differently about the issue of control and choice during independent reading. In general, most teachers will agree that children should be reading books that make sense to them; that is, teachers want children to spend most of their time reading books that are, roughly speaking, "on the child's level." The difference of opinion revolves only around whether teachers believe that children can be taught and trusted to choose books wisely and to read with comprehension.

Teachers who don't believe children can choose books for themselves tend to micromanage their students' reading lives. They may tell children which books to read to be certain they are at an appropriate level, and also keep track of every book a child reads in order to monitor the child's comprehension with lots of question-and-answer worksheets. Other teachers may direct which books are to be read independently to ensure that children are reading a steady diet of the classics.

In classes where teachers control children's reading choices, the younger children at least will often be stepped through a sequence of progressively more difficult books. The advantage to this is that children will not attempt books that are too ambitious for them. On the other hand, children in these classrooms will be less likely to be passionate, independent readers than those in classrooms where individual choice is supported. When teachers teach children how to choose books wisely, children can create their own paths through the world of books; they develop "tastes" as readers. One may adore historic fiction; another will devour mysteries.

Teachers vary the way they divide their own time during independent reading periods, too. Some will expect the class in general to read on its own, while the teachers work with a small group of readers who need special support. Other teachers will be actively involved in what their students are doing during independent reading, moving among children as they read, perhaps encouraging two to read together, or prompting another to look over a book before he reads. These teachers usually take observational notes on children, and then bring several children together for special work or support as needed. Still other teachers act as overseers during independent reading, perhaps talking with children when they finish a book to check that they understood what they have read.

Finally, teachers link independent reading and the home in various ways. As Lucy mentioned, ideally books will travel between the home and the school. Preferably, a child who starts a book in school will bring that book home, continue to read it there, and follow through the next day in school. Some teachers, however, are reluctant to allow books to leave their classrooms. They're justifiably worried about losing books. Instead, they expect children to have parallel texts going: a school book and a home book. Obviously, this poses some difficulties for many children. Regardless of how a teacher approaches independent reading, parents should expect some connection between what their children read in school and the reading they are asked to do at home.

Reading Children's Literature in Partnerships and Small Groups

When I was a child, reading discussions were led by the teacher. The students all would progress through the chapters of the class book assigned as homework, and the next day during reading time we'd talk about the previous evening's reading. We'd define and spell vocabulary words, and answer our teacher's questions: "How would you describe the character?" "Has the author shown us personality traits?" "On what page?" "And what do you infer from that?"

This sort of instruction is still dominant during reading time in many classrooms. The questions may be written by the teacher or provided by teacher guides. Regardless, what children are doing in the name of reading is to answer someone else's questions.

More often, however, teachers recognize that children need to pose as well as to answer questions. When teachers always control the topics of discussion in a reading class, the children must passively wait for a teacher to ignite their thinking. It is much more important for children to learn that, as readers, they can think with texts. Thus, frequently today, children are asked to work in partnerships or small groups, deciding on their own how to reflect on texts, while teachers model ways of thinking about books. A teacher might, for example, use class discussion about the whole-class read-aloud book to demonstrate that it's helpful to notice how characters change as a story progresses, followed by a prompt, "This may be something all of you want to think about with your partners or in your small groups today." Later this same teacher might draw up her chair alongside two children who, side by side, are reading as if on cruise control—they read, read, read, and never pause to talk. The teacher might suggest they spend some time discussing what they've just read. If the children squirm uncomfortably, unsure of how to begin, the teacher can model how to get started or pose a direct question like, "What are some of the things readers often think about when they look up from their books?" Together, the teacher and the children can assemble a list of strategies for reflecting on a book, and the teacher might include the strategies demonstrated during the whole-class instructional time. The teacher then can leave once the children are, for instance, comparing their lives with that of the main character or effectively using one of the other strategies on their list.

Parents who watch such literature discussion groups might wonder why teachers support so much talk about books. They might prefer that children just read, read, read. But teachers know that the challenge of teaching children to read has everything to do with promoting thoughtfulness; and that when children have conversations about books, they often, as Lucy said earlier, become internalized.

Basal Reading Series

Although greater numbers of teachers in the United States teach reading through literature-based approaches, many still use a basal reader. A reading series usually provides both the materials and the philosophy behind that teacher's reading instruction.

In a basal reading program, specific anthologies are designated for each grade level. The earliest levels, called the preprimers, are usually used at the start of first grade, although in some schools these might be used in kindergarten. Thereafter, usually two books are used for each grade level, one for each half of the school year. Readers are often supplemented with a vast number of workbooks and books of master worksheets.

In basal reading programs, children are assigned particular books in the series, based on their abilities. The teacher generally determines these abilities through the use of the publisher's test, which reveals how accurately an individual can read. Thus, in a very real way, the publishers who produce basal readers control a child's life in school.

Usually, a teacher will form three different ability groups, and each will use a different text. One group will probably be above-grade level, another will be called average or on-grade level, and a third will be the below-average group. Once these groups are aligned, instruction is given according to plans prescribed by publishers in the teacher's manual, which is composed of scripts as to what teachers are to say and what answers they are to expect.

Reading series programs focus on three kinds of instruction: decoding, comprehension, and language skills. The skills in each area are defined, and the order of instruction is preplanned for the teacher. Regardless of the grade, every teacher is expected to follow the same sequence, determined by the reading series publisher. Teachers using a basal reading series generally focus on one or two skills a week, then students practice those skills. The time teachers spend with a group each day can vary from 15 to 25 minutes, which usually includes deskwork. Since behavior management is important and the work is not always interesting enough to hold children's attention, teachers will use the assignment and completion of workbook pages or worksheets as practice of the new skill, while they meet with the groups. In addition, there are numerous subskills to be taught, questions to be answered, and words to be discussed. Consequently, it can often take a full week for a group of children to get through a very short story.

Basal reading series are usually not written to encourage teachers to skip the less interesting stories or to move students in and out of ability groups based on a student's individual growth and progress. The idea is to move along the continuum of skills as scripted by the publisher. This hierarchical model of reading instruction assumes reading is a process of extracting information from a text for the purpose of answering questions. The text is the sole source of information, and the child's ability as learner and thinker is not taken into account.

Traditionally, all basal reading series were similar. The reading selections were written with controlled vocabulary, and the recommended skills were virtually the same. Today, when a school says it uses a basal reader series, the books may be anthologies containing some full-length selections or excerpts from quality children's literature. Teachers no longer necessarily group their students according to a publisher's tests; and in some cases they do not purchase all the supplementary workbooks. Nevertheless, many educators would argue (and I agree) that as long as control of the curriculum is in the hands of publishers and not educators, instruction will often be inappropriate and not match the needs of the individuals.

Readers of this appendix will rightly feel that there are broad differences between the approaches different school districts adopt to the teaching of reading. If a district uses a basal reader, parents will want to examine the books and accompanying materials, and will want to ask about their child's placement within the class. But even if the classroom uses a basal reader, it is possible that independent reading of children's literature may still be a significant component in a particular teacher's reading curriculum.

Testing and Assessment in Classrooms Today

When parents think about assessment, they usually focus on the formal high-stakes national and state tests. As a parent, it was the formal tests that always made me the most anxious. I knew the test scores would be printed on computer labels, permanently fastened to my child's cumulative record folder, and passed from grade to grade as evidence of his learning. I imagined opening my son's school folder and seeing a long row of computer labels with numbers, percentile ranks, and growth curves alongside the miniature-sized school picture of Michael, stapled in the corner of the folder. I remember receiving the impersonal and official-looking computer printout of his test scores. It felt like a judgment of me as a parent, as well as a judgment of my child. I would pore over the numbers in each subtest category, unclear what the scores meant and how I was to respond to them.

In the 1980s many parents and educators were feeling the pressures of high-stakes testing, particularly the standardized achievement tests. Few seemed to object to the idea of students taking tests, but they wondered: "How much of what was being tested matched what was being taught in classrooms? What did schools do with the results of the tests?" They were also concerned that tests could not or did not measure attitude or creativity, nor reveal children's strengths as learners or their intellectual habits. Nor did the tests do justice to the wonderful ways children differ from one another. Everyone seemed to agree that these tests were not enough.

As a result, many school systems in the country began to talk about "authentic assessment" rather than testing. Although testing is an assessment tool, the word *assessment* was thought to be broader, referring to many ways of knowing about students' learning lives. Thus, assessment doesn't usually mean simply reading test and quiz scores to graph one child's progress against another.

Assessment continues to be a topic of major reform, but meanwhile, standardized tests are still pervasive in many schools. Therefore, parents need to better understand how and why school districts use them.

National and State Tests

Although there is no one official national test, well over 100 million children take achievement tests every year in our nation's schools, and thousands of other children take state tests, which are often called competency tests. School districts purchase these national tests from commercial test publishers.

Tests are referred to as standardized when the same conditions are used to measure student performance across every test situation. Every student supposedly takes the test under the same conditions, and each student's performance on a standardized test is compared to a "norm group" of students of the same age or grade who took the same test. Some standardized test publishers provide school systems with different norms depending on whether the test is given in the beginning, middle, or end of each grade level. But parents should realize that despite all efforts to the contrary, in actuality, students never take the tests under the same conditions.

While certainly there are students whose teachers and parents give them confidence about taking these tests, others are intimidated by warnings, or harassed with advice. Some students may take the tests in their own classrooms, with their teachers nearby to help if a pencil breaks or the paper rips; while other students are herded into cafeterias and monitored by teachers they do not know. Furthermore, the content of the tests may or may not match the content of the courses given to students in the preceding year. Students who have been doing more advanced work in a particular area may come up short on test areas that adhere strictly to the curriculum. Personal capabilities, too, must be taken into account: Some students have long attention spans and have no problem reading numerous passages on a variety of subjects. Others may respond by not paying attention.

In these and other ways, the format of standardized tests can be more problematic to certain students and less so to others. Usually, tests are written in a multiple-choice format because it is easy to score and can be administered to large groups of students at the same time. But students who have not spent most of their time in school answering batteries of questions will not always fare well with these problems.

Most educators would agree that standardized tests can be used effectively to reveal certain broad trends in a school system. They may even provide information about children with learning difficulties or those who may be potentially gifted. But most educators will also agree that the content of standardized tests rarely match what they teach, and therefore do not convey accurately what students know and can do. Finally, the test may also be normed against groups different from any particular local population. And because of the short-answer format, standardized tests do not convey a child's ability to think critically and creatively, to integrate information from a variety of sources, to shape new problems, to work collaboratively, or to imagine other possibilities.

With an annual cost of over $900 million, many educators question whether the money spent on test preparation materials and the actual testing materials is the best use of resources. Some point out that if standardized tests were designed only to reveal broad trends in the district for the state or the board of education, and not to inform teachers about individual students, then it would be less costly in time and money to test every other year. Many schools, for example, spend hundreds of hours drilling children on the procedures for taking standardized tests. The result of this is that tests are also costly in terms of time and anxiety. In many classrooms, the entire environment must be altered every time the class practices for a test and again when the test is administered. Seats are lined up, children are separated, and pencils are passed out. Children are prohibited from talking with the teacher, and they are not allowed to ask questions once the test is underway.

Early childhood experts in particular have expressed strong opposition to the use of standardized testing in kindergarten, first, and second grade. Parents should find out what their children's school considers to be appropriate methods of assessment and how the results are used. If school systems use some form of testing in the K-2 grades, parents will want to ensure that children are also assessed throughout the year using many "authentic assessment" measures, which are discussed later in this appendix.

Of course, standardized tests can be beneficial. Supporters of tests emphasize that they provide an objective measure of how one child is doing compared to another. But the danger in this kind of comparative testing is that parents give too much power and credence to the results. Parents must remember that numbers represent one test, one time, and the content may have been biased or may not have been representative of their children's classroom curriculum. Alternative assessment work is crucial if parents are to gain a full picture of their children as learners.

In addition to the results of national standardized tests, school districts may also report annually on how students score on state tests. Although the focus may vary from state to state, the purposes of state tests are to check on the progress of individual students in each school or to evaluate the effectiveness of school programs. Some state tests are competency tests, intended to ensure that students are minimally competent in areas such as reading, math, and writing.

While national tests provide information that helps districts report trends, some state tests are intended as a way to identify individual students who fall below a designated state reference point. These students are then provided with support services. Unfortunately, these support services may cause children to be labeled as inferior. Furthermore, since many of these services take place outside the classroom, children often must be removed from the rest of their class, causing them to feel set apart and stigmatized. To alleviate these problems, parents are usually included in the process by which the school decides which support services to give to which children.

Parents need to feel confident that this is the best way to meet their child's needs, and that the benefits will outweigh the potential disadvantages.

State competency tests are also under reform. Requiring schools to make sure everyone is minimally competent is now regarded as a very low expectation for children. Educators are turning their attention to issues of establishing higher standards in curriculum and assessment, while moving away from establishing levels of minimum competency.

Again, as long as standardized tests are prevalent in schools, parents must learn how to help their children. Both schools and parents share a role in preparing students for these tests. Ideally, teachers begin test-prep about a month prior to the test, although test preparation can occur as early as September and run through March. Such excessive preparation effectively takes over the curriculum, and reduces opportunities for higher-level thinking and learning. Test preparation for reading must not be confused with the teaching of reading.

Proper test preparation teaches a child how to use the machine-scored answer sheets and to fill in answers. Test prep also helps children anticipate the special language used on tests. Children should be taught, for example, that a question that reads, "Which one of these things is not true," really is asking, "Which sentence is false?" During test preparation work for some reading tests, children will be encouraged to read all the questions before reading the poem or story. They may be told that it's okay to underline and write in the margins on the test booklets, even if the written instructions contradict this.

The most important way a parent can help is to have a positive attitude toward these tests, and, at the same time, impart the seriousness of the test. Parents should never create stress for their children about failing. When children don't score up to expectations on a test, parents cannot let the result alter their confidence in their children. Recently, a group of my colleagues joined Lucy and me in observing several fourth graders taking a test. The "best reader" in the class was a girl who had scored only in the seventy-first percentile. The teacher wondered how this could have happened. "Was she perhaps not such a good reader after all?" she wondered. The child, too, had many insecurities based on her seventy-first percentile score. She talked a lot about not being a good test-taker. Since receiving the seventy-first percentile score, the girl's parents had told her many times that she would never be the sort of person to do well on tests. Upon further investigation, we learned that if she had answered just one more question correctly, she would have been in the ninety-first percentile as a reader. This girl's one score from third grade may have jeopardized her educational experience. How helpful it would have been if the girl's parents and teachers had assured her that their day-to-day knowledge of her abilities were trustworthy.

There are, however, a few things parents can do to help their children score better on tests. Parents can help by inviting children to spend some time reading and talking about reading in ways that stay close to the text. At home, some parents might try helping their child follow printed directions. Whether playing a board game or assembling a birdfeeder, paying close attention to the text and following directions are skills some teachers believe are necessary for success on some reading tests.

Parents can also help build their child's stamina for sustained reading. So often we say to children, "Read for 15 minutes and then take a break," or "Spend a few minutes on math now and then do the rest later." But since these tests require that children pay attention for a long period of time, parents might try encouraging children to read and work on math for longer stretches of time.

The schools that do little or no preparation for these tests either feel that their standards are higher than those in the tests or they believe that test prep wastes valuable time. If this is the case, parents may want to ask teachers about tests. They can often find out some characteristics of a test by asking questions such as "What is the format of the test? Is it better to guess on a question, or to leave it blank?" Then they can prep their children themselves. While they shouldn't overemphasize the importance of the test, it can benefit children to have a sense of the ground rules. Other parents want to know about the value of purchasing commercial materials to help their children prepare for a test. These materials, despite their labels, often do not match the test format children will face in school.

Those parents who regard the annual results of the standardized test as the way to measure and assess the sum of all their child's learning for the year give far too much credence to the tests, which can lead to serious harm to their child's self-concept and motivation to learn. We all know someone who has confided that a test score they received 20 or 30 years ago altered their entire experience as a student and a learner from that day on.

It is much wiser to regard the results of a test as just one measurement. No one could possibly measure in a few hours all that any of us knows. Parents have known their children all their lives, and should not let a score from a single test alter this knowledge. Reading test scores cannot reveal how much their child enjoys reading, nor can such a score measure a child's persistence and ingenuity in wrestling with problems in math.

In summary, standardized test scores represent just one facet of school accountability. Thus, parents will also want to know how else their child is assessed in school throughout the year. Such tools as report cards or progress reports will reflect their child's everyday school performance.

Authentic Assessments in the Classroom

Authentic assessments are measures of learning, but their goal is not so much to measure as to improve learning. When teachers assess their students, they gain information that guides instruction. And when parents come to parent-teacher conferences, this is the kind of information that teachers are apt to share; they will tell parents about their standards and talk about a child's progress toward reaching these standards.

Parents who don't see the usual number of letter grades on daily worksheets or homework assignments may wonder whether teachers are keeping track of their children. This is a reasonable question, but usually teachers will keep anecdotal and observational records, which are far more helpful than rows of scores could possibly be. If you were to visit some of the teachers I know, you might stand in their classrooms and watch for an hour and never see anything that looks like assessment. If you were to talk with the teacher, however, he would probably tell you and demonstrate that he was assessing the entire time. When a student looked puzzled and asked a question to clarify why a particular word had a certain pattern, the teacher was assessing. When a small group of students gathered to edit or proofread their final drafts, the teacher was assessing.

In many school districts, authentic assessment is accompanied by a revision of progress reports and report cards. Teachers who have the chance to create their own authentic systems for assessing students are then able to ensure that there is a congruence between teaching practices and assessment. These assessments reflect what teachers value, not what a testing company directs teachers to value.

Parents whose children are in such an environment may be surprised when they receive their child's first report card or progress report. Instead of number grades, they see narrative comments. Instead of the traditional grades of A, B, C, or D, children may receive D for developing, I for independent, S for sometimes, or A for always. Samples of a child's work are often included in the progress reports, which parents receive at parent-teacher conferences.

Many school systems recognize the fact that the term *authentic assessment* and all that it represents may be an entirely new concept to parents. Administrators and teachers know that reform is not possible without public support and understanding, and to that end many schools offer parent workshops or presentations at board of education meetings to help parents understand new testing and assessment practices. It is important for parents to realize that whether a school system is just starting to examine the issues of assessment, or whether it is steeped in assessment reform, such changes mean that the administrators and teachers are working hard to ensure that students are learning in more rigorous and authentic ways.

APPENDIX E

Building a Partnership with Your Child's Teacher

In the days and weeks before a new school year begins, parents try to get children ready for school. We do this not just by buying sneakers and school supplies, but by talking about the new teacher to help our children feel comfortable with the idea of a new adult in their lives. During the last fleeting weeks of summer, teachers too are busy preparing for the new term. Even if they are still vacationing with their families, every teacher's thoughts turn toward school.

In the midst of all these separate preparations, thought should also be given to how to form a good partnership with our child's teachers. What do teachers want and expect from parents?

Probably, if teachers came together to speak honestly and openly about what they want from their students' parents, most would say they want parents to begin the school year in the spirit of partnership and cooperation. As a principal, I know I want parents to feel this way. I want teachers and parents to agree that when something doesn't go well in class or when a child says he hates school, there will probably be many reasons behind these problems. Knowing this, we won't blame anyone. Instead, we'll try to get to the bottom of the problems together. Teachers and parents should also expect to disagree on some issues—and that's okay. This kind of spirit requires mutual respect and ongoing honest communication.

Each year the school schedules occasions for formal communication between teachers and parents. The first is usually the school's

Open House or Meet the Teacher evening. Teachers prepare carefully for this meeting; and regardless of how experienced they are, most feel anxious about this first encounter with their new parent group. First impressions matter; teachers are aware that some parents will judge them for the rest of the year based on this first meeting. Consequently, teachers need our support, particularly in public forums of this sort. Parents, of course, come to this meeting with varying degrees of confidence in the school and the teacher, and with different attitudes. One parent may make negative comments and express her anger or general dissatisfaction with something about the school, the teacher, or the class. In such a situation, other parents need to publicly support the teacher. This is not the occasion for this type of encounter. This first meeting is meant to launch the school year in the spirit of cooperation.

When parents have concerns about a teacher, they should voice these concerns directly to that teacher and not to others. Teachers often make this possible by writing letters to parents encouraging them to call or write at any time, and to feel free to ask questions or share their concerns. Yet parents often complain to other parents instead. While this may initially alleviate anxiety, it is no way to solve a problem.

I don't think parents who socialize first about their concerns do this to sabotage a teacher. In fact, I think often they go to others because they are afraid that if they bring their concerns directly to the teacher, the teacher may feel angry and take it out on the parent's child. It's with good intentions, then, that these parents talk to each other rather than talk to the teacher.

But there is no doubt in my mind that this indirect approach backfires for the parent. Teachers usually hear about these conversations and inevitably feel that it would have been more helpful if the parent had come directly to them. This is how misunderstandings and miscommunications develop.

No doubt, the structures of schools can get in the way of effective communication. Usually, there is little opportunity to orient our children or meet our child's teacher before the school year starts; and when the first day dawns, there is no time to stop and talk with the teacher beyond a moment or two at the classroom door before or after school. Unless parents arrange a specific appointment, there may be no time to talk with our child's teacher until parent-teacher conferences.

When parents have not had the opportunity to meet or talk with the teacher, they sometimes arrive at the classroom door intent on having a one-on-one conversation with the teacher. They may even bring their child in late, and walk into the classroom, expecting the teacher to talk with them then and there. Another parent might bring a forgotten lunch or snack to the classroom, and when the teacher comes forward to accept it, the parent launches into a serious discussion. This puts teachers in a very difficult situation. It is not possible for the teacher to integrate the late child into the classroom or hand over the forgotten lunch, continue supervising all the children in the classroom, *and* talk with the parent at the door! If you can imagine what it's like to have a big birthday party for your child, and then try to picture that while all the children are there at the party, one parent tries to talk with you about setting up a playdate for the following week, you'll have some image of what this situation is like for teachers. Both teachers and the other children in the class deserve respect, and this means finding a more appropriate occasion to confer with the teacher.

Perhaps the most important way to begin to form a mutually supportive partnership with our child's teacher is to speak respectfully of the teacher, even in the face of disagreement. We need to do this with other parents, but especially in front of our children. This is essential if we expect our children to be productive and have a positive attitude about school.

Matching Teacher to Child

When I was a child I remember having feelings of excitement and anticipation, heavily underlined with fear of the unknown, on the day my classmates and I were told who our teacher would be for the next school year. I usually knew who these teachers were—I'd seen them on the playground during recess, or glimpsed them teaching as

I scurried past their classrooms with my hall pass clutched in my hand. There were some teachers who everyone wanted to have, and others who were dreaded.

As a parent, I again felt some of the same anticipation and fear, waiting to hear who my children would have for their teachers. For weeks in advance of the announcement, I'd run over the list of teachers. I usually had my hopes pinned onto one or two possibilities. But I always felt alone and powerless in my concern. It was hard to believe I had no part in this decision, that it was out of my hands. Up until that point, I had been able to choose my child's nursery school, his camp, even his friends. To have something this important decided for me was difficult.

Schools today, like the schools I knew when my children were young, still let parents know their child's new teacher sometime between the end of the school year in June and the opening of school in September. The matchmaking process of placing children with teachers is a complex one. But the truth is there are ways that parents can have some voice in choosing their child's teacher. To do this, wisely, however, parents need to learn something about all the teachers in their child's school.

Parents can learn about teachers simply by talking with other parents. But what parents need to remember is that the judgments they hear from other parents reveal something about those other parents and their children, as well as about the teacher in question. Each person's evaluation of a teacher is really an evaluation of the experience someone else's child had with the teacher in question.

In general, parents tend to prefer teachers whose style parallels their parenting style. A parent who likes a lot of activity will probably be dissatisfied with a teacher who doesn't. Some parents put a premium on teachers with warm, nurturing, and loving natures; others prefer teachers who are strict or strong. That said, parents may want to consider whether it is wise to request teachers similar to themselves. Children often benefit by learning from someone very different from the parents; this provides a balanced approach. Perhaps nurturing, gentle parents need not worry so much about the teacher who contrasts with them; the warmth and assurance they've given their child will put that child in particularly good stead for the taskmaster teacher.

In any case, parents must learn more about the teachers in their child's school if the student-teacher match is to succeed. To this end, most school districts publish a newsletter of some sort. Parents can look through back issues at the local public library or in central school offices to gain insight into the ways different teachers run their classrooms. There may be photographs of two teachers reading outdoors to their classes, for example, pointing out that two classes meet regularly to share books. Or there may be a photograph of a teacher sitting on the roof of a building in a sun chair, with a caption explaining that when her students collectively read 300 books a month, that teacher always does something outrageous and funny as a reward. Of course, it's not possible to draw global conclusions from such photos, but it is possible to assume, for instance, that the first two teachers believe in literature and in collaboration across different age groups; or that the third teacher also values children's reading, but believes that they need incentives to lure them to read. Let's say I noticed that for several years in a row a particular teacher was pictured in one of these newsletters with a class trophy for winning one contest after another—a spelling bee, a geography contest, a math competition. I might infer that this teacher values competition, particularly the type that requires fast quick answers to isolated questions. This might lead me to wonder whether this teacher also allows children to spend sustained time on inquiry projects. It's important to read these newsletters with a discerning, open-minded attitude to determine which teachers share our values.

Another way to learn about teachers is through parent orientation sessions, in which each teacher takes a part of the curriculum or the school day and presents it to the parents. Teachers may bring charts or examples of children's work or talk with parents about the schedules they are planning for the year ahead. In my school, these orientations are intended to relieve parents' anxiety over which teacher their child will receive because the teachers show parents that although different things may be emphasized in each classroom, all of the teachers generally do the big things in similar ways.

Sometimes, however, an orientation will reveal significant differences between teachers and parents, in which case the parents should meet with the principal or director to talk about these differences and the implications they might have for parent or child.

Usually parents who do not have a student in the class are not invited to visit classrooms during the school day without an administrator accompanying them. It is disruptive to students to always be on display, and many people feel that parents who visit classrooms put the privacy of children at risk.

Parents can also learn about teachers by meeting with or talking with the principal of the school. A principal might explain the studies particular teachers are engaged in, committees teachers have served on, or the different teachers' areas of interest and expertise. When parents worry that a teacher may not be "experienced," principals must explain that new teachers bring new perspectives and new teaching theories and practices to the school, and often serve as valuable resources to other staff members. New does not mean unqualified.

Bulletin boards in the hallways outside a teacher's classroom also can give parents an idea of what teachers care about. For example, in one class, each child's piece of writing bears the title "My Trip" and each piece is carefully edited. One parent will think, "What neat and careful work the children in this class do," and another will think, "Must every piece of writing be copied over perfectly before it can be celebrated and put up on the class bulletin board?" Parents may notice differences among these bulletin boards, which can serve to highlight a teacher's methods and personality.

The Placement Process

Deciding which children to place in which class is one of the most complex tasks for school administrators to accomplish each year. Although parents can supply input, in most schools, the following procedures take place:

1. Placement is determined through the joint effort of many staff members. The principal alone does not decide where students

are placed. Each child is considered as an individual as well as a member of a class as a whole. When the students of one school feed into another school—for example, when fifth or sixth graders are placed into the middle school or junior high school—this process can become even more complex.

2. School principals may write a letter notifying parents when the placement process is scheduled to begin. If parents have information relevant to their child's placement, that should be conveyed to the school personally, by mail, or by phone.

3. Parents are asked to refrain from requesting a specific teacher. This is one of the most difficult aspects of the placement process. The principal may tell parents that requests are accepted, but that there is no guarantee they will be honored.

Principals regard teachers as the most valuable source of information during the placement process. Even during kindergarten placement, when children are unknown to the school, the principal relies on input from others, usually from parents, as well as the team of teachers and other professionals who have had a chance to meet the children.

When parents tell me what they want for their children and what they think their children need to learn well, I convey this information to the appropriate teachers. School administrators welcome specific, accurate information and consider it thoroughly to determine a child's placement. Conversely, it is not helpful when parents request or demand particular teachers. In addition, it is very difficult to entertain questions from parents who want to know if a particular teacher is "structured" or "creative" or "warm." Such questions are almost impossible to answer because what one parent thinks is structured is different from every other. Misperceptions are rampant, and cannot always be corrected.

Naturally there are situations that require sensitivity and special handling if children are to be placed correctly. Administrators need to know, for example, about a bad experience a particular child or family has had with a particular teacher.

A school typically weighs the issue of placement over the course of many meetings that include classroom teachers; reading or learn-

ing specialists; and special-area teachers including physical education, music, or art teachers, and school administrators. Remarkably,
in many schools, the receiving teachers are not present at the placement meetings; in fact, the receiving teachers usually don't find out
who is in their classes until the placement process is complete.

In the end, the placement process is one that affects teachers and
families long before school begins. All parties realize the significance of matching students with teachers, other students, even philosophies. To be successful, parents, teachers, and administrators
need to understand and consider the many disparate factors that
must come together if children are to have the best possible learning
experience.

The Importance of Parent Involvement

A mother in my school told me that when her son Jed started kindergarten, she was more surprised by the expectations the school had for her than for her son. "I thought once Jed started school, he would have a lot to do but that my job would be lightened, that I'd have time on my hands. Instead, life has become a series of events, expectations, and permission slips flying at me from all sides. "Will I sew costumes? Come into the room and read with kids? Organize the wrapping paper sale? Drive on the field trips? Volunteer in the school library?"

Many parents are caught off guard by the number of expectations schools have for them, because while schools go to great lengths to help children know what to expect of school, they do very little to orient parents. Kindergartners are often invited to look around the school before the year begins, to visit with their teacher, and even to take a trial ride on the school bus, but the parents are left without a clear idea of what to do next. Suddenly, the year is underway and they find themselves inundated with requests for involvement. When there are so many ways to get involved in the school it's hard for parents to know what to choose or how to choose. And if parents know that they don't have much time, they may think it is wiser to just stay out of the way.

My first message is this: It truly helps when parents become involved in the life of their child's school. *Parents' involvement in school tells their child that they endorse the school and that they regard themselves as partners in their child's education.* This is an important message to send to the child, to the child's teacher, and to all the people who comprise the school. A school is really a network of relationships, with the principal, classroom teachers, special teachers, parents of other children, and the children themselves.

There are many different forums for involvement, and each has its particular benefits.

- Parents can become active in the parent-teacher organization and in events it sponsors.
- Parents can be active during school hours in their child's classroom and in the special-area classrooms such as art, music, or the library.
- Parents can be active at home in ways that support classroom work.
- Parents can use their particular talents and interests to make a contribution to the school.
- Parents can be part of school-based teams of decision-makers who work through issues that affect the school community.

Being Active in Parent-Teacher Organizations

The parent-teacher organization is the most official form of parental involvement in a school. At the beginning of the year (or when a new family moves into the district), I always let parents know about our school's parent-teacher organization. I tell them the names of the officers of the organization and often encourage them to phone these people. Information about the parent-teacher organization is also available during meet-the-teacher nights in the fall. Because the invitation to become involved in this organization comes from the principal and often is the first invitation, parents sometimes interpret that the parent-teacher organization represents the highest form of parental involvement. Consequently, they may feel guilty if they can't be active participants. When my children were in elementary school, usually I couldn't attend the parent meetings, and I remember wondering whether I would be judged harshly by my child's teachers.

I encourage as many parents as possible to join the parent-teacher organizations, to pay the dues, and to feel entitled to speak out on issues that concern them; whether active or not, all members are entitled to vote and to speak their minds to the organization. Moreover, the school *needs* your voice. Too often, a very small clique of parents assumes the authority as spokespeople for all, when in fact these parents may represent a radical fringe group. Just because these people spend weeks organizing a festival for the school should not mean their views about curriculum or personnel carry more weight than other parents' views. It's important, therefore, that *all* parents realize they have as much right to speak out at parent-teacher meetings as do other parents.

In general, parent leaders and people who are active in the parent-teacher organization offer extraordinarily valuable services to schools. Two of the most valuable contributions of the parent-teacher organization are the fund-raising and community-building events they plan and sponsor. Every school sponsors events such as book fairs, annual carnivals, plant sales, or school plays; often the success of these endeavors depends on parent volunteers. And because the funds raised by a parent-teacher organization need not go though the red tape of a district's budget, they can be put to immediate use. Many schools have used these funds to purchase playground equipment, musical instruments for the band, books, or computers. Parent leaders and parent organizations also do an enormous amount of work to foster goodwill in the school community. In my school, parent leaders host welcoming teas for parents of kindergartners, guest storytellers for family evenings, and frequent parent education workshops. The community comes together around these occasions. Often, working parents are able to cochair such events, since many of the arrangements can be made outside of the school.

Parent leaders of parent-teacher organizations also use their positions to act as advocates for the school. They often serve as representatives on school or district committees, collaborating on behalf of the school with community members and parent leaders from other schools. On these committees, parents often initiate ideas for events that become districtwide events.

Involvement in the school's parent-teacher organization can be individually rewarding as well. These parents have the opportunity to forge a close working relationship with the school faculty and principal, and to get to know parents of children from every grade. When these parents visit the school, they are recognized and feel valued by staff and student body alike. They are regarded as people who care about the education of all children.

Being Active in Your Child's Classroom or in Special-Area Classrooms

Parents who help out in the classroom value the opportunity to gain an insider's perspective on the environment, the teacher, their child's school life, and perhaps most important, classroom learning.

One way to be active in classroom life is by being a "class parent." This involves helping out in the social events that take place in the classroom. The class parent may help the teacher with a party or celebration or may organize transportation for a field trip.

Other parents serve their child's classroom by sharing their work life, their knowledge, or their expertise. A parent who has an exciting career may visit to talk about that; or, a parent who is an origami artist may teach children to fold paper birds. It is also possible to work alongside the teacher to offer help during instructional time. In my school, some teachers invite parents into their classrooms every month to help out with math, science, reading, or computer lessons, usually according to a schedule made far in advance. A parent who offers to help by listening to individual children read must be available during the class's regularly scheduled reading time, while other parents may be given the flexibility to come for a half hour at the beginning of the school day to do whatever they wish with the class. Or teachers may prefer to assign a small part of the lessons to the parent, perhaps reading with a pair of children or helping students to complete a project. This wide variety of options enables working parents to arrange their schedules in advance and plan what to do with their children or the class as a whole.

Parents agree that one of the benefits of working in their child's classroom is that they get to know their child's teacher. Teachers benefit, too; they often remark that, otherwise, their only opportunity to talk with some parents is at parent-teacher conferences or when there is a cause for concern about their child. Parent visits also help to familiarize parents with school programs. One parent told me, "Most parents aren't teachers, and it's so helpful to see how the teacher works with the children. So many things have changed since I went to school, and watching the teacher, I learned so much about how to help my son." But parents say that seeing their child in the school setting, especially in her own classroom, has made all the difference in their conversations at home. Parents who have met the class gerbil and have worked in a math center have a lot more to talk about with their child. They know the right questions to ask in order to hear more about their child's life in school.

Parents with particular interests or talents may want to help out in the "special" areas in their child's school: art, music, the library, or physical education. Special-area teachers (also called "cluster teachers") often have no assistance and are grateful for the support of volunteer parents. In many schools, parents regularly help the librarian reshelve books, or work with the art teacher to keep the bulletin boards or art displays updated with current student artwork.

One word of caution: Parents who help out in their child's classroom need to be sensitive to issues of confidentiality. When a parent spends time in the classroom, they will learn new things about their child's schoolmates. Perhaps three children will get in a fight over who will sit near the teacher. Or the visiting parent may discover that Abby has trouble understanding fractions, or that Scott needs special help reading. When teachers open their doors to parents, they must be able to trust that parents will respect all the children and not interpret or judge anything that they may see or hear while sharing these experiences.

Being Active at Home to Support Classroom Work

Teachers always need time and assistance to prepare for classroom projects and instruction; therefore, they are indebted to those parents who are willing to help from their homes. Parents can help "publish" children's writing by typing children's poems and stories, then binding these into small books. Parents can research a field trip to ensure that it goes smoothly. One parent I know sewed six police uniforms for a fifth-grade production of the play *Oliver*.

Another benefit to parental involvement at home is that the children see firsthand how parents support their class. The child may even become involved in the work. Parents say that when they have helped in this way at home, their child's interest and excitement in the project grew surprisingly high. And for many working parents who are unable to help in their child's classroom during the day, these at-home projects are a wonderful alternative.

Making a Single, Major Contribution to the School

Parental involvement need not be on a day-to-day basis. Parents who tackle significant individual projects also leave a lasting imprint on the school and in children's minds and hearts.

In my school, when several parents wanted to start a Saturday basketball league for first graders, they raised money, purchased child-sized basketball nets and backboards, and initiated Saturday games. One parent, after noting that her child's teacher encouraged children to bring books between home and school each day, offered to sew corduroy drawstring bags for each child in the class. The bags hang on the backs of every child's chair in the classroom. Another group of parents, together with the children and the art teacher, painted a hopscotch board on the playground. Parents also make flags, start gardens, build tables and bookcases, and donate paintings. Parents who support their child's teacher or school in these ways are always remembered by everyone in the school because their support was so personal and unique.

Joining School-based Teams

In many states, school districts are mandated to form school-based committees or decision-making teams composed of parents, teachers, administrators, and sometimes community members. Parents often serve on these teams for one or two years, and meet to work with the other members on issues such as school citizenship, communication, and researching community resources related to the school curriculum. Schools and school districts also form committees around issues that arise in the district: "Should the kindergarten be extended to a full-day program? Should the district close an aging school or refurbish it?" When issues such as these are on the front burner in a community, members of the boards of education or administrators will often ask for parent representatives to participate in the decision-making process. Parents with a particular expertise in, say, law or politics can be invaluable assets in following through on these issues.

Many districts also have districtwide committees made up of parents from each of the district's schools. In my district, a group of parents supports each school's relationship to the cultural arts. With the help of the school district and the parent organizations, this group helps to sponsor and organize performances by visiting artists and musicians throughout the school year. We also have a board-approved districtwide nutrition committee composed of parents, teachers, administrators, and several students. This group meets each month to assess the quality of food in the school lunch program.

Most school or district meetings involving parent volunteers are open to the public. When parents are considering whether to volunteer on a committee, they should first observe the committee in action.

Knowing the different ways they can get involved in schools helps parents to make wise decisions regarding the contributions they can make in their child's school life. By choosing the form of support that matches their interests and family life, parents can become valuable members of the school and the community.

ACKNOWLEDGMENTS

No figure looms larger in my learning life than Lucy. My first thanks, then, go to Lucy Calkins, who makes all things seem possible. I am grateful to Lucy for her generous and painstaking help with my writing and for encouraging me countless times to follow my insights. Lucy's energy and brilliance have always been an inspiration to me and I thank her for our friendship and for the honor of joining her in writing this book.

I also want to thank the community of teacher-educators I have worked with at the Teachers College Writing Project for the past ten years. It has been my privilege to teach and study alongside these people who have become lifelong friends.

I especially want to thank a few members of the Teachers College community, past and present. Shelley Harwayne has taught me about the grace and craft of good teaching. It was a privilege to work and learn alongside Shelley in many New York City classrooms. I am grateful to Randy Bomer for his intelligence and thoughtfulness. He has enriched my understanding of literacy more than I can say. Many thanks also to Joanne Hindley whose respect for children and deep love of teaching have always been an inspiration. I want to especially thank my friend and colleague, Laurie Pessah, who encouraged me to keep writing. She listened to each draft and generously gave her insights. I am grateful for the years of collaboration and for the respect and honesty we share as friends and learning partners.

My thanks to Phil Carolan, Deborah Blair, Ed Blair, and Richard Koebele for their trust in children, and for the intelligence and courage they always demonstrated as principals and educational leaders.

I want to thank the Cold Spring Harbor Board of Education for their wisdom and dedication to our entire community. I am grateful to our superintendent of schools, Raymond Walters, for his wise and caring leadership and to the entire Cold Spring Harbor community. You have created a wonderful place of learning for children and I am honored to be a part of it.

But the teachers, staff, and parents I am most indebted to are those of Goosehill Primary School. My thanks above all to the teachers for inviting collaboration and for countless hours of conferring about teaching, children, and schools.

I am especially grateful to all the parents who have served as presidents and executive board members of the Goosehill Parent-Faculty Association. I am indebted to them for their insights and belief in schools and school people. I particularly want to thank several parents who offered their ideas and graciously agreed to read early drafts. Thank you to Karen Bingham, Lori D'Alessio, Ellen diBonaventura, Debra Duffy, Jane Holden, Bill Mammone, Jean Thatcher, Suzy Vecchio, and Bea Wall.

A special thank you to Karen Berger and Scott and Lydia Wegman for their encouragement and for generously giving their time to listen to many drafts of this book. I am also grateful to Fran Berger, Martha Campanite, Eileen Hood, and Scott and Carolyn Lindenbaum who offered their ideas and support on the earliest drafts.

My thanks to Ellen Best-Laimit who gave honest advice and encouragement from the start and graciously read and commented on many drafts throughout the writing of this book. I also want to thank Barbara Grieco for sharing stories of her children and generously supporting me by patiently reading many early drafts.

Susan Levy, a brilliant friend, has always helped me to ask big questions about teaching and learning. Her advice and support helped through many pages of my writing. A special thank you to my colleague and good friend Rochelle DeMuccio who offered her intelligent insights and generously gave her time to carefully read many drafts and think through ideas with me.

I am grateful to Liz Maguire, John Wright, and especially to Sharon Broll for the wisdom and patience she invested as she read through every section of this book. My daughter Michelle will never forget the thrill of meeting a real editor when she delivered the final drafts to Sharon.

Finally, I will always be grateful to my husband and best friend Tony and our children Michael, Marissa, Michelle, and Kristyn. They have been extraordinarily understanding and patient with me throughout the living and writing of this book. I thank them for their constant love, for their sound advice, imagination, endless jokes, and for allowing me to share every literacy event of their lives from their earliest scribbles to their high school essays. My life would not be the same if it weren't shared with them.

L. B.

NOTES

Chapter 1

1 Smith, Frank, *Reading Without Nonsense* (New York: Teachers College Press 1985)

2 Heath, Shirley Brice, *Ways with Words* (New York: Cambridge University Press 1983)

3 IBID

4 Weiner, Harvey S. *Talk with Your Child: How to Develop Reading and Language Skills Through Conversation at Home* (New York: Viking 1988)

5 IBID

6 Trelease, Jim, *The Read-Aloud Handbook*, Revised Edition (New York: Penguin Books 1995), p. xxi

7 IBID

8 Wells, Gordon, *The Meaning Makers: Children Learning Language and Using Language to Learn* (Portsmouth, NH: Heinemann 1986), p. 87

9 Armstrong, Thomas, *Awakening Your Child's Natural Genius* (New York: Putnam's Sons 1991), p. x

10 Meek, Margaret, *On Being Literate* (Portsmouth, NH: Heinemann 1992), pp. 103, 105

11 Wells, Gordon, *The Meaning Makers: Children Learning Language and Using Language to Learn* (Portsmouth, NH: Heinemann 1986), pp. 194, 195

12 Smith, Frank, *Reading Without Nonsense* (New York: Teachers College Press, 1985), p. 64

13 Meek, Margaret, *On Being Literate* (Portsmouth, NH: Heinemann 1992), p. 54

Chapter 2

[1] Anderson, Richard C., Elfrieda H. Hiebert, Judith A. Scott, and Ian A. G. Wilkinson, *Becoming a Nation of Readers: The Report of the Commission on Reading* (Center for the Study of Reading: Champaign, IL 1985), p. 23

[2] IBID

[3] Trelease, Jim, *The Read-Aloud Handbook*, Revised Edition (New York: Penguin Books 1995)

[4] A profile of the American Eighth Grader: National Education Longitudinal Study of 1988, National Center for Education Statistics (Washington, D.C.: U.S. Department of Education, June 1990)

[5] Anderson, Richard C., Linda Fielding, and Paul Wilson, *Growth in Reading and How Children Spend Their Time Outside of School*, Reading Research Quarterly, Summer 1988, pp. 285–303

[6] *Reading the Difference: Gender and Reading in Elementary Classrooms*, Edited by Myra Barrs and Sue Pidgeon (Maine: Stenhouse Publishing 1994)

[7] MacNeil, Robert, *Wordstruck* (New York: Viking 1989), pp. 23–24

[8] *Reading the Difference: Gender and Reading in Elementary Classrooms*, Edited by Myra Barrs and Sue Pidgeon (Maine: Stenhouse Publishing 1994)

[9] Pipher, Mary, *The Shelter of Each Other: Rebuilding Our Families* (New York: Grosset/Putnam 1996)

[10] Baum, Frank, *The Wonderful Wizard of Oz*, illustrated by W.W. Penslow. (New York: William Morrow and Co., 1987)

Chapter 3

[1] Paterson, Katherine, *Gates of Excellence: On Reading and Writing Books for Children* (New York: Elsevier/Nelson Books 1981), p. 20

[2] Baylor, Byrd, *I'm in Charge of Celebrations* (New York: Charles Scribner's Sons 1986)

Chapter 4

[1] Meek, Margaret, *On Being Literate* (Portsmouth, NH: Heinemann Press, 1992)

2 Smith, Frank, *Reading Without Nonsense* (New York: Teachers College Press 1985)

Chapter 5

1 Howe, James, "Reflections." The Writing Project Quarterly Newsletter 1:3 (spring): 12. 1987

2 Pipher, Mary, *The Shelter of Each Other: Rebuilding Our Families* (New York: Grosset/Putnam 1996), p. 15

3 Trelease, Jim, *The Read-Aloud Handbook*, Revised Edition (New York: Penguin Books 1995)

4 Pearce, Joseph Chilton, *Magical Child* (New York: NAL Dutton 1992)

Chapter 7

1 Gardner, Howard, *Artful Scribbles: The Significance of Children's Drawing* (New York: Basic Books)

2 Anderson, Richard C., Elfrieda H. Hiebert, Judith A. Scott, and Ian A. G. Wilkinson, *Becoming a Nation of Readers:* The Report of the Commission on Reading (Center for the Study of Reading: Champaign, IL 1985)

3 Allington, R. and A. McGill-Franzer, 1989 "Different Programs, Indifferent Instructor." In *Beyond Separate Educator: Quality Education for All.* Edited by D. K. Lipsky and A. Gartner. Baltimore, MD: Paul H. Brookes Publishing Company.

Chapter 8

1 Shaughnessy, Mina, *Errors and Expectations* (New York: Oxford University Press 1977)

2 Gardner, Howard, *Artful Scribbles: The Significance of Children's Drawing* (New York: Basic Books)

3 Baylor, Byrd, *The Other Way to Listen* (New York: Charles Scribner's Sons, 1978)

4 Elbow, Peter, *Writing with Power: Techniques for Mastering the Writing Process* (New York: Oxford University Press 1981)

5 From *Jamboree Rhymes for All Times* by Eve Merriam. Copyright ©

1962, 1964, 1966, 1973, 1984 Eve Merriam. © Renewed Eve Merriam and Dee Michel and Guy Michel. Reprinted by permission of Marian Reiner.

Chapter 9

[1] Curriculum Evaluation Standard for School Mathematics National Counsel of Teachers and Mathematicians, 1989, pp. 6 & 18

[2] IBID

[3] IBID

Chapter 10

[1] Quindlen, A., *Living Out Loud* (New York: Random House 1988) Copyright © 1987 by The New York Times Co. Reprinted by Permission.

[2] Reprinted from Robert Francis: *Collected Poems, 1936–1976* (Amherst: University of Massachusetts Press, 1976), copyright © 1976 by Robert Francis.

[3] Duckworth, Eleanor, *The Having of Wonderful Ideas* (New York: Teachers College Press 1987)

[4] IBID

[5] IBID

[6] Elstgeest, Joseph, *"Encounter, Interactions, and Dialogue"* in *Primary Science: Taking the Plunge*, W Harlem, ed. (London: Heinemann Educational)

[7] Duckworth, Eleanor, *Evaluation of the African Primary Science Program*

[8] Duckworth, Eleanor, *Evaluation of the African Primary Science Program*

[9] Roe, Anne, *The Making of a Scientist* (New York: Dodd Mead, 1974)

[10] Huxley, Julian, *Memories* (New York: Harper and Row, 1970)

[11] IBID

[12] Duckworth, Eleanor, Jack Easley, David Hackines and Androula Henriques, *Science Education: A Minds-on Approach for the Elementary Years* (Hillsdale, NJ: Lawrence Erlbaum Associates, Inc., 1990)

[13] IBID

Chapter 11

[1] Fritz, Jean, "The Known and the Unknown: An Exploration into Nonfiction" in the Zena Sotherland Lectures, (New York: Clarion Books, 1993) p. 161

INDEX

non sequiturs, conversation and, 24–25
nonfiction reading, 39–41, 106, 222–27
nouns, 179
Numeroff, Felice, 50
nursery school. *See* preschool(s)

O

observation. *See* everyday miracles,
  awareness of
O'Dell, Scott, 154
"old math," 182
"one-to-one" pointing, 93
oral language development. *See also*
  conversation(s)
  children's talk, importance to, 7–9, 12,
    14
  early writing and, 53–58
  improving, 26–30
  kindergarten readiness, 253–55
  parent's role in, 7–8
  reading, importance to, 28– 29
organized activities. *See* lessons and sports
Owl Moon, 49, 51, 201
Owls in the Family, 39

P

paper and writing tools, providing, 63–64,
  66, 116–17, 169
parent-teacher conferences, 284, 287
parent-teacher organizations, 294–96
parents. *See also* home; oral language
  development
  involvement in school, 19–20, 237–38,
    293–99
  math education, 181
  play/playthings, 108–11
  reading, early, 83–86, 95–96
  reading, middle years, 142–44
  science education, 199–201
  social studies education, 215–16
  spelling skills, extending, 71–73
  standardized tests, preparing child for,
    281–82
  teachers, in partnership with, 285–92
  time spent in talking with children, 11
  writing, early, 53–58, 77
  writing, middle years, 162–65
"particle approach," writing curriculum, 259
partnerships. *See* collaborative work
Paterson, Katherine, 37, 77, 154
"pattern approach," writing curriculum, 260
Paulsen, Gary, 37, 154
Pearce, Joseph, 121

Peck, Robert Newton, 153
Pee Wee Scouts, 151
Peet, Bill, 50
pets, 131, 132, 133
phonics, 97–100, 269, 270
picture books, as read-aloud selections, 49
pictures, "reading" the, 89, 91–92, 98–99
Pipher, Mary, 43, 113
play
  cultural values, impact on, 112–14
  deepening/extending, 119–27
  importance of, 108–11, 126–27
  losing/winning, learning how to, 124–25
  playthings, selecting, 115–18
  playthings, storage of, 118–19
  resourcefulness, encouraging, 111–15
  science education and, 202–6
  taking turns, learning how to, 124
poetry
  emergent readers and, 106
  as read–aloud selections, 39, 49
  writing, early, 65, 79, 80
  writing, middle years, 166
pointing, to words, 92–93, 94
Polacco, Patricia, 50
politeness. *See* social graces
prefixes, 29
preprimers, 274
preschool(s)
  child-centered, 240
  cognitive, 241
  combination (middle-of-the-road)
    approach, 241–42
  early writing curriculum, 52–53
  selecting, 7–8, 239–42
pretend reading
  emergent readers and, 85, 86–88, 90–91
  kindergarten readiness and, 250
  writing, early, 61
primer readers, 96
principals, 290, 291
problem solving, in math, 183–90, 196
"process approach," writing curriculum, 259
progress reports, 283–84
projects/hobbies, 131–38
pronunciation, 29–30
published curriculum programs, 258, 262,
  274–75
"pullout" for support services, 244, 251,
  280
punctuation, 85, 259

Q

questions (parent's/teacher's). *See also* drill-
  and-skill

school(s). *See also* teachers
  group discussions, teaching the art of, 23–24
  matching teacher to child, 287–90
  oral language development and, 13
  parent involvement, importance of, 293–99
  parent-teacher organizations, 294–96
  phonics, debate over, 97–100
  placement process, 290–92
  play/playthings and, 126–27
  read-aloud book selections in, 49–51
  use of "known-answer questions" in, 27–28
science
  creativity, encouraging, 201–6
  curriculum, 263–65
  interest in, deepening, 206–9
  parent's role in, 199–201
  sustained research, promoting, 209–14
Science-in-a-Box program, 202, 209, 210
screening. *See* standardized tests
Secret Garden, The, 33
Seldon, George, 36
self-concept
  reading, early, 85, 102–4
  writing, early, 59
  writing, middle years, 164–65
self-discipline, work habits and, 128
self-esteem, 168, 255, 280, 283
self-initiation
  of chores, 140–41
  of corrections, in reading, 93, 94
  of reading, 88
semantics, of a sentence, 99
Sendak, Maurice, 50
separation anxiety, 244, 245
series books, 49, 151–53
Shaughnessy, Mina, 163
Shaw, Charles G., 95
Shiloh, 45
Sign of the Beaver, The, 32
signatures, writing and, 59, 166
signs, writing and, 166
Sim Farm (computer manual), 224
Slote, Alfred, 149
Smith, Frank, 10, 28, 99, 100
Smith, Robert Kimmel, 39, 153
social awareness, motivating, 221, 231–33
social development, 239, 250
social graces
  conversation and, 25–26
  interrupting, teaching not to, 24
  lessons/sports and, 136
  turns, taking, 124
social studies
  curriculum, 261–63
  explore, helping to, 216–20

facts, teaching, 220–21
  importance of, 231–33
  interest in, encouraging, 225–31
  issues of, 221
  nonfiction books, reading, 222–27
  parent's role in, 215–16
Something Queer series, 153
sounding out words. *See also* phonics
  alphabet work and, 100–102
  reading, early, 90
  spelling skills, extending, 74
  writing, early, 60, 61
Speare, Elizabeth, 32, 154
special-area teachers, 292, 297
speech and language. *See* oral language development
spelling
  phonics and, 100
  reading, early, 83, 85
  skills, extending, 71–76
  writing, early, 60–61, 62
Spinelli, Jerry, 153
spiraling curriculum, 196
sports. *See* lessons and sports
SSR time (silent, sustained reading), 270
standardized tests
  achievement, 277–84
  competency, 280
  kindergarten readiness, 243, 248, 251, 252–55
  math ability and, 198
  national and state, 278–83
  oral language development and, 14, 30
Steig, William, 38, 50
Stevenson, James, 50
Stone Fox, 39
stories, children's
  importance of, 8, 42
  oral language development and, 18
  writing, early, 64–71
stories, shared family. *See also* memories, shared
  early reading development and, 95–96
  oral language development and, 9–13
  teach life values, 16–17, 43
storying, defined, 18
Stuart Little, 36, 38
subtraction. *See* math
"Summons" (poem), 200
Superfudge, 151
support services
  in kindergarten, 244, 246–47
  in reading, 161
  standardized testing and, 280
Surprise Island, 152
sustained reading, 147–50, 270, 282
syntax, of a sentence, 99